THE SELECTED WRITINGS
OF
ZOLTÁN KODÁLY

WE ARE INDEBTED TO MRS. ZOLTÁN KODÁLY FOR HER
INVALUABLE ASSISTANCE IN PREPARING THIS BOOK

THE SELECTED WRITINGS
OF
ZOLTÁN KODÁLY

BOOSEY & HAWKES
MUSIC PUBLISHERS LIMITED
LONDON · PARIS · BONN · JOHANNESBURG · SYDNEY ·
TORONTO · NEW YORK

Selected from the Hungarian original: VISSZATEKINTÉS I–II,
ed. by Ferenc Bónis, Zeneműkiadó Vállalat
First Hungarian edition © 1964 by Zoltán Kodály
Translated by Lili Halápy and Fred Macnicol
Binding and jacket by Klára Rudas
Photographs by László Vámos, reproduction of
archive photos by István Glavák

First published by Boosey & Hawkes Music Publishers Ltd.,
295, Regent Street, London W1A 1BR
© 1974 by Mrs. Zoltán Kodály
For distribution throughout the world with the exception of
Hungary, Albania, Bulgaria, China, Cuba, Czechoslovakia, the
German Democratic Republic, Mongolia, North Korea, North Vietnam,
Poland, Rumania, the Soviet Union and Yugoslavia
In co-operation with Corvina Press, Budapest
Printed in Hungary, 1974
ISBN 0–85162–021–3

CONTENTS

III. ON MUSIC EDUCATION

IV. ON HIMSELF AND HIS WORKS

APPENDIX

I
ON FOLK MUSIC

HUNGARIAN FOLKSONGS

Foreword

There are two objectives to folksong publication, two different approaches. One is to bring together all songs originating among the people; here, comprehensiveness is the most important consideration, and the intrinsic value of the songs irrelevant. Such a collection is a sort of "comprehensive dictionary of folksongs". The best arrangement for this is also that of a dictionary; the Ilmari Krohn edition of Finnish folksongs *(Suomen Kansan Sävelmiä,* four booklets up to 1906) is an example of this type of collection. The songs are written down carefully and authentically for one voice and all known variants are indicated. Only a collection of this type can provide the basis for all aspects of folksong research.

The other objective is to introduce the general public to folksongs so that they can be taught to appreciate them. A "comprehensive dictionary" is unsuitable for this purpose since it includes both first-rate and much poorer material. The best must be selected and then to some extent adapted to public taste by some form of musical arrangement. Folksongs must be dressed to be taken from the fields to the city. In urban attire, however, they are awkward and uncomfortable. Their apparel must be cut in a fashion that will not hinder their breathing. Whether for chorus or for piano, the accompaniment should always be of such a nature as to make up for the lost fields and village. As far as the authenticity of the tunes is concerned, the popular edition should not fall short of the complete one.

Of course, the first kind of publication is possible only after all the material has been collected. Here, where this work has scarcely begun, it will be some time before we can even think of such a thing. Even in the very early stages of collecting, however, the cream has been selected. This publication has been prepared for the general public from such a selection of songs, and, as the income from it will be used for further collection, it serves the first purpose as well.

Some of the twenty songs come from the recordings of Béla Vikár, who has worked long and zealously in the cause of Hungarian folklore—here we have to thank him for his kind permission to publish the songs; the others come from our own recently begun collection. In view of the conditions prevailing in Hungary, we have included the melody in the accompaniment too. In the forthcoming volumes (when they will appear depends on the results of our collecting), we shall not always adhere to this. We are presenting something to be sung, not to be played on the piano.

If only these expressions of the spirit of our people, often very ancient in origin, would meet with even half the affection they deserve. It will be a long time before they can take the place which they ought to take in our musical life, public or private. The overwhelming majority of Hungarians are not yet Hungarian enough, no longer naive enough and not yet cultured enough to take these songs to their hearts. Hungarian folksongs in the concert hall!—Today this still sounds strange. Equal in rank with the masterpieces of world literature and foreign folksongs! But the time will come: a time when there will be Hungarian music in the home, when Hungarian families will not be content with the most inferior foreign music-hall songs or with the products of domestic folksong factories, when there will be Hungarian singers, when not only the lover of rarities will know that there are Hungarian folksongs other than *"Ritka búza"* and *"Ityóka-pityóka"*.

(1906)

THE PENTATONIC SCALE
IN HUNGARIAN FOLK MUSIC

Anyone who is aware of the scantiness of the material presently in print in Hungarian folksong collections, and knows that even what has been published is based on superficial observation of the songs of only a few Hungarian regions, cannot be surprised if further, more systematic and wide-ranging collecting work reveals much that is new and teaches us many things of which there was not even a hint in the collections of Mátray, Szini and Bartalus.

Since 1907, when Béla Bartók first found several examples of it among the songs of the Székely region of Transylvania, we have known that the pentatonic scale—the basis of the music of so many ancient peoples, perhaps even of all peoples—is alive and flourishing here, too.

Where can it be found? As far as we have been able to discover since then, the entire Székely region, among the Bucovina Csángószékelys, is the home of the pentatonic-type melody; traces of it are found in Transdanubia and among the Hungarians of the Uplands—in short something of the older Hungarian folk culture has survived everywhere. The surprising analogies between fragments of folk culture discovered in widely separated parts of the country indicate the strong probability of an over-unified folk culture.

The so-called "Hungarian scale" was once considered the most characteristic feature of Hungarian music. This was disproved long ago. Today, if we are looking for some trait which distinguishes the music of the Hungarians from that of all neighbouring peoples, we find it in its rhythm and in its use of the pentatonic scale.

Its structure. The Hungarian pentatonic scale is a "natural" (or descending "melodic" minor) scale from which the second and sixth degrees are missing. If, for example we choose G for the tonic, the scale is: G–B♭–C–D–F. In addition to these five notes most melodies reach the F below the tonic as well as the octave of the tonic, the G; very occasionally the upper third, the B♭, a tenth above the tonic, also occurs. Thus, the widest possible range is: F–G–B♭–C–D–F–G–B♭ and the narrowest is: G–B♭–C–D; for some tunes are content with four notes, and thus we may actually have cases of tetratony. But these are exceptions. As there are no semitones in it, our scale belongs to what could be called "anhemitonic"-type pentatony.

Tempo of the songs. As concerns the tempo, we can find lively tunes consistently in dance-step throughout; the majority, however, are rubato, and rather slow.

11

Accordingly, we find gay texts only in the dance-songs—though not even all of these are gay. Moreover, the text of slow tunes is always serious, indeed, very sad. The Székelys call this type *keserves* (complaint); as they warm to the melody, they produce a veritable flow of stanzas, each sadder than the preceding one. Rubato does not so much mean sudden changes of tempo as different lengths of fermata, the pauses between the lines; the time-value of parlando sections does not generally show much variety. In some of the following examples an attempt has been made to indicate the rubato as exactly as possible.

Rhythm. The tunes are isometric (they consist of lines of equal length); the lines have 6, 7, 8, 11 and 12 syllables; in dance-songs, lines with 11 syllables are the most frequent and in the "complaints", lines with 8. The stanzas, with one or two exceptions, have four lines. To match the tunes, the texts have a pattern of four-line stanzas; two-line fragments are also heard quite often, however, especially in eight or twelve-syllable lines. In some regions, two lines of text go with four lines of the tune, each line being repeated. Much observation is still needed to clarify the relationship between tune and text.

Ornamentation. Rich ornamentation is a striking characteristic of the slow, sad songs. It would be a mistake to consider this either a cantor's mannerism or a Rumanian feature—to mention the two opinions most often heard. We know that from the end of the sixteenth century almost to the beginning of the nineteenth, ornamentation prevailed in composed music all over Europe; in fact, it was a separate, intricate branch of the art of performing. It is not known at present to what extent Székely, and old Hungarian ornamentation in general (for to this day elderly people all over the country apply some amount of ornamentation in their singing), is a relic of this style and to what extent it is related to similar phenomena in oriental music. Whatever its origin, however, it is certainly an interesting relic, every note of which deserves attention—the more so as we shall not hear it much longer. Today's twenty or thirty-year old can no longer sing in this way, and does not even want to. The change in taste is an almost tangible process taking place before our eyes. And as the style of performance disappears, the melodies themselves usually disappear as well.

Living folk music is thus losing something of great value. To anyone who can rid himself of his bias towards western (chiefly German) music, it offers the greatest artistic delight; even as performed by untrained singers, it gives an impression of clarity, maturity and perfection—that is to say, of a finished style.

In performance, ornamental notes and groups of notes are always a soft, glissando-like portamento, even if the separate notes are distinctly audible in the group. To get some idea of the sound of these songs, we must always try to sing them, never merely play them on the piano.

It should be pointed out that in the ornamental notes, the second and sixth degrees are also sounded for a moment in passing without in the least affecting the special pentatonic character.

Melody. The clue to the melodic structure is most quickly found by examining the last note in the lines; they are the four pillars which support the edifice of the melody. Comparison is facilitated if we reduce all melodies to a common final note. The most suitable note for this purpose is the G above middle C.

1

These eight notes constitute the whole tonal system of Hungarian songs and provide their marvellous variety, beauty and strength. Substituting numbers for notes, we can express the ends of the lines of every four-line tune with a three-figure signature. For example, the first line of a 1 4 5 tune ends on G, the second on the C an octave above middle C and the third on the D, a ninth above middle C. It is superfluous to indicate the fourth because it is always G.

The most frequent line-endings in pentatonic tunes are:

	usually	seldom	never
First line-end	5,7,4	VII,1,♭3,8	♭10
Second line-end	♭3	VII,1,5,7	8, ♭10
Third line-end	♭3,VII,1	4,7	5,8, ♭10

The greatest variety is found at the end of the first line, the least at the end of the second. The tenth B♭ never stands at the end of a line and even apart from that it is seldom heard at all.

Let us now examine some characteristic examples and observe the melodies of the separate lines.

Examples. We shall begin with the dance-songs. (C.=the collector's name.)

2

In dance-style ♩=108-120 Structure: 5,1,1.   Méra (Kolozs County) 1912.C.: I.Balabán

Hat ö-kör a föl-det nem magá-nak szántja, É-dës any-ja lá-nyát sem magá-nak tart-ja.

(Six oxen do not plough the earth for themselves; / Mother dear does not keep her daughter for herself either.)

This is a very widespread tune, although there are few six-syllable ones in dance-songs, (another example: in Bartók's *For Children*). The majority have eleven syllables.

The following songs, Nos. 3 and 4 are also widespread, as is shown by their numerous variants and they are known to practically everyone in the Csíkszék and Marosszék regions.

3

In dance-style Structure: 7, ♭3,7.   Gyergyócsomafalva, 1907. C.: B. Bartók

1. Ha ki-mëgyëk arr' a magas te-tő-re, Ta-lá-lok én sze-re-tő-re, ket-tő-re
2. Nem kell nékem sem a ket-tő, sem az egy, Hadd szeressen a-ki ed-dig sze-re-tett.

1-2. Ej, baj, baj, baj, de nagy baj, Hogy a ba-bám szí-ve o-lyan, mint a vaj.

(1. If I go up to that high top / I'll find a lover, or eenv two. / Oh, what a pity, what a great pity / That my love's heart is just like butter.
2. I don't need the two, or the one either, / Let the one love me who has loved me until now. / O what a pity, what a great pity / That my love's heart is just like butter.)

4

In dance-style Structure; 5, 1, VII.   Gyergyóalfalu, 1910. C.: Z. Kodály

Föl-szántom én a sze-be-ni nagy ut-cát, Ve-tëk be-le pí-ros pünkös-di ró-zsát,

Én is be-le - ve-tëm magam pa-lánt-nak, A-ki sze-ret szakit-son le ma-gá-nak.

(I plough up the main street in Szeben; / I plant a red peony rose in it. / I plant myself in it, too, as a seedling. / Let him who loves me pluck me for his own.)

This kind of song is not for the moment threatened with extinction. The change in tastes mentioned above affects only the slow, rubato, ornamented melodies; pentatonic thinking itself still has strong roots even among young people. The following little song, probably of more recent origin, also shows this. (It is the nostalgic sigh of a Csík County housemaid.)

5

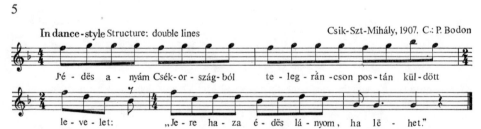

In dance-style Structure: double lines   Csik-Szt-Mihály, 1907. C.: P. Bodon

J'é - dës a - nyám Csék-or-szág-ból te - leg-rån -cson pos-tán kül-dött

le - ve - let: „Je - re ha - za é - dës lá - nyom, ha lë - het."

(1. My good mother sent a message by wire from Csík: / "Come home, if you can, my good sweet daughter".)

2. Second stanza:

Honne mennék, j-édesanyám
Kietekért akár hogy is,
Négykézláb is, mezítláb is,
Bocskorban is, zekében is,
S vonaton is, taligán is,
Szekeren is, tránvájon is, de nem lehet:
kéredzettem asszonyomtól, nem enged.

(2. Of course I'd go, my good mother, / For you somehow or other, / On hands and knees, or even barefoot, / In sandals, or in a jacket, / By train, or by wheelbarrow, / By cart, by tram, but it's impossible: / I've begged leave from my lady—she will not let me go.)

(In the second stanza the first bar is repeated five times.)

Next, the slow ones. It is very difficult to write them down exactly, mainly because of their many irregular values, which our present notation cannot express. Any attempt can only be an approximation, more or less close. There are many degrees to which a note can be lengthened, and we must content ourselves with indicating only two: ⌒ means a shorter pause and ⌒ one twice as long or even longer. A fermata in brackets means an indefinite pause—which may even be omitted. A certain shortening of the value of the note is shown by the mark ⌣ above it.

6

Poco rubato ♩=72-76 Structure: 5, 1, ♭3.   Bodok (Nyitra County) 1906. C.: Z.K.

1. Csak azt szá - nom bá - nom, tő - led el kёll vál - nom,
2. Csiz-mám el - szag - gat - tam, pat-kóm el - kop - tat - tam,

Sok u - tán - nad va - ló já - rá - som saj - ná - lom.
Még-is é - dёs ru - zsám tő - led el - ma - rad - tam.

(1. I'm only sorry I have to part from you, / I regret the time I spent going after you. /
2. I wore my boots to shreds, I wore out my heel-iron, / And yet I still did not get you, my sweet rose.)

15

7

Gyergyószárhegy, 1910. C.: Z.K.

Slow parlando Structure: ♭3,♭3,♭3.

1. Is - te - něm, Is - te - něm, . (de) Ki - nek tě - gyek pa - naszt, (Ej)
2. Ha más - nak měg- mon-dom: An - nak hí - rit hal - lom, (Ej)

Az i - de - gě - něk közt Ki - től kér - gyek vá - laszt?
Ha ma - gam - ba tar - tom: Szí - vem el - fony - nyasz - tom.

(1. My God, my God, / (but) Who can I complain to / (O) Among the strangers / Who can I ask for an answer? /
2. If I tell someone else / They will gossip about it, / (O) If I keep it to myself I sear my own heart.)

Both revolve round the first four notes of the scale, not counting the F in No.7—which is sometimes even omitted.

8

Gyergyóujfalu, 1907. C.: B. Bartók

Rubato, parlando Structure: 7, VII, VII.

Annyi bá - nat a szü - ve - měn, Két-rét haj-lott az e - ge - kěn

Ha még ěgy - gyet haj - lott vol - na Szüvem ket - té ha - sadt vol - na.

(So much sorrow in my heart, / It fills the sky twice; / If it had filled it up once more / My heart would have split in two.)

Two tunes of this kind can be found on pp. 48 and 109 of *Ethnographia,* 1908.

9

Gyergyószentmiklós, 1910. C.: Z.K.

Rubato, parlando Structure: 4,♭3, VII.

(Aj) Tő- lem a nap úgy te - lik el (Aj) Ha fěl - jő a - lig ha - lad el.

gliss.

Nem vir - ra - dok ö - rö - möm - re, Nem sö - té - tü - lök ked - vem - re.

((O) The sun passes so from me, / When it comes up, it scarcely moves away. / I do not dawn for my delight / I do not darken for my pleasure.)

Slow parlando Structure: 4,♭3,VII.   Gyergyóalfalu, 1910. C.: Z.K.

El-in-dul a há - rom ár - va,   Hosszú út - ra,   buj - do - sás - ra

Azt kérdte a   szép szűz   Már - ja: „Ho-va mëntëk   há - rom   ár - va?"

(Three orphans set out / On a long journey, into exile. / Then asked the lovely Virgin Mary, / "Where are you going, you three orphans?")

Actually a variant of the previous song—and yet how very different!

11

Fogadjisten, Bukovina, 1914. C.: Z.K.

Rubato ♩=54-56 occasionally, certain lines 60-63 Structure: 8,♭3,♭3.

Mënyëk az ú - ton le-fe-lé   Senki se mond - ja: gye-re   bé!

Gye - re bé   ró - zsám, gyere bé,   Csak magam   va - gyok i - de-bé!

(I'm going on down the road, / No one says to me—come on in! / Come in, my love, come in, / It's only me alone in here!)

One of the most often heard A variant: p. 112 of *Ethnographia,* 1908. The following, No. 12, is fairly widespread, but of course, like Nos. 8–11, only among elderly people.

12

Kisgörgény (Marostorda County) 1914. C.: B. B.

Parlando ♩=92 Structure: 1,♭3,1.

Ár-va vagyok, mint görli-ce,   Mint   a-ki-nek nincs sen - ki - je   Ár -

- va vagyok én ma - gam is,   Ár-va   az én ga-lam-bom is.

(I'm an orphan like a turtle-dove, / Like someone who has no one. / I am an orphan myself / And my lover is also an orphan.)

Here, among the ornamental notes, we find the missing second and sixth degrees. The first note starts off from an uncertain pitch, somewhere around C–D. This also occurs frequently at the beginning of lines. It may be a physiological necessity to support the emphasised note from in front, and since the Hungarian language does not provide syllables preceding the stressed ones, the singer assists himself in this way. We can nearly always hear indeterminate subsidiary notes before the first note of the song, such as a, m, n; if the first syllable begins with a vowel, glissandos are common. In many cases these supporting notes are clearly discernible—at the beginnings of lines two, three and four of the above song, No. 12, for example.

We are presenting two examples of the twelve-syllable line. These are the longest, and this may be why they are sometimes recited in a more lively manner, with only a very short pause after the first line, or none at all; the fermata comes only at the end of the second.

13

(Aj)Sirass, él-dës anyám, míg e-lőt-ted já-rok, Mert az-tán si-rathatsz, ha tő-led el-vá-lok

(Aj)A jó Is-ten tudja: hol tör-tént ha-lá-lom? A jó Is-ten tud-ja: hol tör-tént ha-lá-lom?

((O) Mourn me, dear mother, while I am here before you, / For then you can mourn me if I part from you. / The good God knows where was my death. / The good God knows where was my death.)

But the twelve-syllable line can also be heard slowly, with rests after every sixth note.

14

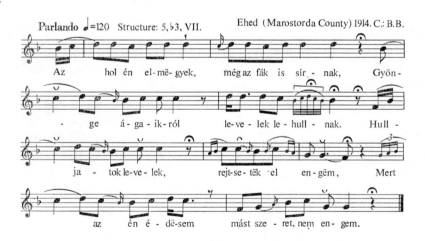

Az hol én el-më-gyek, még az fák is sír-nak, Gyön-

-ge á-ga-ik-ról le-ve-lek le-hull-nak. Hull-

ja-tok le-ve-lek, rejt-se-tëk el en-gëm, Mert

az én é-dë-sem mást sze-ret, nem en-gem.

18

(Where I'm walking even the trees weep; / From their frail branches leaves fall. / Fall leaves, hide me away, / For my sweetheart loves another, not me.)

This tune—one of the best-known Székely melodies—was published in three variations as early as 1883, in Vol. III of Bartalus (pp. 12, 14 and 66); its fourth variant is on p. 7 of Vol. VI. Of course, it is only now that we notice its pentatonic nature. The variant in Vol. VI is pure; in the others there is the odd transitional note here and there.

There is no trace of ornamentation whatever in Bartalus's written transcriptions; the free recitative is crammed into uniform $\frac{4}{4}$ time, and there is no mention of the manner of presentation: the written notations do not give even an approximate picture of the original. And it must be said that this is not the only case. It was necessary to resume the collection of Hungarian folksongs not only because so little material had been collected previously, but also because even what was available was almost useless as a result of the deficiencies of the written transcriptions.

Pentatonic phraseology. No doubt the peculiarities of rhythm, ornamentation and structure all contribute to the particular effect which distinguishes these songs from any other music. With regard to structure, we should mention that the end of the second line stops strikingly often on the third, in our notation B♭. The relationship between this and the real final note is like that between the semicolon and the full stop. It gives a natural phrasing division, particularly to pieces of a recitative nature. (E.g. Nos. 7, 9, 13 and 14.) It often occurs when the first half of the song is in a higher register than the second; it begins high and then becomes lower and lower.

15

(Have you heard what happened in Pálfala? / They killed a poor gendarme for someone's money. / At seven he took coffee around Korond. / At ten his red blood spilled out.)

(See also Nos. 2, 3, 5, 6, 9, 11 and 12.) But this is a general characteristic of Hungarian tunes, in that it does not have a fugue-like (fifth sequence) beginning.

The special atmosphere of our tunes as presented here is created mostly by the combinations of intervals stemming from the pentatonic system. Most often we hear a major second coupled with a minor third or a fourth; it is from these three kinds of intervals that the special pentatonisms originate:

19

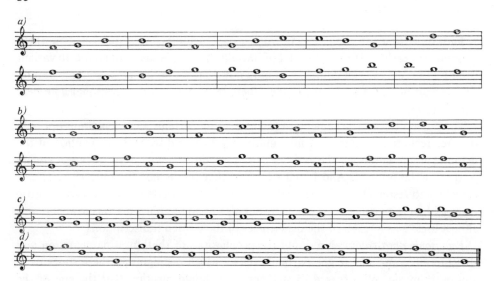

Only once is there occasion for two major seconds and major thirds: B♭–C–D; B♭–D. The patterns under *d)* can be increased at will from published songs.

Relationship between pentatony and the major-minor system. In view of the fact that even our villages have long been overwhelmed with music in major and minor keys, it is surprising that the pentatonic system survived in a completely pure state, even if only in a dozen or so examples. The pentatonic foundation has remained unaffected, however, even in songs influenced by the seven-note scale. In turn, songs based on heptatony have adopted some pentatonisms.

Songs belonging here can be classified in four groups. 1. Purely pentatonic (the majority of our examples). 2. Songs in which the two missing notes appear here and there as transitional notes or grace notes (Nos. 7, 9, 10, 12 and 14 of our examples). These usually have pure pentatonic variants as well. 3. Songs in which the notes outside the system are given a separate syllable (indicated with an asterisk: No. 15). The evidence of these examples shows that groups 2 and 3 do not differ essentially from groups 1 and 4. Songs in which some phrases of the melody point to a pentatonic origin, but in which the influence of the major and minor, the tonic-dominant relationship, has more or less obliterated the basic pentatonic structure. Most examples belong to this—transitional—group. They show clearly how songs gradually move farther and farther from the pure type, until at last only one or two pentatonic characteristics indicate that even under the changed system, the older kind of melody-weaving has still been at work.

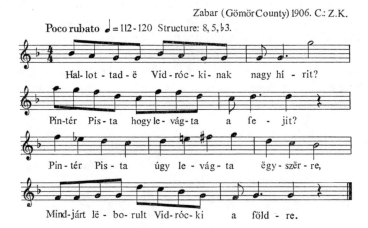

Zabar (Gömör County) 1906. C.: Z.K.

Poco rubato ♩ = 112-120 Structure: 8, 5, ♭3.

Hal- lot - tad - ĕ Vid - róc - ki - nak nagy hí - rit?

Pin- tér Pis - ta hogy le - vág - ta a fe - jit?

Pin - tér Pis - ta úgy le - vág - ta ĕgy - szĕr - re,

Mind- járt lĕ - bo- rult Vid- róc- ki a föld - re.

(Have you heard the great news about Vidróczki, / How Pista Pintér cut off his head? / Pista Pintér cut it off at the first go, / Vidrócki stumbled to the ground straight away.)

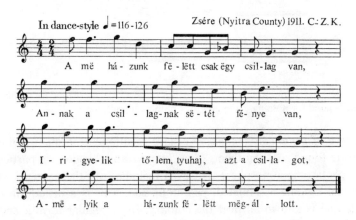

In dance-style ♩ = 116-126   Zsére (Nyitra County) 1911. C.: Z.K.

A mĕ há - zunk fĕ - lĕtt csak ĕgy csil - lag van,

An - nak a csil - lag- nak sĕ - tét fé - nye van,

I - ri - gye- lik tő- lem, tyuhaj, azt a csil- la - got,

A- mĕ - lyik a há- zunk fĕ - lĕtt mĕg- ál - lott.

(Above our house there is only one star. / That star has a faint light. / They envy me, oh hey, that star / Which has stopped still above our house.)

In these two examples we find the pentatonic system combined with the modern minor and even with the major scale (No. 18). The later stage of evolution has not displaced the old one, and the present system, barely two or three hundred years old, lives as a peaceful neighbour of one which the Greeks had called archaic in 350 B.C., and which had been used long before that by the Chinese.

In the Transdanubian region, the old system fights the new in a peculiar way. It is no doubt the effect of the major scale that old songs of a purely pentatonic structure may be heard with the third and seventh higher. This height sometimes reaches that of the major scale, so that we seem to be dealing with a purely major song. (Bartók, example 244.) If, in this example, we lower the third and the seventh by a semitone, we get a pentatonic scale. *And the tune exists in this form, too!* In countless cases the thirds and sevenths are not definite enough; they are neither high enough nor low enough to be grouped either here or there. They float between the two. Sometimes the same singer will intonate them higher one time, lower the next. But the whole pattern of these songs proves beyond doubt that they are rooted in the pentatonic system.

19

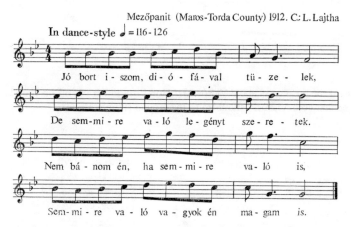

Mezőpanit (Maros-Torda County) 1912. C: L. Lajtha

In dance-style ♩ = 116 - 126

Jó bort i - szom, di - ó - fá - val tü - ze - lek,

De sem - mi - re va - ló le - gényt sze - re - tek.

Nem bá - nom én, ha sem - mi - re va - ló is,

Sem - mi - re va - ló va - gyok én ma - gam is.

I drink good wine, I use walnut wood for heating, / But I love a lad who is good for nothing. / I don't care even if he is good for nothing, / I'm good for nothing myself, too.)

The influence of pentatonic regions. We have mentioned the main regions where our songs were found. Among them, some Transylvanian regions in particular have so strong a pentatonic atmosphere that even melodies of other systems which find their way there become assimilated, pentatonicised. This is a melody in the usual major mode and is known all over the country. In its regular form it ends on B♭. But this variant becomes pentatonic in the last six or seven notes of the third line, and its ending renders the whole tune similar to examples Nos. 3 and 14, whose first half apparently remains in B♭ major while the second gradually moves into G minor. (It should be pointed out that pentatonic melodies should not really be approached with the concepts of modern harmony; they have nothing to do with major and minor, with heptatonic scales. It is only in the interests of clarity that we have used the terms of today's music.)

Epilogue. However interesting it would be to pursue the struggle between pentatony and more recent systems with hundreds of examples, enough has surely been said to arouse interest. We would only add that in recent decades pentatony has made many inroads into European music. The most varied genres, the highest as well as the lowest, are full of it. This is the origin of a certain kinship of idiom between works otherwise very distant from one another both externally and internally. The sources are different, in some cases it was the exotic, in others the ancient or the "folk" which was being sought; and everywhere imitation dulled it to the point of monotony. A phenomenon frequent in the movement of ideas can be observed here: independently of each other, various people set out from different points with different purposes and achieved similar results. No doubt, with its primitive but virile energy, pentatonic melodics provided a refreshing novelty after the over-chromaticised melodies of the previous period.

We cannot attempt to go into the essence of pentatony nor into comparing the pentatony of different peoples. We consider that pentatony is a key which can open many locked doors in the Hungarian melopoeia. A glance at the above table of motifs will show that many of the favourite phrases of Hungarian melodies are rooted in the pentatonic system.

One further point should be mentioned however. Although we cannot find pentatony in the music of the neighbouring peoples—where at least it is not such a basic phenomenon as it is in ours—there are nevertheless traces of it in the music of related peoples. To follow in the footsteps of Hungarian comparative linguistics by systematically comparing melodies would hardly be feasible today: we have too few reliable examples of the music of related peoples. On the other hand, the correspondence between Hungarian pentatonic tunes and the Cheremis tunes published in the Appendix (p. 87) of Bartók's book, or tunes of the Votyak and highland Cheremis peoples published by Ilmari Krohn, cannot be considered accidental.

Faced with these surprising correspondences we cannot but think that, however far the Cheremis people's country is from Csík and Zala Counties, there are ancient elements in the soul of a people that cannot be changed either by time or by distance.

(1917–1929)

HUNGARIAN FOLK MUSIC

This fairy-tale prince has many enemies—more than once have we felt their poisonous breath while trying to help him regain his realm—and they say that he is not a genuine prince at all. His peasant attire is not a disguise, but reality. Pretty little songs, they say, half praising and half disparaging, which express the primitive feelings of simple folk in a primitive form. A tulip-embroidered cloak—pretty on a peasant lad, but a "cultured" person could not wear it. Fields with wild flowers, etc.

Well, Hungarian folk music is much more than that. To begin with, it is not a "class" art. True, it is alive today only among the tillers of the soil—but it has to do with the whole of the Hungarian people. In the course of a thousand years, a great many rivulets flowed into it, as into a great reservoir. There is not a single experience of a single segment of the Hungarian people which has not left its mark on it. Therefore it is the mirror of the spirit of the entire Hungarian people.

Once, every people—and the Hungarians not so very long ago—formed an undivided unit. Even the increase in the number of social levels did not mean a greater cultural separation. As little as three hundred years ago, the same song could be heard in castle and hovel alike. Since then the castle has crumbled; if it still stands, its inhabitants are aliens or have become unfaithful to Hungarian songs. They have preserved some old treasures, the festive garb and the weapons, but they have forsaken the songs. The hovel has remained faithful: of the old treasures it has preserved that which is most precious—the ancient furniture of the soul. And of the whole Hungarian people... its own and also that which it had received from above. Songs sung three hundred years ago in the Esterházy palaces are not known there any more. But in the small village of Kolon in the Zoboralja region, Zuza Szalai, a wizened old woman still knows some of them. And, in Transylvania, so do some old white-stockinged Székelys. Rural Hungary has preserved the continuity of traditions. It is our job to take over from it and to cultivate them further.

The fire must not die out.

Hungarian folk music is an organ with a hundred tones; there is a tone for everything, from gentle jokes to tragedies. An entire evening is not long enough to sound every one of them. Today I want to refer to only one of its less familiar registers.

Even a layman will realise that the texts of groups II and III differ from what is

24

considered folk style in the strict sense of the term. In fact, they are remnants of our literature's first golden age of lyric poetry. From Balassa to Amadé, a great many anonymous poets of remarkable talent have left their mark here. Access to this literature is difficult: it is hidden in old manuscripts, even Thaly's popularised versions having become rarities now. Although most were songs and not just reading matter, scarcely a dozen of their tunes have survived. And those which have were written down by dilettanti. (Even then dilettantism weighed heavily on the destiny of Hungarian music.) It is an exception for one or another of the written transcriptions to indicate rhythm and key clearly. As a rule, even such exceptional cases are not really definite. Here is a tune from a manuscript of about 1767 found in the National Museum:

20

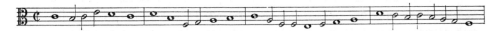

This key makes no sense. The beginning has been written down correctly by a later hand, one third higher:

E D E G F E F D A B C D

with the remark: *sic delineatur* ("thus it should be written"). But whoever wrote it still says nothing about the rhythm.

In 1902 Béla Vikár was lucky enough to record the following tune on the phonograph, sung by the old people of a small village in Udvarhely County:

(Béla Bartók transcribed it from the phonograph recording):

21

(It was sorrowful for me / To be born into the world, / That I have to suffer these things / Which I did not deserve.)

One glance is enough to show that the two melodies are essentially the same. But what a difference: first the skeleton, and even that is uncertain; here living flesh-and-blood reality. Pitch and rhythm are accurate. Old notations do not even attempt to write down the ornamental notes, although they are the essential seasoning of the whole period's music. Composers took this into account when writing their music and this is what the performers learned as the principal element of their craft (diminution). Only beautifully elaborated ornaments were needed to bring music to life. (This is easily understood by anyone who has heard Handel's *Suite* in D minor played by Edwin Fischer. The gipsies' flourishes, so often reviled, are to some extent the remains of this ancient ornamental art. More useful than the current criticism, or past enthusiasm, would have been to transcribe accurately tunes precisely as played by eminent gipsies.)

In addition to the nine songs of this kind presented today, there is a number of others whose texts originated from old written poetry. In most cases they were badly mutilated and only one or two stanzas survived. This also indicates that it is oral rather than written traditions which have kept them alive. For performance purposes it was necessary to complete them by drawing on old sources, with the stanzas in brackets.

I know the fact that one or two stanzas of an old poem are sung by country people does not prove that they had the same melody in the past. In fact, the same text is sometimes sung to two or three different tunes. But, as long as a certain text is connected with only one melody, it can be assumed that it was also sung with that melody in the past. This is almost certain in the case of No. III. 4, Ádám Horváth's manuscript (1813) presenting it with the same text. He had, however, no known contact with the Székely people of Transylvania.

No. II. 1 has two variants from different places. The text is in all probability by Balassa.

Zsigmond Móricz also found Rákóczi's *Complaint* with a similar melody at Nagy-ecsed. A few other songs of the *kuruc* period were also still alive about 1910. It is a pity that Kálmán Thaly, that tireless collector of texts, did not see to having the melodies written down exactly, since many were still widely known at that time (about 1860). Káldy's *kuruc* songs, which have become widely known since 1890, are not original but second-hand collections, taken partly from printed material. We can see that even today this song lives in a much fresher and more original form among the people of Szalonta than it does in Káldy's notes.

According to Thaly the *Gyöngyösi körtéfa* (Gyöngyös Pear-Tree) refers to Rákóczi's field hospital at Gyöngyös, and therefore he considers it contemporary.

Thus, while only the texts of our old poets' works were known to have survived, folk traditions had preserved the melodies as well. In addition, these traditions explain the hieroglyphics of some old notations of melodies.

The more valuable part of the Hungarian *Monumenta Musicae* springs not from the dust of archives, but from a living source—the memory of the people. How far back this memory can reach we do not know even today. Surely much farther than the sixteenth century. *This* is the history of Hungarian music—one has only to learn how to read it.

For twenty years now, in the course of our collecting, we have had to listen to many remarks about the uselessness of this work. One of our elderly well-wishers grumbled about the fact that someone who could himself compose should spend his time in rural areas searching for songs that every servant-girl knows.

Is it not the symptom of a grave illness that the most beautiful songs, created by Hungarian musical genius over the course of a thousand years, were known only to servant-girls and old people? Was it not an urgent duty to learn these songs from them and to hand them back to the whole Hungarian people? Rural areas are now bidding farewell to the old traditions; their young people are not carrying them on any more. It is our turn.

The fire must not die out.

(1925)

WHAT IS HUNGARIAN IN MUSIC?

When I was asked to answer the question appearing in the title, a series of articles came to my mind which I read a good thirty years ago in a French periodical. The music critic Paul Landormy put a similar question to some outstanding personalities of French music who were then still alive, namely d'Indy, Bruneau, Duparc, Dukas and Debussy, and also to Romain Rolland, who was then known only for his excellent work as a French music historian and critic.

I read the replies with even greater interest, for the question had greatly occupied the attention of our generation, too. We were most surprised that this question had also been raised by the great French nation. For in the course of its musical life, dating back several centuries, the French nation had created a music that was original and different from everything else; in other words, French music.

The contradictory answers show how difficult the question was. In the opinion of one of them, for example, Berlioz had written music that was the most French of all, while according to others Berlioz was the least French. Yet one would think that it would not be hard to reveal the fundamental characteristic elements of a nation that has a recorded history of one and a half thousand years, and then to find in its music those elements that best reflected these characteristics.

Here in Hungary the difficulties are even greater. We have known Hungarian music, or music that can be termed Hungarian in its style, for barely a hundred or a hundred-and-fifty years; and so far it has been impossible to form a homogeneous picture of the Hungarian character from the history of the nation. It has, therefore, hardly been possible to reveal the connection between the Hungarian character and Hungarian music.

Besides, it is easier to *suggest* national characteristics in works of art than to approach them by way of analysis.

We do have a firm point, however, which is based precisely on music, where we can dig our toes in and seek for "what is Hungarian in music", and this is folk music, in its most ancient layers.

If we select and set aside all pieces from the songs of the people that we have in common with neighbouring nations, or originate from Hungarian or foreign composed music, or reveal the influence of any European culture, what we are left with

28

can hardly be anything else but the ancient, natural music of the Magyars, who once conquered the Hungary of today.

We have direct evidence of this, for similar music can be found even today in the regions where the Magyars lived prior to the Conquest, among peoples whose ancestors they had met or perhaps intermarried with.

We know that the conquering Magyars did not constitute a homogeneous racial formula; but they were much more than that, for they were a people of superior values—a military, political and cultural organisation of tribes of different origins, and even different languages. The music of these tribes may also have differed from one another originally. But as a uniform language emerged, it is quite probable that a uniform music developed, too, perhaps by the equalisation of principles of form that were once contradictory. Two such principles appearing together and separately have survived up to this very day in our folksongs. One is the principle of pentatony, the other that of parallel structures. Our first example demonstrates one of them, while the second demonstrates both:

22

(My dog Rajna is barking, / My lover, the brown one, is coming. / Though he's brown, he's no gipsy, / He really does love me truly.)

23

(Fly, peacock, fly / Up onto the County Hall / To bring freedom to the poor prisoners.)

Here we have two types of tunes, isolated and unknown in today's Hungarian environment, but closely connected with an old Central-Asian musical culture, and representing its outermost branch, which reaches as far as the Lajta river.

29

Hungarians have a great many kinds of songs, but this type is never missing where Hungarians live. If we marked it in red on the map a darker hue would find its way to the Székely region, Transdanubia, and the area where the Palóc ethnic group lives, but there would be no spot inhabited by Hungarians that would not be marked, even if diluted to pink, to indicate the traces of ancient Hungarian music.

What do these traces reveal? That the spiritual foundation of the Hungarian people has not altered in a thousand years; that links with other peoples did not shake their original system of music nor change their musical way of thinking.

The Turks stayed here for a hundred-and-fifty years. We do not know what music they brought; if it was Southern-Turkish, its Arab–Indian–Gipsy scales have left only scattered traces.

For five hundred years now gipsies have been begging for bread, lamenting and playing music here. The Hungarians listened to them, tolerated them and fed them, but they did not adopt their music. The Hungarians only warmed to the gipsies when the latter learnt, with clever mimicry, to reproduce Hungarian music for the Hungarians.

Like their language, the music of the Hungarians is also terse and lapidary, forming a number of masterpieces that are small but weighty. Some tunes of a few notes have withstood the tempests of centuries, as if they had been carved in stone. Their forms are so final that they do not appear to have changed in a thousand years. The exact counterpart of one song and another has also emerged among the related peoples, as if they had only stopped singing together yesterday.

The Hungarians have therefore an original and singular musical mother-tongue. It is a living music in which all Hungarians—except the middle and upper classes—still meet and understand one another today. Indeed, anyone who does not want to exclude himself from the musical community of a nation has either to re-learn the forgotten musical mother-tongue of his ancestors, like István Széchenyi, who had to learn the Hungarian language again, or, if he has come from another country and wants to live here, to learn it as a new language as Ankerschmidt did.

"But how can we advance from the short songs to higher art forms?" the doubting Thomas of thirty years ago would ask. Just think of the mustard-seed, "which indeed is the least of all seeds: but when it is grown, it is the greatest among herbs and becomes a tree, so that the birds of the air come and lodge in the branches thereof".

Three things are essential for a national literature of music to come into being: first, traditions; second, individual talent; and third, a spiritual community of many people that accept the manifestation of individual talent as its own.

There is no fertile soil without traditions. On the other hand, traditions in themselves do not create higher forms of art, however much alive they may be.

In one of his lectures Elek Petrovics spoke about paintings in which the faces, weapons, and garments were all Hungarian, but the pictures themselves were not. There are certain pieces of music in which all the motifs are Hungarian and yet the piece as a whole is not.

It is sure that the putting together of folk motifs will not produce a higher organic form. For this can only be brought about by individual talent, possessing greater concepts and special creative powers.

Why was folksong research really necessary thirty to forty years ago?

Because even the greatest talent is unable to flourish in a vacuum. During that period there was no homogeneous musical awareness or public spirit in music here. We had just reached the peak of half a century's import of foreign music. Our musical life was swamped with foreign music, particularly Italian and German.

It is true that we had made considerable progress in musical culture. But together with the implements of culture we also imported the substance and whole atmosphere of an alien culture that penetrated into everything. All Hungarian experiments were dwarfed beside this.

At about this time dilettantism in music began to monopolise the guise of national-ism. A rift ensued in which Hungarian music was set in opposition to classical, that is foreign, music. Educated people turned a deaf ear to Hungarian music, while the others excommunicated all higher forms of music, under the pretext that it was for-eign. They did not want to know the Shakespeares and Michelangelos of music.

This problem should have been solved long ago, but it still remains unsolved today. Those who are cultured musically should be rendered more Hungarian and the Hun-garians made more cultured in music. As a matter of fact, it is an interminable task requiring a permanently alert and balanced musical policy. This is the only way in which a spiritual community can be created, the active participation of which is imperative in the establishment of a living national art. This is taught by the whole history of culture. In its most flourishing period every nation was unified in feelings and tastes alike. The characteristic feature of periods of decline is that the educated people and the masses fail to understand one another.

The significance of folk traditions in the past thirty years has become common knowledge to such an extent that today there can be no doubt that it is impos-sible for anyone to become a Hungarian composer without having experienced them.

But Hungary is also part of Europe, so she must live among European traditions as well. The purpose in life of a country and a people situated at the point of impact between East and West can only be to belong to both, and to smooth out and blend the contradictions between the two. Seen from this point of view the Hungarian who is not European is worthless; and so is the European quality if it is not Hungarian at the same time.

We can and must learn from the musical culture of all nations. In its character that of Italy lies closest to us because it is also based mainly on singing. But we must learn from the Germans and French as well.

Let us not forget that every great national school is the meeting point of different cultures, and even races. The history of music abounds in examples of this.

In the sixteenth century the Flemish Willaert found his way (from Buda!) to Venice and laid the foundations of the great Italian school. In the seventeenth century the

Italian Lully launched a new French style in Paris. The German Schütz introduced the Italian school into his own country, which resulted in a new German style. In the eighteenth century an Alsatian German, called Johann Schobert, arrived in Paris and created a new style there, acknowledged by every Frenchman as the most French of all. The national styles during the nineteenth century were pioneered by immigrant German musicians in almost every country. This happened in Hungary, as if it was always the touch of foreign genius that aroused the national spirit of a country to new life.

The great personalities, following the pioneers, also combined several cultures in themselves. The greatest among them, like Bach or Mozart, maintained connections with practically every trend of their predecessors and contemporaries with the result that their influence reached far into posterity. And yet, these giants express their national characteristics much more vigorously than lesser talents who rely on national traditions with an exclusive one-sidedness.

However contradictory it may seem, it is true that the more we are linked with European culture the greater our own culture will grow. It is enough just to think of our great poets. By the age of twenty-five Petőfi had learned only German, French and English in addition to Latin. Had he lived longer he would certainly have joined Arany in his studies of Greek and Italian. Self-imposed seclusion and lack of culture will blight national features.

What musical features are characteristic of Hungarian folk music? In general, it is active rather than passive, an expression of will rather than emotion. Aimless grieving and tears of merriment do not appear in our music. Even the Székely laments radiate resolute energy.

Hungarian folk music has a rhythm that is sharp, definite and varied. Its melody has buoyancy and freedom of movement, and does not unfold timidly from a premeditated harmonic basis. Its form is concise, proportionate, lucid and transparent. The form is lucid, for we always know where we are. By examining an extract from a folksong it is possible to determine whether it is the beginning, middle or end of the song. If Hungarian composed music is really inspired by the spirit of folk music, and wishes to continue the traditions, it must contain all these qualities. If its rhythm is diffuse, its melody contrived, and its form dim or too intricate, then it will hardly meet with Hungarian tastes. Of the worlds of "Homer and Ossian" the former is akin to the Hungarian one. The Greek-Latin sense of form is closer to the Hungarian soul than the mists of the North, and therefore it only accepts those German composers who composed following the Latin culture of forms: from Bach to Beethoven and from Schütz to Brahms. Thus, Reger, for example, however much he is admired by the Germans, will have hardly any Hungarian adherents.

With respect to instruments, Hungarians seem to prefer softer string and woodwind instruments to the noisy brass. That is why they have an aversion to brass bands and jazz. True, a symphony orchestra may need all types of instruments, but the Hungarians have been attached to the traditional chamber-music-like composition of gipsy bands for so long that this may suggest a particular preference in their taste for instruments.

If we consider all creations produced so far by Hungarians, they seem in general to be the work of people of ideas and apt originality rather than people of diligent, indefatigable elaboration. For this reason, and also due to their sense of form related to that of the Latin peoples, Hungarians will hardly ever produce mammoth works, cut to the dimensions of pieces by Bruckner or Mahler. It is quite probable that even Wagnerian longwindedness will remain alien to them.

On the other hand, Hungarian audiences simply must be raised from their present primitive state of musical comprehension. For today an average Hungarian can neither comprehend nor follow the musical structure of any piece that is longer than a short song. Is this also a national characteristic? No, it is purely musical ignorance, a musical wasteland, the breaking up of which should be the mission of the schools.

To enable the national spirit to express itself in a higher art form as well, it is necessary to raise the cultural level in the music of the whole nation.

Then the nation would not be frightened away from really serious classical music by wishy-washy, insipid pieces. The erroneous belief that only light music can be Hungarian would then come to an end; and the antagonism of ideas when referring to Hungarian and classical music on an either—or basis would be terminated.

As a rule the character of a piece of music can be Hungarian to varying degrees. As when wine is mixed with water: a strong wine even if diluted with double the quantity of water will still retain its wine flavour; on the other hand, a chemical analysis can prove the presence of even a few drops of wine in water that does not taste of wine at all.

In this way even trashy light music can be said to possess Hungarian elements. And what is more, pure dilettantism itself can fleetingly show a Hungarian feature here and there. The durability of Hungarian characteristics, however, is only ensured by complete artistic proficiency.

The present moment in history is favourable: the masses, their senses still sound and unadulterated, must be introduced to musical culture. Why could something good, in fact the very best, not be offered to them right away?

The broader the masses who come into contact with genuine musical culture, the more frequently will compositions be created whose atmosphere, content, form and life are Hungarian. Then one will have to ask less and less frequently, "What is Hungarian in music?" For everybody will know.

(1939)

THE ROLE OF THE FOLKSONG
IN RUSSIAN
AND HUNGARIAN MUSIC

Lecture

The idea that even the poor man can mean something in culture first appeared some-where in the intellectual upheaval preceding the French Revolution. Even in its most modest manifestation it was a revolutionary idea, for at that time culture and art existed only for the well-born, well-dressed, rich and leisured classes.

From the time of Rousseau and Herder attention turned in the direction of the poetry of the poor. For the time being, the only aspect of it that was emphasised was that it could have something to say, even to the cultured man. But this, too, was something new and spread only gradually. Even a century and a half later, when we set out to collect folksongs, there were many cultured people who queried, "What can these stupid peasants possibly know that could be of any interest to a cultured man?"

First of all it was the literary and linguistic significance of folk poetry that was re-cognised. Everywhere it was only after one or two generations that musical interest followed literary interest. But its significance was not the same in every country.

In France, Germany and Italy, where a great literature had already been created long before through the musical culture's blossoming, folksong had already been absorbed into art music in earlier centuries, or at least enriched some branches of it. Here the interest aroused in folksong at the turn of the eighteenth-nineteenth cen-turies did not for the moment have much influence on art music.

However in countries where old art music hardly existed, it did have an immediate style-forming effect. Starting from their folksongs, the Slavonic and Scandinavian peoples set about the creation of a national musical style; around the same time we Hungarians also joined in. The reason for their having achieved results sooner than we did is simple: they struck upon their true folksongs sooner.

Russian music set out on this road with Glinka, and with greater or smaller fluctuations has remained on it to this very day.

It is natural that every new generation, if it is talented, does things differently from its predecessors. The reaction to every vigorous national trend is the counter-trend of internationalism. The Rimsky-Korsakov–Mussorgsky period was thus followed by Tchaikovsky, Rubinstein, Skriabin and Glazunov, who wanted to be European rather than Russian and felt they had to make a choice between the two. After these, the Russian voice flared up once more: mainly in Stravinsky. It is true that he then produced in his own person the reaction to himself in his later neutral, international works.

We are not yet sufficiently familiar with the works of the more recent Soviet composers to have an adequate view of them. Some, principally Shostakovich, appear to stand for the international trend; others, like Khachaturian and Kabalevsky, now here among us, do not yet consider the inspirational strength of the folksong to be exhausted.

When we began to journey on this road, the Russian example already stood before us. Liszt was personally acquainted with the Russian composers, he studied their works thoroughly, and even performed them in Weimar. He himself wished to do something similar.

For his *Rhapsodies* however, he was not able to get at real folksongs, and because he lived abroad he was not able to search for them. His collectors made their selections from only the surface layers and so he himself did not manage to delve more deeply.

The Russian composers came closer to their people because they lived among them, they spoke their language. For their own melodies they discovered original forms of polyphony preserving and emphasising the characteristics of the melody. Their own works thus retained the atmosphere of folk music even though they raised it to a higher power, so to speak.

Later, Mussorgsky was particularly stamped as a dilettante, and indeed Rimsky-Korsakov even arranged and corrected his works. Now we know that much of it was not dilettantism requiring correction but inspired originality, which even Rimsky-Korsakov himself did not fully comprehend.

Liszt did understand it, as we know from his letters, but apart from him there were very few who did. It needed the arrival of Debussy to discover Mussorgsky for Europe, and for Hungarians, too. (It was in 1911 at a concert of the New Hungarian Music Society [UMZE] that we first heard a Mussorgsky work: the *Nursery* song cycle.)

After Liszt, and partly during his lifetime, came the international reaction against the Hungarian branch of which it fell to our lot to struggle. It further became our function to carry out here what had been achieved in Russia by the Rimsky-Korsakov–Mussorgsky group. The composers are usually at one and the same time folksong collectors and editors. The overall picture of the style is naturally different on account of the different nature of the melodic material. On the other hand the whole European style has also changed since then and has naturally left some traces on the style of every contemporary. But the relationship between composers and the national traditions can only now develop into such as was already present with the Russians at that time.

What is to follow? That we cannot know. This much is certain: the style-forming strength of folk tradition has not yet been exhausted by us; there is plenty left for those coming after us. All the more so as the impoverished Hungarian will only now begin to enter the cultural world, not merely as giver and inspirer but as consumer as well. It is only in the future that the liberated people can reach higher music as an appreciating public, and there is no question that the basis of their taste for a considerable time (or permanently) will be their own tradition.

For it is indeed true that the setting aside of folk costume and the insatiable desire for the discarding of folk traditions goes hand in hand with the flight from the peasant way of life. But it is easier to put off a coat than either a language or music. And if that desire becomes so great, and with the help of the schools carries the people to a point where they become capable of understanding more demanding music, then there is no doubt that they will prefer those elements in which they explicitly or implicitly recognise themselves.

The ambience of the Liszt rhapsodies was that of the intelligentsia. The relationship between the Hungarian intellectuals and the people is a quite special socio-historical problem. The intelligentsia inhabiting our towns is to a large extent of foreign origin and began to speak Hungarian only a few generations ago. They neither have nor could have any roots in the people whatsoever. The spiritual world and the music of the people is foreign to them. But it also became so for the intellectual with roots in the people, of village origin, and who even lives there among the people. It is partly social consciousness of rank, and partly cultural aspirations that increasingly separated him from the people.

There is a similar phenomenon elsewhere, too. One of the most typical forms of cultural ambition is the import of foreign culture, which is considered to be better; or alternatively home produce developed under its influence.

In the first half of the nineteenth century a style of song with a foreign flavour to it developed also in Russia, the so-called *romance*; we were able to become familiar with the last blossoming of this through the performances of the Stepat Balalaika Orchestra. This kind of song stood in the way of the pioneers of Russian music in precisely the same way as our own town art-songs did with us.

From all this it follows that—at least providing its spiritual content and cultural quality does not undergo a radical change—the intelligentsia can only have a secondary role to play in the formation of public taste in music. For this reason, and also because of the future development of Hungarian music, it is urgently necessary to make the widest range of people participants in music culture.

There are strictly speaking only two kinds of music: good and bad. We have to welcome with open arms good foreign music in appropriate doses, since this is where we meet the masterpieces of world literature without which we cannot live. Bad foreign and bad native music are equally damaging, like the plague. The cure for them has not yet been discovered but the fight goes on against them in every country of the world, with greater or less success. It is a favourable moment in this battle when an opportunity to get to know good music suddenly opens to great masses of people. We are now living in such a moment. Many think that the new, still unspoiled masses cannot reach good music straight away. First they have to get beyond the various kinds of bad music before they can, by a slow purifying process, reach the good. I do not agree with this view. Why can the good not be given straight away to those who do not yet know either the good or the bad? Anyone whose taste is still undefiled will undoubtedly be pleased by the good. And if he once gets to know the good and comes to like it, what is bad will have difficulty in ingratiating itself with him.

It is self-evident that this protective inoculation must be given as early as possible. Good taste cannot be inherited, but it can be corrupted very early. It is for this reason that education to good music must be started in the school or indeed in the kindergarten. It is for this reason that I have for more than twenty years devoted a considerable part of my time to the improvement of musical life in the schools. I do not grudge that time since even, though I have been able to write fewer works because of it, I have to a certain extent contributed to the increase in the numbers of those who understand good music.

If we build up our school system in this spirit and if we make a little more time for music in the curriculum, it will not be without results. We have to establish already in school children the belief that music belongs to everyone and is, with a little effort, available to everyone.

We Hungarians are all the more obliged to travel this road since more costly means towards the popularisation of music—such as we hear of in the Soviet Union, for example—are out of the question for us because of our poverty.

But what can we learn from the Soviet Union? First of all, respect for art and the artist. So far we have respected the artist largely only after his death. We have left him to die and then by means of a splendid funeral we have sought to set right what we had done against him during his life. The artist would gladly dispense with the magnificent Hungarian funeral if we were to afford him more understanding and appreciation in his lifetime.

We have already observed that Russian music was from the outset an encouraging and inspiring example. Here at home, alongside the one-sided German trend, Russian music was scarcely to be heard with the sole exception of Tchaikovsky. To hear Russian music we had to go to Paris. Since then *Boris Godunov* has also reached Budapest, but we are still in arrears. We cannot understand the most recent Russian composers either unless we know what came before them better, just as it is not possible to understand Stravinsky completely without Rimsky-Korsakov. A survey of Russian music can therefore not disregard historical order at least not until the greatest gaps in knowledge have been filled in.

In the large-scale music folklore work of the Soviet Union the music of the related peoples can claim to be of special interest to us. One after the other these smaller peoples are now rising up out of the mists of anonymity; the collection and publication of their folksongs is one of the first signs of their national consciousness. In amazement we notice from these how many ancient elements there are in our own folk music, since everything that coincides with theirs points to ancient times of co-existence, as there is no knowledge of more recent contact which would have made transmission possible.

This knowledge is of great value to us, quite apart from its purely scientific significance. Because of this we know we are a branch of an ancient tree, our roots are deep, and since we differ from so many peoples, we do have something new to say to others.

And even if since the French Revolution the dignity of every man and his right to life are increasingly generally recognised, we believe that sooner or later this will also become true of the human community, so that the rights of the smallest nation will be recognised and it will be left intact with all the elements without which it cannot live its full life and cannot fulfil its cultural function.

The Hungarian has—in defence of his mere existence—for centuries spilt as much blood as would be enough for the whole life of a nation.

Whenever he was allowed to live—for short moments—he set to immediately, so as to speak out in the culture of the world what only he was called to say, so as to build up what no one else could build up in place of him. These semi-pronounced words and mutilated buildings, begun over and over again a hundred times, show that whoever refused to allow this nation to live, destroyed not only men, not only physical life, but murdered a whole culture.

Those, on the other hand, who let us live and protect our life, protect a growth which means joy to more than us ourselves.

Endre Ady did not find a flower on the "Magyar Fallow":

> *I walk on meadows run to weed,*
> *on fields of burdock and of mallow.*
> *I know this rank and ancient ground—*
> *this is the Magyar fallow.*
>
> *I bow down to the sacred soil;*
> *this virgin ground is gnawed I fear.*
> *You skyward groping seedy weeds,*
> *are there no flowers here?*
>
> *While I look at the slumbering earth,*
> *the twisting vines encircle me,*
> *and scent of long dead flowers steep*
> *my senses amorously.*
>
> *Silence. I am dragged down and roofed*
> *and lulled in burdock and in mallow.*
> *A mocking wind goes whisking by*
> *above the mighty fallow.*

(Translated by Anton N. NYERGES, *Poems of Ady*.
Hungarian Cultural Foundation, Buffalo, N.Y., 1969.)

I would contradict Ady's fatal vision. His own work is proof: flowers do grow here. Just don't let them be trampled down, let them blossom, then marvels will be seen. If we were left to live in peace for just one hundred years, this little country would be a paradise on earth.

(1946)

CHILDREN'S GAMES

Preface to the First Volume of
"Corpus Musicae Popularis Hungaricae"

With this volume the Hungarian Academy of Sciences begins paying off the debt of a century. Item 11 of the minutes taken at its session on the 9th of January, 1832, reads of follows: "The letter of the people of Esztergom County has been read informing this Society of a publication, issued on the 21st of November 1831, on the propagation and fostering of the Hungarian language. It requests this Society to meet the need for special expressions and terms used in different crafts; to have folksongs produced with a view to endearing the Hungarian language to compatriots of other tongues and finally to have lessons and lectures written and published on the texts of wedding and other national customs. The President is requested to thank the County of Esztergom, in the name of this Society, for the information it has submitted and for the confidence shown in this Society, moreover, to inform the County of the steps this Society has already taken with respect to the first item, having asked its members living in all parts of the country assiduously to collect the expressions and terms used in all kinds of crafts. This Society has also taken steps with regard to the folksongs and, as soon as a work of merit of this kind has been received, it will be published. Concerning the third matter, this Society remarks that it is not averse to taking up the subject and will, in due time, work on it; however, for this purpose much preparatory work and the obtaining of information from different regions are needed."

The text of the letter itself is as follows: "To the Honourable Hungarian Learned Society. The way in which we endeavour to promote the spread, fostering and flourishing of the Hungarian Language can be examined in greater detail from the statutory decision attached hereto. In order to contribute to the promotion of the Public Weal, we beg the Honourable Hungarian Learned Society to deign to supply the words used in different crafts, since there is a great scarcity in them. Also to have Hungarian songs produced fit to meet the taste of common people in order to encourage those who are inexperienced in the Hungarian Language and thus to cause them to grow fond of same. At the same time to vouchsafe to have short explanations and lectures written on the sayings customary at weddings and other national ceremonies. We remain, the Honourable Hungarian Learned Society's ever ready servants, hearty and benevolent Friends and Brethren, the People of Esztergom County, at our General Assembly on the 21st of St. Andrew's month, in the Year of 1831."

At the session of the Academy held on the 26th of November in the same year, item 400 reads: "The letter of Komárom County's people has been read; in it this Society is requested to compensate for the deficiencies in words used in different crafts and to have songs, suitable to make the language better liked, written and published. In consequence of this appeal it has been decided that the Secretary should apply to the members to collect or to have their acquaintances collect the words of crafts fashionable among Hungarian artisans who live in the various places where the members have their residence or in their regions and also to collect either the explanations of these terms or the words corresponding to them in other languages. At the same time the appeal for the collecting of folksongs should also be repeated. The Noble County of Komárom should be informed that steps have been taken in both matters and that this Society will always bear in mind the County's further requests in the future; moreover, that it hopes that the collecting of folksongs can be commenced soon."

Indeed, the appeal had its results, because the General Assembly of the Academy held on 9th November, 1833, decided on the publication:

"IVth resolution, on Folksongs,
of the General Assembly, 7th session, 9th November, 1833.
Item LIV.

Ordinary members Mihály Vörösmarty and Ferencz Schedel having reported that from the ten collections of folksongs handed over to them for perusal they had already selected the material for a couple of volumes... the Session has laid down the following principles on which an agreement has been reached. A collection of folksongs can be prepared either for the people in order to ennoble their taste and morals or else for the psychologist, who will be able to deduce the people's character from such original manifestations. Included in the former can be (1) real folksongs already popular among the people, with such changes as would serve the above-mentioned two purposes and yet would be produced in the spirit of the people so as to endear them to the people; or (2) such songs as, though written by writers, are similarly inspired by the spirit of the people. With respect to these latter it is particularly desirable that national virtues and the heroic deeds of the nation be borne in mind. In the second kind of collection exclusively such songs are to be included as have come into being among the people, moreover songs in their original form without any embellishment or improvement. On the grounds of the appeals of the Counties of Komárom and Esztergom and by its own convictions, this Society, at present, gives priority to the former for its useful purpose and recommends the printing of a collection to be compiled in this spirit. The collection would appear in two kinds of publications: (a) in small booklets economically printed for the people and (b) in better print and with music for cultured readers. Appointing ordinary members Mihály Vörösmarty and Ferencz Schedel as editors, the General Assembly submits the matter to the Honourable Directorate for appropriating the costs."

And yet, nothing happened for eleven years but a further appeal. Item 313 of the session of December 11th, 1837: "In sending out the *Name-Book* it has been decided that a circular letter should be attached to same. In this letter the old members are requested again and the new ones called upon by the present session always to pay close attention (a) to the words and idioms of dialects as well as to terms used by craftsmen and to proverbs, (b) to folk tales, folksongs and customs", etc.

In item 29 of the session held on 2nd January, 1844, we can read the following: "The letter of Baron Miklós Jósika, President of the Kisfaludy Society, has been read. On behalf of that Society he declared the intention to publish a collection of Hungarian folksongs and folk tales. He knew that, about ten years ago, this Learned Society had planned a collection of folksongs, in which the living songs are published in a somewhat *nobler and more attractive form* so as to spread good taste among the common people and that, in response to its appeal, this Learned Society had received smaller or bigger collections from several places. On the other hand, the intention of the Kisfaludy Society was quite different in this respect, for it wished to collect the folk tales and songs *as they really and typically are* and to put them at the cultured reader's disposal rather than to give them back to the people. Therefore they asked this Learned Society not to grudge from the Kisfaludy Society the use of collections of this kind to be found in its archives. After a lengthy argument in the course of which some members wished the collections to be put at the Kisfaludy Society's disposal, the more so as the present financial state of the Academy of Sciences had postponed for long the execution of the plan in question, furthermore, as the plan was quite different from the intention the Kisfaludy Society had intimated, on the other hand, although they did not oppose the submitting of the material in question for subsequent publication, for they considered the plan of the Kisfaludy Society most commendable, other members deemed that to order such a transfer of the collections would be outside the scope of the session. Therefore they proposed that the matter be submitted, with a recommendation, to the next General Assembly— and this has been passed as a resolution by the majority. At the proposal of ordinary member János Fogarasi it has been decided that the Kisfaludy Society be notified that care and attention should also be paid, as much as possible, to the music of the folksongs to be collected, so that several valuable instances of these essential and characteristic accessories of the Hungarian people's poetry be not only saved from oblivion and put at the disposal of the cultured public but that—by being edited by such as understand them in a perfect Hungarian spirit—they be saved from the fate of numerous Hungarian songs already published, and distorted, mainly by foreign musicians."

According to item XIII of the General Assembly held on December 17th "it has been decided that the collection of songs in question be submitted to the Kisfaludy Society for their use..."

From that time on, the Learned Society laid aside for a while the cause of folksongs. In 1846 Erdélyi's first volume appeared, to be followed by the second in 1847 and by the third, the thinnest, in 1848. The texts mostly originated from the manuscripts of the Academy. We have not found any trace of what it was that Vörösmarty and Schedel had selected. Erdélyi did not make mention of this either, thus the selecting and editing must have been his own work. Nobody has ever investigated his sources or his relationship to them, although this should have been a very urgent task—indeed one holding out the promise of extraordinarily edifying lessons—for literary historians. He published only twelve melodies, edited by Fogarasi and Travnyik, tunes with piano accompaniment, which came out in 1847. In these two booklets he published only one stanza of the texts, referring to the rest by the numbers of the songs in volumes I and II, but never to those in volume III. In his prefaces and the enumeration of the manuscripts of the Academy, Erdélyi gave account of over a thousand tunes. What has become of the other melodies?

In 1852 the Academy asked Erdélyi to return the manuscripts. He answered in the following letter. "Sárospatak, November 23rd, 1852. Your Honour, Mr. Secretary, In compliance with your request I am returning herewith the collections of folk poetry received from the Honourable Learned Society, with the request to see to it that the same should not be demanded from me any more. The musical notations that may have been attached to them are not with me. The Learned Society and particularly Mr. Fogarasi suggested that the Kisfaludy Society should take steps with a view to the songs also being put down in musical notation; at that time I handed over half of the musical notation to Mr. Fogarasi and the other to Mr. Travnyik; they are now there. However, very much has happened since then. It would be no wonder if all were lost. I remain, Your Honour's obedient servant, János Erdélyi."

Erdélyi's guess proved to be right: all trace of the music was lost, with the exception of about forty tunes written beside their texts. Evidently, the others were in separate music books. Of them only one has been found so far: Dániel Mindszenty's collection of 88 songs, mentioned in Erdélyi's list under Nos. 52–63. They emerged at an auction in 1941 and found their way back to the Academy's collection of manuscripts after a hundred years' vicissitudes. Although not in the original manuscript but a later copy in the hand of the collector, the collection of Dénes Kiss, a law student of Pápa in 1844 and later lawyer at Komárom, has also been found. This collection figures in Erdélyi's list under No. 44. The 122 texts in it fit to perfection the series of melodies preserved under No. 1097 in the manuscript archives of the National Széchényi Library.

Thus, the publication of melodies came to naught. And yet, from the thousands of melodies at Erdélyi's disposal a large-scale collection of abiding value could have been born. And if only a few hundred well chosen tunes had been brought to light before 1848, our music might have set out half a century earlier on the course which in poetry had been pointed to by Petőfi and Arany.

True, publication with piano accompaniment considerably increased costs, and let us not forget that even Erdélyi's first volume could not have appeared unless "a patriot unwilling to disclose his name" had undertaken to publish the collection, which amounted to thirty gatherings. But that age was incapable of conceiving publication in any other way (and this was the curse on folksong publication for the next half-century), so everything, with the exception only of Színi (1865), was burdened with a piano accompaniment, which, on the one hand, hampered the spread of the publications and, on the other, did not contribute to the development of music because it hardly reached an artistic level. The other drawback was that, since the interest in folk music was not satisfied at the right time, it gradually faded. In the beginning the nineteenth-century popular plays about the peasantry propagated genuine folksongs but later they spread more and more the songs of newly emerging composers. The publications, copying one another, reiterated the same one or two hundred tunes and always mixed them with composed songs. The first major collection of a higher standard, the seven volumes of Bartalus (1873–1896) came late and did not bring enough good or enough new songs to revive the fading interest. According to the Preface to his seventh volume Bartalus arranged the tunes in such a way that "on the one hand, the mood of the songs be also expressed musically, on the other hand, that in every one of them not only a subordinate accompaniment but a small and independent work of piano literature should also be provided." He attempted more than he could cope with; and what he could have coped with, i.e. the exact recording of single-line tunes and their separation from composed songs, he failed to do. Thus he could not satisfy the requirements either of specialists or of the public at large. Considering the quantity and cost of the individual pieces in his publication five or ten times as many tunes could have been published. Many a thing happened between 1873 and 1896 and by the time the last volume of Bartalus had been published, a noticesheet put up at the Millenary Exhibition with the melody taken down in notation from Béla Vikár's phonograph recording of the ballad of *László Fehér* meant the dawn of a new era in folksong research.

For want of material no scientific examination of folksongs could be performed. True the Academy supported Bartalus's publication and did much in the field of music besides this: it published first Mátray's and then Bartalus's papers dealing with the history of music, and also assisted Gusztáv Szénfy's folksong research. His collection, allegedly comprising two thousand tunes, has vanished without trace. On the other hand the Kisfaludy Society, which, in Erdélyi's words (Vol. I, p. VII), "was in charge not only of collecting the songs but also of publishing their melodies", more and more regarded folksongs from a biased, literary angle. Although it also supported Bartalus's publication it did not see to a joint—or at least parallel—publication of melody and text, and thus the body and the soul of the folksong became more and more separated from each other. Only in two of the eleven volumes of his collection did Bartalus allow a modest space for tunes. In 1911 he re-edited Kriza's collection *Vadrózsák* (Wild Roses) without the melodies, in spite of the fact that by then the majority of the melodies had been found. Meanwhile music publishers glutted the market with such a mass of different song-books, of "a hundred-and-one, a hundred-and-two, a hundred-and-three" Hungarian songs, into which, here and there, some folksongs also strayed, that public opinion could justifiably believe that the question of folksongs had been solved.

Only narrower circles of specialists took note of Vikár's collecting. The present writer began his collecting tours in 1905 and Béla Bartók in 1906, since studying the printed collections and listening to Vikár's cylinders had convinced us that real folksong research would begin only then. In the meantime the Academy published in 1908 Bertalan Fabó's work, *A magyar népdal zenei fejlődése* (The Musical Evolution of the Hungarian Folksong), but, deplorably, did so without expert revision, which then gave rise to János Seprődy's scathing criticism. Fabó did not know the results of new collections and worked on the basis of old and partly erroneous material without any scientific method. Thus his book in no way promoted the cause of the folksong. In 1913 we thought that the Kisfaludy Society might devote a part of the high amount of state subsidy put at its disposal to the correct publication of folksongs and we submitted to them an application to this end. No answer came to this application but 1914 did come* and for a long time after that nothing of this kind could be thought of. Nor could the idea of the essence of the folksong, namely, that it is a complete work only together with its tune, be brought to prevail in Vol. XIV of the collection of the Kisfaludy Society which was published in 1924.

In the thirties interest in ethnography was revived and such a large-scale work as *A Magyarság Néprajza* (The Ethnography of the Hungarian People) was able to come out in two editions. At Zoltán Gombocz's insistence the Academy of Sciences got in touch with us concerning the publication of recent collections and in 1933 (exactly a hundred years after it had passed its first resolution) it decided to publish the material. For the purposes of preparatory work it put a room and appropriate equipment at our disposal and undertook to cover the costs incurred. At the request of the Academy of Sciences Béla Bartók was relieved of his teaching duties at the Academy of Music from September, 1934, and was occupied in an official capacity with the preparatory arrangement of the material and the revision of the phonogram records. The present writer was meanwhile in charge of having old manuscripts of folksongs in public collections copied and then comparing the copies with the originals.

At Béla Bartók's initiative the Academy of Sciences had gramophone records made; this was later continued by the Radio. Having shortly surveyed the links between Hungarian folksongs and those of the neighbouring peoples, Béla Bartók was investigating and classifying the Ukrainian and Polish material. After his departure in October, 1940, the present writer continued the work, an official assignment up to June 1942 when he retired, and then voluntarily after that. In October 1943 an inevitable break ensued due to air-raids and the material had to be packed and put in a safe place. The material has fortunately been preserved, but the reconstruction of the badly damaged building of the Academy took a long time and the actual work could be continued only in the autumn of 1949; and it was only

---

* The outbreak of the First World War.

45

from January 1950, that the Academy could temporarily secure a small room in which the work could be pursued.

Since from 1945 the Academy of Sciences had no funds whatever for publishing purposes, from the autumn of 1946 the Ministry for Religion and Public Education and subsequently the Ministry of Public Education provided for the noting down of music to be started, for the payment of one collaborator at first and then of several, as well as for the costs of paper and printing.

From the collected material the volume of children's games was prepared for the press first; but also as a matter of principle, it seemed expedient to begin with this.

> *The fragment of a song several centuries old that can be heard*
> *sung by Hungarian children up to this very day:*
> *'Lengyel László, our good king,*
> *even he is but an enemy'*
> *proves that in bygone days the poet of the people looked farther*
> *back to the history of the motherland...*
>
> (Kölcsey, "National Traditions", 1826)

Ever since 1792, when *"Kis pillantás"* (Little Glimpse) was published in the *Magyar Hírmondó,* and since Kölcsey's admonition, literature has kept an eye on children's singing games but has not dealt with them with the care their significance deserves. Sporadically texts noted down fragmentarily have appeared here and there. But we do not know of any notations of melodies dating back to before 1865. Before 1878 there was no publication of the text, tune and game together. Both from a scientific and from a practical point of view the publication of this volume appeared to be the most urgent.

Children's singing games allow a more profound insight than anything else into the primeval age of folk music. Singing connected with movement and action is a much more ancient and, at the same time, more complex phenomenon than is a simple song. It offers much more hitherto untouched material to science for all kinds of investigation than any other branch of folk music, on which its thorough examination can also throw new light.

In the same way as the child's development repeats in brief the evolution of mankind, his forms of music represent a history of music; indeed they afford a glimpse into the prehistoric period of music. From the reiteration of the smallest motif, comprising but a couple of notes, we can observe all grades of musical development up to the average stage of the European folksong: the sentence of eight bars. Here the child's music often touches that of adults. There are bigger structures, too, but in them it is no longer the musical logic that supplies the connecting link but the narrative.

In no other branches of folk music are its specific phenomena evinced so clearly. The naive, ancient, playful instinct, which here operates freely has often vanished from the musical life of adults. If only for the sake of well-rounded texts grown-ups adhere more closely to permanent, stereotyped forms. Here, like tiny crustaceans in

Lake Balaton, the motifs stick together, always in a different way; as in our dreams, when one figure shows the features of two or more people at the same time, the atoms of melodies swarm, unite and become separated again. It is the eternal secret of folk poetry: a miraculous swarming of atomized entities and of heterogeneous elements clinging together to form new entities. This ever seething furnace, in which new syntheses are born and old units disintegrate at the same time, in which what is new is born and what is old dies—though at the same time what is abiding in it is reborn— is a much more faithful mirror of the teeming quality of life than the art of poetry and composed music with their fixed and unchangeable forms: forms which perhaps do not change only because their creator is dead or because the feeling that had brought the work into being has grown cold in him.

Panta rei! And nowhere is this as palpable as in children's games. And yet, this kaleidoscope-like variegation but rarely becomes artistically shapeless; it is rather in one shorter piece or the other that fragmentation or wear is revealed.

A pair of bars, the time equal to two steps, during which each foot touches the ground twice and the heavy and light relationship is repeated twice, is the basic formula of the child's musical form. In musical notation it appears as two $\frac{2}{4}$ bars. This can be realised in three–nine phases (syllables). The tempo of the steps is between 108 and 126 per minute.

This is the form of counting out, a side branch—usually without a melody—of children's rhymes. In foreign countries there is a vast literature on it, with us it has not been dealt with so appropriately.

This is also the form of chanted words to dance to, and here the grown-ups' world of form touches that of children. Their rhythm is not so varied, usually seven or eight syllables, but the manner of their performance is the same as that of counting-out rhymes that have no melody and of other jingles. As a rule, they end on a certain rise of the voice, which coincides with the dynamic summit, on the last stressed syllable. Also in the text of dance chants there are many fragments of songs, thus it is also in the text that the primitive form meets the independent part that had degenerated from developed forms.

Finally, rhythmical exclamations of marching demonstrating crowds are akin in form to children's songs, with verses for counting out and with dance words. They also are pairs of bars, repeated; their rhythm being like the formulae of children's songs from those with three syllables up to those with eight or nine. Here, too, the last stress produces the dynamic climax.

As we can see, childish forms are not restricted to the age of childhood. Many adults are satisfied with them, particularly in their active music-making. Some people listening passively to music can also attentively follow larger forms, but when whistling or humming to themselves while working they are often content with a fragment of a couple of bars or a shred of music of no more than a sentence. On the other hand children can also reach the musical capacity of the average adult (the sentence of eight to twelve bars) as has been proved in numerous instances. The decisive factor is not only age. We have seen children of five who knew over eighty grown-up folk-songs; and there are innumerable adults who remain children as far as music is concerned; their comprehension does not extend beyond a pair of bars, particularly in countries where music is not developed in the primary school.

This is how children's forms in music live on in the world of grown-ups. And if the songs of the latter find their way down to children, they usually submit to the separate laws of that world. Sometimes we seem to recognise a fragment or a characteristic phrase, floating on the fabric of childish pairs of bars as a leaf will on the surface of water, or when it appears like a face reflected by rippling water, blurred but still recognisable. At other times a cell, becoming detached from the songs of adults, grows into a new, independent and closed small unit. Children will dissolve the bigger units into smaller ones that suit their sense of form. In the same way as they will endlessly repeat a word, they will also repeat pairs of bars or even single bars. As a rule children's songs afford a much deeper insight into the biology of folk music than those of adults; indeed, they will even illuminate a number of phenomena of adults' songs. The physical consistency of children's songs can be of various kinds: loose, "colloidal" forms, half-way towards crystallisation into closed forms; or, in the opposite direction, disintegrating from crystallised forms towards colloidal or even liquid states. It is most instructive to observe these changes on the same material (see Nos. 166–183). We can observe the same tune amidst protean variations; it disintegrates into its component parts only to become crystallised for a time into other different forms. Its elements, the pairs of bars, are united, then divided, only to be united again, all with the greatest resilience. We do not yet have a sufficiently clear picture of the permanence of these changeable formulae; this will be clarified by further close scrutiny.

The formation of variants is much more many-sided than in the closed forms of the songs of adults. In the latter the range hardly undergoes any transformation; it is mostly a case of variation in the melody or rhythm. In children's songs there are hardly two variants with the same range; there are more faulty reproductions, gaps in memory, and they feel less restriction in tune and text alike. The variants more frequently become fixed as new, permanent formations. Children's songs are the perfect models and the richest thesaurus of examples of the formation of variations.

Anyone who does not like the Hungarian people will come to like it most quickly through children, while watching and getting to know their hundred faces from impish cockiness to tender emotion, all radiating towards him from the magic kaleidoscope of these games. No teacher can do without a thorough knowledge of these games. Anyone who did not take part in them as a child will bear the traces of his sad childhood till the day of his death. It should be his most urgent task to learn them subsequently, to enter into their spirit, for without doing so he cannot get close to the soul of the children. Only here will he see how the world is reflected in the soul of Hungarian children.

48

Ever since *Flóri könyve* (Flóri's Book) (1830) most of our Hungarian teachers lived in the tragic delusion that to educate people meant to pervert their true being, to teach them something different, something better, that is—something foreign. This was intensified after 1850 when the Austrian method of teaching was introduced. Through channels both on the surface of the earth and underground there was a bountiful influx of German taste, but not the good one that would have paved the way for the great; it was the low one, the precursor of botched work and trash.

If one has not perused the collections for schools and kindergartens of the past half century (no critical history of them has yet been written), one cannot have an idea what an odious attempt had been prepared here against our children, and, in them, against the whole future of the Hungarian nation. Wherever these collections found their way, they destroyed surviving traditions. Among other things, they were the last straw in the alienation of the educated intelligentsia from national traditions, a process already started by the crop of songs of the *biedermeier* era, a period of German taste, these songs being termed folksongs of the nobility by Szini. Fortunately, their effect was limited to the sphere of schools. In this way traditions survived more or less safe and sound among the people scarcely touched by school and kindergarten. They flourished most luxuriantly in places to which the desert air of educational matters of those times did not even reach.

Áron Kiss's collection (1891) tried to oppose the alien current by taking a firm stand on the ground of traditions. Not with complete success: even half a century after his time the un-Hungarian, taste-perverting trend was rampant. The kinder-garten-teacher poetry of the paper *Kisdednevelés* deserves a separate study. At times it was smiled at, Andor Kozma wrote a mock-poem about it but nobody has fathomed its disastrous effect. Anybody may observe that a fairly bright village child who has attended four or six forms of the primary school, has stored in his memory several hundred useless and worthless verses, quite enough to blunt him to real literature for ever. Let alone music. As a reaction to the folk tunes propagated by Áron Kiss, schools were overwhelmed by worthless and un-Hungarian melodies produced by authors from whose souls the basic Hungarian foundation was lacking. This music has not yet found its reviewer either.

There are foreign elements in the games of this volume, too, and we have tried to point them out as much as possible. But it is a different matter if a child living on the linguistic border learns a game or two from his neighbour, whose mother-tongue is different, and then sings it in the distorted foreign language he perhaps does not even understand (see No. 1070); and again another matter if a game or song, though Hungarian in its language but alien in its spirit and of bad taste, is officially imposed upon him by a central authority.

A foreign element, as in the life of the language, either becomes assimilated or remains alien. In vain would we demonstrate, for example, of *"Ég a gyertya"* (Candles burning) that it is of foreign origin. It has become naturalised and merged among Hungarian songs; it does not sound foreign. If, on the other hand, we hear in the Budapest playgrounds the melody of *"A gazda rétre megy"* (The farmer's in his field), we may think, from a distance, that it is German children playing.

Although from the very beginning Hungarian collections of folk poetry have sporadically published a game or two—without their melodies—prior to Áron Kiss they were not collected as they deserved. It was as a result of his proposals that the national meeting of teachers adopted in 1883 the following theses:

"1. Games and the songs that may go together with them are to serve the cause of Hungarian national education and therefore the Hungarian character of the games is to be preserved. 2. Children's games and their tunes are to be collected in all regions of this country." The *Magyar Gyermekjáték gyűjtemény* (Collection of Hungarian Children's Games), 1891, is the result of their efforts. It was a formidable collective work, which brings credit to Hungarian teachers. True, it was in the same way that the Academy of Sciences had obtained half a century earlier the material of János Erdélyi's collection; but Kiss enumerates 214 collaborators from 48 counties; neither before nor since has there been such large-scale, nation-wide collection with us.

Áron Kiss pursued, first of all, a practical purpose. He wanted to provide schools with a Hungarian stock of games to replace the host of alien songs, of the Fröbel kind and otherwise, that had gained ground. He had no scientific aim but a great part of the material collected was also suitable for such purposes. It would have been most valuable if, side by side with the games published, he had mentioned in what different places the same games were known. As he pointed out in his foreword, "Volumes of identical games, or hardly differing variants, have been found. Thus I had to lay aside whole volumes. Similarly I have laid aside the games collected among compatriots whose mother-tongue is not Hungarian (Germans, Ruthenians, Slovakians)". So far our quest for these volumes which were laid aside has proved fruitless, although it would be extremely interesting to hold another inspection on their basis with sixty years' perspective. We have made some tests and succeeded, by going to the spot, in correcting some notations that seemed erroneous. Games in foreign languages would be similarly interesting. It would not have been so arduous a task to explore the origin of *"Ispiláng"* if we had had some of its German variants.

Today Kiss's collection is extraordinarily rare. It was printed on such poor paper that a great many copies disintegrated because of that rather than because of having been used too much. In the hands of kindergarten teachers and school teachers, for whom it had been intended, it is hardly found at all, not even in its abbreviated editions (1891, 1910). For this reason alone, a great comprehensive collection was urgently needed.

All the available material is contained in our collection, only that with completely uncertain notations being left out. We do not take responsibility for every note. Our doubts and proposals for collections have been indicated in the notes. In numerous cases only further checking on the spot would offer certainty. This will be the task of future research, for the investigation of children's singing games is not to be brought to an end with this volume but to be launched by it.

50

It is amazing that, following so many eminent examples from the Finns, there appear again and again collections with tunes written down in different keys. The publishers delude themselves by stating that they are rendering the original key. This is only an illusion, for their notation can indicate only the twelve tempered notes, whereas in reality there are many more. We have no notation for a sound between C and C sharp. We do not deny the importance of absolute pitch; in fact we have established it from the beginning in our collections with the phonograph and later also with those performed without a phonograph, but this is not sufficient either: the singer's compass should also be examined because only then would it become clear whether he (or she) uses rather the higher or the lower part of his range; and whether the break of the melody (when the upper or lower limit of his voice is reached the singer breaks back to another octave and continues there) is conscious with him or whether he does not even notice it.

The time of unsystematic folksong publishing is over. Comparative research is impossible if, in turning the pages of a collection put together without any musical system, we have to seek similarities by relying merely on our memory. Only by finding a common basis for melodies is their quick comparison possible. For this reason here, too, the G above middle C is used as the common key-note. We may be able to convince our readers that the letters of relative solmisation also do useful work in the comparison of melodies. Many experiments have been made to arrange melodies in a dictionary-like system. No unified system has been found, nor ever will be found, on account of the diversity of the melodies. From its own characteristics every body of material has to develop its most suitable order so that similar melodies will be side by side, and everything can easily be found. This is what we have attempted in the present volume. Some of the children's games consist of so many elements that in order to facilitate the finding of related motifs, we have had to set up detailed reference tables.

There are relatively few phonograph recordings. The expensive cylinders had to be saved for complicated melodies with grace-notes and ornamentation; the games, relatively simple but sometimes very long, would have taken up too many. That is why the notation of small rhythms within the bars is sometimes sketchy. Older collections, thus including Áron Kiss's, suggest that children's games consist of similar quavers and crotchets. But data recorded with the phonograph show that up to a point the length or brevity of syllables asserts itself here as well, though not so much as in the more declamatory singing of grown-ups, which stresses more the meaning of the words. But the melic-rhythmic element predominates to such an extent in children's songs that in them a short syllable is freely lengthened or a long one shortened if this is demanded by the symmetry of rhythm. Phonograph recordings evincing a more precise application are not decisive either, particularly if they were sung by merely one person, for the singing sounds different if produced by a group in the heat of the game. The frequent spoiling of texts and the distortion of meaning show that the sense of the text is only partly conscious; and that is why, even in the

51

pronunciation, the shortness or length of the syllables does not come across accurately. Anyhow, the enunciation of a child is not so definite as that of an adult.

One more word about the faulty intonations to be found here and there in the phonograph recordings. Strictly speaking, if examined by instruments, every performance, even that of trained singers is full of little faults in intonation; and with folksingers, unless their hearing is especially uncertain, we do not find relatively more mistakes. This is how the fluctuations of pitch and the irrational rhythms occasionally occurring in the phonograph recordings must be evaluated. The fluctuations of rhythm are chiefly due to the fact that the recordings were of necessity made in a resting position, without any movement.

It is a well-known fact that in folksongs published without their melody there are many errors; in many cases the rhythm cannot be established for certain, the tune taking care of the completeness of the text. This is even more true of children's singing games. Here, on account of the freedom in the number of syllables, the rhythm is often uncertain; without the melody we cannot ascertain whether the text is erroneous or not. In all probability there are even more mistakes in the texts of children's songs published without their melodies than in the texts of folksongs. That is why nursery rhymes, even such as have no tunes, or counting out jingles must be written down in notation because even so they have rhythms though not always unambiguous ones. Their genuine, alive-sounding form is provided only by the notation of rhythm written above it. Indeed, attention should be paid to their tunes, too! For the intonation of jingles without melodies often differs from ordinary speech; so it must be noted.

We have good reason to believe, even if we cannot prove it with variations, that most of the singing games now without melody used to be linked with tunes, even if the performer declares that it is only "spoken" (our people "tell" a song, too).

The phonetic inconsistencies of the texts could not be eliminated; the data had to be published as we found them; arbitrarily we could not insert dialect forms, even if we knew the dialect of the region in question. There were scarcely any collectors who noted these features down accurately. But nobody is to be shocked at the inconsistencies of the phonograph recordings either. Collectors have observed for a long time that even if in their everyday speech all peculiarities of the dialect are alive, in their singing people try to enunciate according to "educated" speech and, in front of the phonograph, they are mostly embarrassed and take particular care. This is the cause of the unevenness even within the data on the same singer. The pronunciation of the people has in any case been strongly affected by schooling, reading and radio. In most places it is only the layer of the population least touched by these three factors that speak their dialect consistently. In indicating dialects we have generally followed the decisions of the Conference on the Vernacular (1942). Where we obtained more detailed data, we have naturally retained them. When the more recent indications of the Institute of Linguistics appeared the greater part of our book had already been set.

52

The remarkable new feature of our book, the systematisation of types of games, the work of György Kerényi, is the first experiment of this type in world literature. On this basis comparative research of games can now be launched internationally; a work up to now based, apart from memory, on a few rough and ready categories only. The book is otherwise the fruit of collective work in which, apart from György Kerényi and Ilona Rácz—Bartók's old colleagues—the chief collaborators were Pál Járdányi and Lajos Kiss. In addition to them we had to avail ourselves of the work of several proof-readers and translators; these latter we needed to learn the contents of some handbooks in foreign languages. In the question of typography the experience of Gyula Kertész was of great help, and in some cases he made tape-recordings on location.

The inadequacy of our libraries restricted comparison with foreign material as did the paucity of special books on the subject. We are particularly indebted to all who assisted us in obtaining such works. We came by some foreign books through the National Centre of Libraries. Professor Victor Belyayev (Moscow) put at our disposal a photo-copy of a rare Russian collection. At our application the Czechoslovakian Embassy had a Prague library send us Orel's work, which was otherwise unavailable. The French Institute in Budapest helped us in a similar way. Professor Adolf Chybiński (Poznan) and Professor Walter Wiora (Deutsches Volksliedarchiv, Freiburg i. Br.) were kind enough to reply to requests for information submitted to them by letter.

Having jointly discussed the proposals about the many possible ways of arranging the book, we eventually decided upon its final form. We could not find any more suitable one or one more easy to handle. For this I take responsibility, aware of the fact that all the collaborators strove with profound devotion from good towards better and that from the summary of results achieved so far our book will provide a firm foundation for further research. Future researchers will find enough encouragement with regard to what to collect and how; and in what way to avoid the mistakes of previous collections and correct their deficiencies. Our index of places shows from what regions there is as yet little or no material. The comparison with the games of other peoples will reveal in what direction further connections can be sought. We repeat that with the present book we do not want to terminate the study of singing games but to start it. Thus it will be up to the future researcher to examine to what extent and in what manner the social differences in villages are reflected in children's games; so far our collections have not supplied any data on this.

What Kiss failed to achieve we can now begin again on a broader basis and with richer material: to bring Hungarian children back to their own country.

Anyone for whom the treasury of folksongs is not a dead museum but a living culture, which has only been checked in its development, will peruse even such unassuming tunes as these with the excitement of constant discovery. They are full of bustling life; a child's imagination and ingenuity clothing some simple basic forms into a thousand guises.

Hungarian folk poetry is like a mountain brook into the bed of which a huge boulder has rolled; the water can continue its course only by flowing around it. In front of the rock it swells into a lake and seems not to flow at all. To roll the boulder out of the bed of the brook lest its free flow and growth be hindered by anything— this is the chief task of our public education, of our scientific and cultural policy.

(1951)

CALENDAR CUSTOMS SONGS

Preface to Volume II of
"Corpus Musicae Popularis Hungaricae"

The *Corpus Musicae Popularis Hungaricae* series began with children's songs, the most ancient and primitive musical activity of our people. The tunes of folk customs appeared to be the next stage. Some of them have already become, and others are now in process of becoming children's singing games. The kinship of their melodies is conspicuous. Minstrels' songs are so close to children's singing games that they were not published together only because the first volume was already too bulky. On the other hand, their relationship to other folk customs connects them rather with the material of this volume.

The many-sided material of Hungarian folk music cannot be constrained into a single, rigid system. Each of its branches must find its own separate order in which it can be most easily surveyed. The volume of children's songs is such an attempt at arranging the material in a manner springing from its very nature. The tunes of folk customs are so varied that they do not have sufficient common features for a purely musical systematisation. Both scientific and practical viewpoints suggested an arrangement according to their contents.

Pursuing the calendar year this volume takes the customs which are accompanied by singing according to their sequence. This order seems to be a purely external formality: but it shows well the relationship to the changes of the seasons of man living close to nature. It is well known that Christian holidays are adjusted to the times of ancient, pagan, nature holidays (winter and summer solstice) and we do not know how many ancient pagan elements have been hiding up to this very day underneath the external religious overcoat. The rigorously scientific exploration of pagan elements still awaits research. The difficulties to be faced are revealed by Gyula Krohn's book: *A finnugor népek pogány istentisztelete* (The Pagan Services of Finno-Ugrian Peoples), although there, in some places, paganism is still alive up to this very day, whereas we have but infinitesimally small data on Hungarian paganism. It took Christianity several centuries to abolish it, at least formally. How much of its spiritual contents has survived in the people would be difficult to state exactly, but it seems to be more than a little.

Even the tenacious adherence to some customs is a sign of the pagan element having survived. Church and secular authorities alike, shoulder to shoulder, persecuted and eradicated them if they did not adjust themselves to the new order. We do not have in mind only our old laws of the eleventh–twelfth centuries. Even in the 1900s a village parish priest tried to put an end to the jumping over the fire at midsummer by persuading his congregation to offer this "pagan custom" as a propitiation for the conflagration that had raged in the village. Thus the clinging religious elements did not save them from the curse of the church.

The remains of shamanism are sought for by researchers in the minstrels' songs and the last traces of magic in children's songs. We are probably not mistaken if we think that the *"lebeke tárgy"* (*lebeke* object) (see: *Középkori magyar verseink* [Our Medieval Hungarian Verses] 1921: 204) and other incantations against evil used to have tunes that could be put down in notation. Their rhythm points to this and who knows in which of our melodies some of their traces are hidden. Krohn mentions that in some of the pagan rituals of Finno-Ugrian peoples there was also music. If the Hungarian people has preserved tunes that can be proved to be two and a half thousand years of age, it is not impossible that these are also among them.

Greetings in rhyme, delivered from door to door, by now appear to be practically nothing but a kind of begging for charity. But could they not once have been social events, almost ritual in their character, which reminded people of turning points in the seasons? For civilised people good wishes are mostly empty words, but for people of the past they may have been of virtually magic value, which they were glad to return as well as they were able to. I shall never forget the happiness with which an old woman of Transdanubia gave me an account of the fine words with which her forty-year-old son had greeted her on New Year's Day. The various festive greetings for namedays are relics of a friendlier, warmer, more brotherly and loving way of simple people's life. The life of the people of old times was surrounded by a dense forest of folk customs. Every episode of life was adorned and rendered memorable. It is characteristic of the age of these customs that, for example, among the twenty separate details of the celebration of a wedding in Kalotaszeg, the religious marriage ceremony is but one—the fifteenth. (*A Magyarság Néprajza* [The Ethnography of the Hungarian People], II, p. 400.) Civilisation has destroyed a great many of them. Their roles have partly been taken over by other institutions. The unwritten "old law" has been ousted by many written "new laws". But even in their present remains they afford a deep insight into the history of our culture.

The significance of their melodies is similar. Perhaps they do not offer much from an artistic point of view: they are all the more noteworthy from the scientific point of view. And although the order of this volume has not been determined according to the musical systematisation, the music researcher can also easily find what he is looking for with the help of the comprehensive tables. Here we cannot go into the numerous unsolved mysteries in the research of customs. Earlier in our scientific life the fabrication of theories based on insufficient and faulty material was a frequent phenomenon. The presentation of exact data was pushed into the background. What a mass of badly published material had to be published again! The most brilliant theory will go down like ninepins under the weight of a single new piece of information. Theories will become obsolete but material, published without mistakes, never will. Anyone who has wandered about for a time in the maze of the many variants of texts and tunes will rightly ask the question: which, then, is the faultless material? When does the variant of equal value end and where does deterioration begin? What is the touchstone of authenticity? We have not yet reached the stage where we can answer these intricate questions with a few words. If we compare the two forms of the Whitsun customs of Vitnyéd—the one recorded by gramophone and the other by phonograph—the former can be compared to a snapshot which, however faithfully it has recorded the situation of the moment when it was taken, does not give a genuine picture of the character of the subject. The other one is nearer, having retained more of the essence of its original, which we happen to know.

And here we have come to the special significance of our volume in the research of variants. From older sources we know the original of several pieces contained in it. In such cases we stand on firmer ground when investigating the direction and trend of the people's transformation work. As soon as we have made sufficient observations in this field we shall not be so confused by the greater or lesser divergencies between melodies without prototypes, or by fluctuations appearing in the performance of the same singer. It is often difficult, if not impossible, to establish the most authentic and most permanent form of a melody. The more we become able to observe all objective and subjective circumstances of the recording or the writing down in notation—that is to say the more well-trained collectors we have—the closer we can get to it. In the interests of completeness for the time being, we had to include tunes written down by dilettantes' hands. Question marks call attention to their mistakes, unless they could be unequivocally corrected. We do not really know a song if we do not know its distribution in space and time. A stage is reached at which we can pursue the life, the development and changes of a tune over a long time, in fact through centuries. The history of songs and the comparison of songs is here of the same importance as are the history of language and comparative linguistics in linguistic science.

In this volume we could not even begin a comparison with the material of foreign songs, because of the vastness of the material on the one hand and the lack of foreign sources on the other. Nor could our aim be such lengthy studies when the publication of the material is our most urgent business. When the material is in circulation there will be more scholars to undertake this work, which demands a thousand eyes: a work without any end.

This volume, too, is the common work of the well-proven collaborators and ancillary personnel of the first. Máté Pál, a new collaborator, performed the phonetic revision of the texts. We have to pay particular tribute to the music specialists of the Museum of Ethnography for the transference into notation of numerous recordings and for comparing them. Here the names of László Lajtha, Benjámin Rajeczky and Lajos Vargyas are to be mentioned with particular gratitude.

(1952, published in 1953)

57

WEDDING SONGS

Preface to Volume III/A of the
"Corpus Musicae Popularis Hungaricae"

Among the customs of every people the celebration of the wedding, this greatest turning point of human life, occupies a special place.

Singing and music stand out from among the thousand ways in which a wedding is rendered memorable. Like every people, ours has its special songs connected with nuptials. It seemed expedient to lift them out of the general musical systematisation and put them into a separate frame of their own. In this way their characteristics are thrown into relief more forcefully, thus facilitating comparative research into their origins.

Included here are, first and foremost, songs closely connected with the different phases of weddings and not used at other times. That is why they can be identified by their tunes alone.

Side by side with the strictly ceremonial songs there are a great many others sung in the course of a wedding. Numerous songs are said by their performers to be customary at weddings, although their texts have scarcely any connection with nuptials or even no connection at all. The host of drinking and revelry songs may have been used for other occasions as well. But considering that poor people, particularly in regions where no wine is produced, had but few opportunities for drinking wine and for revelry apart from weddings, we can well believe that a number of songs were performed only at weddings even if their texts revealed no reference to nuptials. Thus drinking songs and dance songs became wedding songs for those who only met them at weddings.

Although we have omitted the overwhelming majority of such songs, we had to publish some examples, because without them the musical picture of weddings would have remained incomplete. For this reason they will appear in their own place in the musical systematisation and in the groups of variants, being either published again if necessary, or merely referred to.

The musical material of today's wedding is rather heterogeneous. Old music blending with the new or with the very newest faithfully mirrors the social transformation the Hungarian people is undergoing. Two opposing powers are fighting here, too: on the one hand adherence to what is old and traditional and, on the other, social "capillarity", the imitation of more educated classes, at least as far as circumstances allow.

58

The weddings of Hungarian aristocrats of long ago, which lasted a year or until the child first moved, could not be imitated by the tillers of the soil. But we have heard about weddings lasting several days quite recently. Within one's means, and even beyond it, one would try to render memorable the wedding of one's son or daughter. This has found its way even into laments:

"Oh, dear father, my dear father, why did your wish not come true? Oh, how often you had said: don't you worry, daughter mine, I'll make for you a wedding such as nobody has had before!"

In the process of trying to outrival one another, the gentlefolk's customs that could be aped have more or less succeeded in penetrating old traditions. The features which gentlefolk's weddings of old times have in common with those of later peasant weddings suggest that in music, too, we may look for features transferred from higher strata. What they were and how many of them have been adopted may be revealed by the efforts of future research.

The music of weddings spans the whole register of human feelings from weeping and sobbing to wild revelry. Civilisation has muted down extremes and has deprived the majority of rituals of all colour, reducing them to void formalities and finally discarding them altogether. By this the spontaneous activity has become gradually reduced and so has faith in the importance of traditional activities. However, ancient rituals reach far into civilisation, and many of them have survived even during the rule of written laws, not to say in spite of them. Ever since Herder it has been customary to complain about the ruin of folk poetry and traditions. Instead we might rather be surprised that so much is still extant at the present level of civilisation.

A number of new and valuable finds prove that traditions have not perished, but former collections were superficial and incomplete. This refers among other things to wedding customs and songs; this volume, too, shows that there are many more of them alive than we would have thought even quite recently.

One of St. John Chrysostom's sermons provides valuable ethnographical data in this:

"Thus, if you exorcise the Devil, chase out lewd singing and lecherous songs, indecent dances, shameful words, Satan's pageantry, boisterousness, unbridled laughter and all disorderliness and show in the holy servants of Christ; through them Christ will be wholly present, together with His mother and brethren. He who fulfils my Father's will says [the Scripture] is my brother, sister and mother. Well do I know that for many it is burdensome and unbearable that I advocate this and exterminate old customs. Nor do I care about this, because I am not striving for your approval but for your good, not for your applause and praises but for your welfare and your better understanding. Nobody shall tell me that this is the custom. Where we commit sin we shall not mention customs; but if the custom be sinful—even though ancient—stop it. But if it is not sinful—even though not a custom—introduce it and make it strike roots. And that such monstrous behaviour is not an old custom but some harmful novelty just remember how Isaac wedded Rebecca and Jacob Rachel. For the Scripture, too, mentions these weddings telling us how these brides were conducted to the house of the bridegrooms, but does not mention anything like this. The reception of guests and the feast had been prepared with greater solemnity than usual and all relations, too, were invited to the wedding. But there was no word about flutes, pipes and cymbals, drunken dancing and any of the present shameful things. Nowadays the dancers sing hymns to the praise of Aphrodite. They sing about lewdness, adultery, secret love-making, unbridled copulation and many other odious and disgraceful songs. Having become drunk and involved in so many monstrous things they conduct the bride publicly, in a celebratory procession, delivering immoral jingles."

(*St. John Chrysostom,* Sermon I., Cor. 7.2 Montfaucon edition, Vol. III, pp. 234–235.)

Reading this the investigator of wedding customs will naturally think of today's peasant weddings. What four hundred years of Christianity was unable to eradicate among the Greeks has survived with the Hungarians after twice as long a span of time.

When the serious part of marriages with legal significance was taken over by religious authorities and then by secular ones, the spontaneous activity of the people was relegated more and more to the merry and jocular. By today's educational standards these jokes are often coarse, indeed obscene. But we have to turn back the pages of the history of morals and manners by only one or two centuries to find this tenor among the most educated classes up to the royal courts themselves.

If compared with their neighbours and other peoples of similar culture, the Hungarian people definitely belongs to the better behaved ones. There are a great many euphemisms in their language and often they speak even about dumb animals like this: "By your leave: a pig."

The scandalous scenes to be seen in Dutch pictures are virtually inconceivable at Hungarian peasant weddings. Viewing these pictures it is not difficult to imagine their acoustic accompaniment.

Some regions of Hungary seem to be more inclined to obscenities. Thus, for example, the western group of the Palóc people; here such songs are called *"kórdé"* (Pázmány's *kardé*). So far the fewest obscenities have originated from the Székely people. It needs further close examination to reveal in what way this inclination is connected with other characteristics in the different ethnic groups.

It is natural after all that weddings call attention more intensely to sexual life. The unwritten laws of propriety are loosened, but only for the time being. The Dionysian mood of nuptials releases a lot of things that are forbidden on normal days.

There's a wedding, so no wonder
All the women now are drunken,

says one of our songs from the Zobor region. Apart from at a wedding an intoxicated woman would be greatly disparaged and despised.

This is quite different from the erotic jokes which are, and were, common in a company of cultured males, jokes in which in certain periods, for example, in the Renaissance, even cultured women participated. Poggio, a characteristic writer of those times brushed aside objections with the following saying: *"Ipocritarum genus pessimum est omnium, qui vivant."* Phenomena of practically pathological cacology, which were by no means rare in our cultured bourgeois circles, were never to be found among country people.

But nuptial mischievousness and obscenity among the people in general may have another origin, reaching far back into the past. The magic meaning of different forbidden words may be sought there, in the same way as traces of fertility-magic are suggested by wedding customs. There are data pointing to this both in peoples of ancient cultures and in primitive peoples.

The Chinese bride is conducted into the nuptial chamber for a day; there she is visited by the bridegroom's friends who overwhelm her with the choicest obscenities, although in general Chinese rules of conduct are very strict (Funk & Wagnall: *Dictionary of Folklore,* New York, 1949. pp. 210 and 810). The bride's behaviour is watched most closely by the groom, his mother and his friends.

Other data mention something similar in connection with the rain-magic of the Bantus: "obscene words, which are usually forbidden, are customary and legitimate on these occasions". (Frazer: *The Golden Bough,* Vol. III, p. 154, cited by Funk, p. 940.)

Our obscene texts are also to be made available for research, the task of which will be—to use Sylvester's words quoted so often—to find "gold in ordure".

This volume, too, is, the common work of the board of editors, raised by ministerial decree 2059/17/1953 to the rank of Folk Music Research Group of the Hungarian Academy of Sciences. Edited by Lajos Kiss, the volume has been brought into being with the participation of all members of the group: Margit Fleischhacker, Pál Járdányi, György Kerényi, Gyula Kertész, Judit Lévai-Gábor, Károly Mathia, Géza Paulovics, Máté Pál, Ilona Rácz, György Szomjas-Schiffert. From the point of view of ethnography our volume has been revised by Ákos Szendrey. With this volume we have given a complete picture of the musical part of peasant weddings according to data available up to now. We present the volume to the public with the dual wish that, with the emergence of further data, the details hitherto unclarified may be illuminated and completed as far as possible and, secondly, that a complete description of the non-musical part of weddings be produced with the use of all available data.

(1955)

PAIRING SONGS

Preface to Volume IV of the
"Corpus Musicae Popularis Hungaricae"

Hungarian country people prepare practically from their childhood onwards for their marriage. A child of four to five years of age will look out for a mate and will give a serious answer to elderly people's jocular question: "Who is your sweetheart?" And even if it is not the person chosen in childhood who will become his or her spouse, it is no rarity to find a married couple who are former playmates. Children's marriages and early betrothals—as is usual with some primitive peoples and was customary with royal families—are unknown with us. (The only published data is to be found in *A Magyarság Néprajza* [Ethnography of the Hungarian People], Vol. IV. p. 157.)

However, in every phase of life, rural people will take the matter of mating seriously and consider it topical all the time. Perhaps the urban population does not differ from it very much in this respect. But country folk embellish this—like everything else—with the gloss of poetry. Urban children do not know the host of wedding games of village people. Young people in rural parts of the country keep on playing weddings up to the time it does indeed arrive. This is how so many pairing songs have come into being: their texts and music alike mark them off from other kinds of songs; they demanded a volume of their own.

The summer solstice song (see Vol. II. of *Corpus Musicae Popularis Hungaricae*) is the relic of an ancient mating festivity; the minstrels' song inserts mating among good wishes for the New Year. In places where these have sunk into oblivion—or had never existed at all—in their stead, or side by side with them, match-making, mating, pairing-off songs flourish. There are regions where they are connected with special occasions, such as the spinnery, or with the game "The basket's going round". But goose-girls in the fields know them and will sing them by the dozen without any special occasion. They are not only interested in their own mating but also that of their friends. Nobody will sing a pairing song about herself but only about others. There is only one instance where a woman sings herself together with a young man: it is our oldest data, a mating-song which survived in the minutes of a criminal suit of 1750. Its particular circumstances provide the explanation.

Mentioning names means a peculiar personal involvement and excitement for those whose names have been mentioned: a pleasant or unpleasant feeling depending on whether their emotions have been correctly guessed, or whether couples not suited to each other have been ordered together, as mockery or as a joke.

The ancient magic of calling names may also be concealed in these songs, as if the pronouncing of names might contribute to the two persons coming together, in the same way that an incantation helped only if the patient's name was included in it. To write up the names of a couple, to carve them into tree-trunks or benches gives the impression of optical magic.

Be that as it may, by reading the texts we cannot but remember Sylvester's words, so often cited: "Well may any people admire the keenness of the Hungarian people's mind in hitting upon images, which is nothing but Hungarian poesy." Two hundred and eighty different images establish a connection between the two people! This is apart from the peculiar image of summer solstice songs and minstrels' New Year's greetings, not to be found anywhere else.

We do not know other peoples' songs of this kind well enough. However, the few we know do not resemble the Hungarian ones in their texts or in their tunes. (Here we should pay tribute to the helpfulness of the Deutsches Volksliedarchiv.)

A certain lightness and simplicity, without any particular emotional saturation, are common characteristics of the tunes. This is only natural, for here the text is the more important component, whose features, often jocular and playful, would not go with a weightier melody. Moreover, the majority of the singers are young, mostly children, with one foot still in the world of children's games.

The material of our volume demanded a special arrangement. After a lot of experimentation, we have succeeded in putting the material into an order easy to follow, thus facilitating future research work.

Like the previous ones, this volume is also the collective work of the members of the Folk Music Research Group of the Hungarian Academy of Sciences, who all took part in it under György Kerényi's editorship. The way the melodies of Chapter One are arranged and profoundly analysed is the fruit of the individual work of Pál Járdányi.

(1958, published in 1959)

MESSAGE TO THE INTERNATIONAL FOLK MUSIC COUNCIL'S QUEBEC CONFERENCE

I am sorry that the state of my health forces me to miss the occasion to be present at the Conference and to thank you all personally for the honour you have paid me by nominating me as your President.

All I can do for the moment is to confirm my conviction that the Council is today more necessary than ever. We see daily more and more and better and better published collections of many people's folksongs, results of many years of collecting.

What a multifarious field of study and comparison lies before us! Many workers are needed to examine and master the daily increasing material. The harvest truly is great but the labourers are few. We need endless time to know thoroughly each other's treasures and to distil the common humanity from the hundred different faces of national form and expression.

Years ago somebody asked what would happen if some unforeseen catastrophe were to annihilate all the printed music of the great classics. The answer was obvious: it could easily be restored since a great many musicians know most of the music by heart. If Toscanini discovered misprints in the Bayreuth score of Tristan, played for so many years, it means that the work had become for him practically a kind of "oral tradition". His attitude to the work was nearly the same as a peasant's to his folksong.

On the other hand, all over the world there are new collections of folk music, and through recording and printing our folk music is now saved from the threat of oblivion which is due to changing times.

The artistic value of the best folksong is in no way less than that of any great work of art. To propagate this idea alone, it would be worth while to build a Society.

All the work that has to be done completely justifies the future existence and expansion of our Council.

May the Quebec Conference make a fruitful contribution towards clearing up ideas and solving some of the mysterious problems of our beloved subject: the folksong.

(1961)

II
ON PREDECESSORS
AND CONTEMPORARIES

CLAUDE DEBUSSY

He died at the age of fifty-six—perhaps before his time, since even in his later and more tired works, he still appeared to be developing—the finest composer of his generation, the most productive in his influence. At this moment we cannot have a complete picture of him because there are still some works unpublished, or others which have not found their way to us; nonetheless, we can give a general indication of his significance as it had taken shape up to the outbreak of the war.

There are three great obstacles to be surmounted before one can understand Debussy. The first is the relative newness of his music, the second the present predominance of German traditions and the third, Debussy's close connection with the French spirit.

In the course of the short evolution of music there have not emerged as many heterogeneous values of equal rank as there have in other, older arts. And the compositions of ancient periods, so radically different from the present ones, have not become a matter of common knowledge, and cannot therefore effectively counterbalance musical ideals based on today's prevailing one-sided traditions. That is why it is more difficult in music than in the other arts to blaze a trail in a new direction.

In the works of great German composers, music reached heights previously unimagined. But their decadent successors, forgetting that this great rise was the result of a felicitous blend of Italian and German traditions, despise all non-German music as a matter of course *("welscher Tand")*; their assessment of all new music is based on the assumption—and in this respect they agree with their non-German colleagues—that the style created by the great classical composers and fossilised by their imitators laid down laws, eternal and unchangeable, for all future pieces of music. That is why Wagner's struggles were so hard and why Berlioz did not live to see his triumph.

In the same way that the supremacy of the Latin language was eventually challenged by national literatures emerging one after the other, German music, too, will be compelled to give way to modes of expression other than its own. National attempts during the nineteenth century were overshadowed by the German spirit.

Perhaps only Berlioz and Liszt began something essentially different. French music's second attempt at liberation began with Debussy.

Those who have no connection whatever with the French spirit face it with a striking lack of comprehension. An increase in international contacts before the war may have helped to surmount these difficulties. Even so, there will always be artists more difficult for foreigners to approach. In this respect the French compare Debussy with their Racine.

Viewing things from this angle we can find the explanation for most of the objections to him. His melodies seem unnatural, exotic and sickly to the person who does not know, or does not acknowledge melodic possibilities other than the Italian–German ones. His homophony seems that of a dilettante to the person who does not consider that in one way or another every new master "knows" less than his predecessors, because in other ways he knows more. Haydn's polyphony is also that of a dilettante compared with Bach's; and Bach himself is much simpler than the Dutch masters. Nor can we find any "thematic work" in Debussy, because this was not a means of expression suitable for his purposes.

Constructing forms also lay outside the scope of his endeavours. The question is whether he was able to accomplish what he wanted—in which case he cannot be criticised for setting aside tools which were of no use to him. To record a mood in precise, evocative images, to pursue the evolution of an emotion, to catch the line of the soul's fluctuations; this is what he wanted to do and was able to do. Certainly, this is something like Impressionism in painting. But given the antecedents and the rules of evolution this had to come, and it will bear fruit as did that trend in painting.

Is this music lacking independence because it often relies on titles (mostly visual notions)? The French relate to the world by means of their eyes, so it is no wonder they want their eyes to share even in the hearing of music. This and nothing more is the significance of his titles. If this is "programme music" it is sublimated in quite a new way and on a much higher level than Strauss's almost tangible programmes.

In harmonies he often renounced the advantages of combining chords in a customary way, thereby increasing the expressive force of the chords he used. His melodies move in the fresh currents avoiding chromatics. At this point his music touches both ancient and folk music. But it is the culture of tone colours which owes most to him. He discovered previously unsuspected colour possibilities with the orchestra and piano alike. His works are conceived in terms of colours. Strauss emphasised that Berlioz had been the first to do this and that the symphonies of the classics still completely reflected the spirit of chamber music. The further development of composition for orchestra was still unforeseeable; but Debussy took a great step forward, creating hitherto unimagined sound patterns.

In his own country, however, the reform of the language of French dramatic music—the revival of the recitativo—is considered to have been his greatest accomplishment. No one had ever been able to turn the natural rhythms of the French language into music the way he did. His solution of the opera problem might not suit many dramas, but *Pelléas et Mélisande* could hardly be imagined in any other way. Non-French people find too little music in this opera; they are bored by the monotonous murmur of the recitativo since it is not important for them to understand every word. Even if the text did allow—as it does not—a stronger musical expansion and loud bursts of passion, we must still find quite natural this reaction against heavy Wagnerian pathos on the one hand, and the affected bathos and vapid lyricism of French opera on the other. Here, too, Debussy may have discarded the usual means because he was aiming at something different.

He who goes his own way to such an extent will not meet with easy success, and it is possible that for a long time, perhaps for ever, Debussy's music will belong only to the few. But already his influence is widespread and beneficial, possibly residing less in his compositions themselves than in the stimulus they provide to others. Perhaps his educational effect is more and greater than all his works. His compass points the way to a purer and superior art. Now, through him, we are beginning to understand what people meant when praising Mozart's taste—a word which seems to have lost its meaning since then. But now, when so much distorted noise is passed off as music, the first timid rays of beauty, Latin in its lines, seem to shine forth again from Debussy's works.

The course on which he set out leads towards freedom and beauty. And it does not matter how large a part of this new world belongs to him. His realm is not large, not to be compared with that of the few greatest composers. But he is a poet in his own world and nobody can be more than that.

(1918)

THIRTEEN YOUNG HUNGARIAN COMPOSERS

This year the compositions of thirteen pupils of mine have been performed at the students' concert in the Academy of Music. The fruit of four years' serious work, with six string quartets among them. In the same way as inexperienced performing artists have to become accustomed to the platform, it is the school's duty to give an opportunity to budding composers to acquire the experience that can be gained only by a public performance of their works. Only on the platform will the composition become absolutely complete.

With this the composers did not want to appear before the public at large. Usually the press does not discuss students' concerts. But this time prejudiced and malicious communications on some of the works have come out in the press, writings which partly turned into attacks against my whole work as a teacher. I owe it to the attacked young people, who are now entering into life, as well as to the good reputation of the school, to point to the real reasons of this charge. But first a word on what I consider the duty of the training of composers in Hungary.

For a thousand years we have belonged to Europe. If we do not want this to be doubted, we must adopt all values of musical traditions in Western Europe. I spare no efforts to get my pupils to learn, as well as is possible, the polyphonic style, "the Sanskrit of music"—as it is termed by an eminent English writer—"the language of the consecrated priests and sages of music, the language which has been handed down from master to master for centuries, containing all that is imperishable from the past and which will become a means of expression for all great concepts of the future" enabling them to penetrate into the holy books of music as profoundly as possible. In this respect I go further than was usual with us until now; and is, in fact, not customary elsewhere either. But a Hungarian musician, to be able to hold his own, must be better than the average European one!

However, we must rear not only European musicians but, at the same time, Hungarian ones. Therefore they must get to know and absorb our own separate bible of music; I mean the treasures of ancient folk music. Only a blending of European and Hungarian traditions can bring about an achievement that can mean something for the Hungarian people as well. For us folk music means inexpressibly more than does his own folk music to the German, French, or Italian musician. In their countries composed music has, in most cases, absorbed the essence of folk music. The spirit of these peoples is already alive in their composed music. But since Hungarian composed music is still at the initial stages the spirit of the Hungarian people is for all practical purposes alive only in folk music.

For this reason, unless Hungarian musical life is to be restricted to a small circle reared on a foreign culture, it should be saturated with folk music. This idea guided me both when I set out on my tours to collect folk music twenty years ago and when, fourteen years ago, I included folksongs in the solfège teaching of the Academy. That is why I profess that the teaching of singing at elementary schools must be built up totally on the foundation of folksongs.

I do not overburden the students of composition with folk music, particularly not while they are beginners. I do not want to breed artificially "national composers". Some of the pupils lack all traces of Hungarian atavism. If somebody possesses a viable musical germ it manifests itself in its inherited phraseology, mostly in the German manner. I do not disturb this German phraseology, I do not weed it out; I let it grow as it will. (The works of some pupils praised by the press for being composed in the well-known foreign style may serve as evidence.) It would hardly promote the cause of Hungarian music if they, having learned the externals of the Hungarian musical idiom, were to write insincere music which they do not feel in their hearts. "You need to be reborn again"—one may say to them. Meanwhile I am trying to cultivate them on their own roots. When the plant has grown strong it can better endure grafting; when the great transformation, the great internal change matures in them it will find firmer soil.

Individual, inherited inclinations must be the starting points. For even a lesser talent has a definite individuality and it can only develop in the direction of its own internal currents. It is in this respect that I have erred least. I have succeeded in reaching a position where no two of the thirteen could be confused, so much do they differ from one another. But the respect of individuality should extend to everybody. If I do not put them into a Hungarian uniform I must not dress them in a German or any other foreign one either. If I permit one of them to use the style of Brahms, Schumann or other foreign masters as crutches *("on est toujours le fils de quelqu'un")* then I must allow another one to rely on Liszt, Bartók, or directly on Hungarian folk music. And this was done by those decried by certain communications in the press.

As early as February there was a concert at which the works of only two pupils, Tibor Serly (son of Lajos Serly, the well-known song composer and conductor) and Géza Frid, were performed. Serly was born here but brought up in America, which did not influence his musical development beneficially; a few years ago he arrived here with confused, unmelodic experiments. At home he became settled, his mind cleared; in the atmosphere of his own country the love of melody began to unfold in him, he found his soul again. Frid is urban in his nature, with sensitive nerves. He succeeded in ordering his spasmodic eruptions floating on amorphous rhythms into a more disciplined line; if he is able to concentrate his strength he may soon achieve full and free self-expression.

71

This concert was not reviewed in the press. Rightly so. The young composers did not want to collect "critiques" but experience. The others were unable to avoid their fate: unsympathetic disparagement. I consider it necessary to correct with a word or two the picture painted of them.

Those who have been praised rely upon the style of Brahms and German Romanticism or on other European conventions: Antal Deutsch, József Stokker, Emil Fuchs, István Hodula and István Kovács. Of those mentioned, only the first can be considered to have completed—up to a point—his technical studies. The other four still need guidance. Skilful imitation of an existing style is only the first grade in technique.

The other eight, although they too have passed through this school, are setting out on more or less independent courses. Among them Jenő Ádám, Lajos Bárdos, Mátyás Seiber and István Szelényi have acquired a craftsmanship exceeding by far the requirements of the school. But the others, too, have sufficiently firm foundations to escape sinking into the morass of some fumbling experimentation. The warm, individual lyricism of Zoltán Horusitzky is a great promise. Ádám inclines to a style of broad, curving melodic lines. Bárdos and György Kerényi are reticent natures, taking shape only with difficulty and they will need Flaubert's persistence to achieve their aims. If they have the energy for this, then they will achieve it. Following Mozart's course, Seiber has come closest to the style of pure chamber music. The string quartets of the four latter pupils can no longer be considered academic exercises. The consternation caused by Szelényi's *Piano Sonata* shows that his critics do not know Liszt, who has strongly influenced him. His *Sonata* for flute strikes a more individual note. Its moving lament is a document; it affords astounding insight into the soul, which has suffered so much, of the most valuable stratum of Hungary's Jewish youth, from which optimism appears to have totally died out.

Those in the vanguard of proficiency in the craft, the keenest observers of classic masterpieces, the best versed in the holy books of music were, at the same time, most responsive to folk music. The better Europeans were, at the same time, the best Hungarians.

There may be no genius opening up new paths among them; but even the starry skies would be dim if they were lit only by the brightest stars. They all have a love of honest work—anyone who lacks it will soon drop away from me—and the degree of moral seriousness now general among young artists was a rare exception in the happy times before the war.

The attack in a German daily paper asserts approximately the opposite of all this. This piece of writing—*"le style c'est l'homme"*—is an outrage against literary tone and good taste. It oozes the breath of decay. To use Pázmány's words there is nothing in it but "base curses, swearing squabble, ignorant foaming" and so it does not deserve reading, let alone answering. But: *"Sapientibus et insipientibus debitor sum"*; even such occasions must be used to stand up against false teachings, because innocent and well-meaning people may become entangled in their net. Some words are needed to enlighten them.

The hatred streaming from the article is not addressed to one person. Nor is it new. The matter is older and more important.

As much as twenty years ago similar weapons were used from the same directions to assail works which have since taken the place of honour in the treasury not only of Hungarian art but of the whole cultured world. The newness, on account of which they were attacked, was largely ancient: the style of old Hungarian folk music and its new flourishing through the medium of individual creative forces. To a lesser extent the new European style, then unfolding, was the red rag which since then has become "Classicism" all over the world.

As soon as Hungarian folk music, or music nourished on its traditions, appeared on the horizon the attacks were renewed. Again the same tone, the same impotent raging. It is a good omen for the young that the same suspicious armada has been mobilised against them—perhaps a bit prematurely—which, with its poisoned arrows, started a long time ago a war of extermination against Béla Bartók. With no more success, we hope.

In Hungary there is not yet such a homogeneous audience for music as, having grown up in Hungarian culture, would unite the knowledge and love of Hungarian traditions with universal musical culture; one camp still needs only gipsy music. The other, musically cultured side does not know what to make of Hungarian phenomena. But its naive, instinctive capacity will help the audience over these difficulties. Only some musical circles, untouched by Hungarian culture, and a part of the press maintain unchanging hostile battle order against all Hungarian endeavours in music.

Without the effect of foreign culture a national culture will waste away. The very greatest movements in music were the results of great foreign influences preceding them. In Italy Dutch music created Palestrina; Italian music created Lully in Paris and Schütz in Dresden. The rebirth of Hungarian literature was also brought about by the productive influence of foreign literatures. What is more, creators of national art may also spring from foreign blood. Side by side with Lully there are a number of other instances of this. We ourselves have our own artists of foreign origin who have an eternal place in the Hungarian Pantheon. Thus it is not chauvinism if we put some questions to those who have lived among us, only as aliens, like colonisers among savages; to those who do not know anything about Hungarian culture and do not want to know anything about it.

In your opinion only successors of Brahms and Schumann should be reared here. The children of Hungarian music, though they are better musicians, are cast away. Why? Because the Hungarian melos and everything that springs from it is hateful to you. You do not know it, you do not want to know it. Nor do you know, or like, the language and literature. You know Hungarian only for the purposes of everyday communication. In all manifestations of the Hungarian spirit you see something peculiar and alien: Tibet or China. Why do you not try to get to know it? Because you do not like it. And because you do not need it.

Well, live as well as you can. But by what right do you want to forbid us to use our own musical idiom? To teach this language in a Hungarian music school, modestly, side by side with the language of worldwide currency? Within the limits of art we give free headway to all kinds of tastes. But how long shall we tolerate the dictatorial tone with which you want to impose upon us the alien taste of your alien soul?

I confront your conservativism, which is that of a narrow-minded small German town or of international banality, with a Hungarian conservativism nurtured on universal culture. We want to stand on our own feet and absorb from the culture of the whole world what helps us, nurtures us and strengthens us; that from which we can learn how to express our own being as completely as possible. No longer do we want to be a musical colony. We do not want to ape a foreign musical culture. We have our own message and the world has begun to listen to us.

We have not invented Hungarian music. It has existed for a thousand years. We only want to cherish and preserve the old treasure and sometimes, if the possibility presents itself, we want to enrich it.

We can read in the book of Nehemiah that when the Jews, having returned from their imprisonment in Babylon, wanted to rebuild the walls of devastated Jerusalem, they were continually harassed by the enemies surrounding them. Finally, they could only achieve their aim by "one of their hands doing the work and the other holding a sword". There is a long list of those who took part in the building.

The rebuilders of Hungarian music can also work with one hand only; with the other they have continually to fight, to defend themselves. But the wall is being built. I think some names from the thirteen will find their way into the list of the builders. Perhaps the names of those now executed will be the first.

(1925)

TO YEHUDI MENUHIN'S BUDAPEST CONCERTS

Yehudi Menuhin was the first to appear of those globe-trotting artists who have frequented this country. He did not wait for us to invite him once everything was in order again: he himself offered his helping hand. He himself wanted to take part in the reconstruction work, not merely by material help intended for artists. By this he draws attention to the necessity of helping the artist not only with words but also with deeds.

But the intellectual and moral significance of his coming is even greater.

On the one hand it means that Hungary is gradually becoming connected once more to the currents of the cultural world, from which it has been excluded for so many years.

On the other hand, by the fact that he is hastening to introduce us to the unknown work which Bartók wrote for him, he is bringing back to us the spirit of our own lost great man.

This spirit is asking whether there is a square inch of dry ground in this flood-torn country where he can come to rest or must he fly back to Noah's Ark?

Our whole fate depends on how we answer him.

(1946)

ON THE ANNIVERSARY
OF BEETHOVEN'S DEATH

Opening Address at the Gala Concert in the Academy of Music

Ladies and Gentlemen,

If I were to ask, "what have we got to do with Beethoven?" the majority of you present would be scandalised by the question. What, indeed? The same as we have to do with Shakespeare, Goethe, Michelangelo, and every other great figure in European culture. We have been part of this for a thousand years now. For this reason Beethoven's music is also the indispensable nourishment for, and an inseparable part of innumerable Hungarian lives.

But there are still more Hungarians who today, on the 125th anniversary of Beethoven's death, know no more of him than his name, or not even that much. Those people have every right to ask, "What is Beethoven to me? A good gipsy is worth more than any classic."

Can you imagine what sort of work-programme is before us if we set ourselves the aim that there should be nobody in Hungary who would ask what he has to do with Beethoven?

And *this* is the aim we must set ourselves if we do not wish Beethoven to remain the property of the privileged, of the minority, if we do not want the millions to be further excluded from his life-giving, elevating, joyous influence.

But how do we reach this goal? Have we already done enough to come near to it? To this we are obliged to answer with a decided no. There is still much to be done and all the factors have to be related before we can achieve anything. At present no single one is enough; their operation is not sufficiently co-ordinated. These factors are every sort of school, the teaching and educational institutes apart from the schools, concert life and everything which is in the service of musical public education.

But professional education in music itself is still not sufficiently inspired by the idea that music-making is not an end in itself but that it must stand at the service of the whole people.

If we consider now whether Beethoven's personality is suitable for raising an echo in broad ranges of people, perhaps there is no other composer whose whole life-work is such a powerful expression of protest against tyranny, or of world freedom, and of the desire for brotherhood. Hungarians can especially recognise kinship in Beethoven's spiritual temperament as their whole history has been a fight for freedom against tyranny.

But there is one point we must not forget. The spiritual content of a musical work can be understood only through the language of music. Anyone who thinks he understands it when he has read the title and the programme is deceiving himself. It is not enough merely to place Beethoven before the masses. It is also necessary to teach them how to approach him.

It is the right of every citizen to be taught the basic elements of music, to be handed the key with which he can enter the locked world of music. To open the ear and heart of the millions to serious music is a great thing. And we who have been striving for this for a long time now beg for everyone's help so that we may achieve the great goal as soon as possible.

It is with this request that I open our gala evening tonight.

(1952)

IN MEMORY OF HAYDN

For a few years now we have been celebrating the anniversaries of great people, among them those of whom the Hungarian of average culture has not even heard.

We have to do everything to broaden our scope. But if we want to direct the country's attention to those standing less near to us, how can we pass a Joseph Haydn anniversary in silence, one who is not merely great for the whole world but who spent the best part of his life in Hungary and to whom we owe so much?

To begin with he was the first who, by his works with the inscription "all'ongarese", proclaimed to the world that here there is a special kind of musical expression differing from all others. If his employers, the successive Esterházy dukes, had been more Hungarian-minded than they were, and they could well have afforded to be under the circumstances at that time, then perhaps more works of this kind would have been left to us. But even in his works without the indication "all'ongarese" sufficient Hungarian elements are apparent.

To recognise and demonstrate these is the concern of Hungarian research workers, for a foreigner could scarcely obtain such profound knowledge of every branch of Hungarian music as is a prerequisite for this work. Final classification of details can only come about when every work by Haydn becomes available. Because, strangely enough, to this day there is no critical complete edition of this great and popular composer.

Secondly, he was the first to sound the voice of the people, after an aristocratic period, in self-created, highly refined forms.

He did not write for the understanding minority but for everyone. In one of his manuscripts he makes a correction in a few bars and writes the justification beside it: *"Dies war vor gar zu gelehrte Ohren"*. In other sketches he simplifies the first setting, with such observations as *"Und ich sagte Ihm, dass es nicht gut sey interessant zu seyn"*. How many present-day composers could learn from Haydn's remark if instead of *merely* interesting music they tried to express great thoughts in a generally understood language.

For Haydn, however, this was not just a question of style: it came from his explicit interpretation of the purpose of art.

In a letter written in his later years he says: "Frequently when struggling against all sorts of obstacles my mental and physical strength flagged and I found it hard to proceed further on the career I had started, an inner feeling inspired me: there are so few happy and satisfied people on earth, they are pursued everywhere by sorrow and care. Perhaps your work could be sometimes a spring in which the heavy-laden could find for a few minutes peace and rest."

This thought inspired him to further work. He wanted to be the benefactor of mankind. And he achieved this end. There has hardly been any composer who in the past two hundred years has caused more people delight and comfort. Since his death many new fashions, trends and styles have cropped up in music. Great creative artists have appeared, masterpieces have been born. All this has done no harm to Haydn. The best of his work is just as fresh and alive as if it had been written yesterday. No symphonic or chamber repertoire is complete without him.

His music is democratic in three ways. First because he speaks in the language of the people. Then he strives for everyone to understand him (*"Meine Sprache versteht die ganze Welt"*). And finally he once more brings about equality between the parts. Of course he did write works where the other parts are all subordinated to one in particular. But it is when he writes parts of equal rank that he is really in his element. In his eighty-three string quartets he created everlastingly valid models in this genre so that even Mozart confessed him to be his master.

Here in Hungary, considering the musical cirsumstances of the time, his works spread widely soon enough. In 1800 he himself conducted *The Creation* in Buda, and in the twenties and thirties it was also performed in Pozsony (Bratislava), Győr, and Kolozsvár (Cluj). There is indeed one of his works which every Hungarian knows, though to hear it does not make him feel pleasure but bitterness and hatred. This was not directed at Haydn, for the great majority probably did not know that it was by him, nor was it directed at the music, but rather at the political significance of the work—*"Gott erhalte"* was the symbol of oppression, of the denial of Hungarian independence.

In our little country towns, where it was just possible to find a few violin students, civil servants, chemists, who wielded the bow for better or worse, they set to with Haydn's string quartets. For them this was frequently their only route towards better music. But anyone who in this way caught a glimpse of the marvellous realm of music as a young student could never rest until he had penetrated further into it. Thus Haydn became one of the corner-stones of Hungarian musical culture.

His origin and career are for us full of lessons and hope. Here was a child of the people, one of twelve children of a simple village cartwright, born to be a genius but only able to develop into one because sheer chance swept him in among the singing children of St. Stephen's in Vienna.

There is no such thing here with us. But one of our institutions, begun at the cost of many years' struggle, may soon have a similar influence. I am thinking of these seventy-odd schools where the weekly six singing lessons strive to awaken and develop responsiveness to good music.

Anyone might ask why seventy schools when a Haydn is born only once in a century? Well, in spite of the century-old traditions of the Viennese choir, only two Haydns and one Schubert appeared. And a János Richter, too. And the others? They became the public who were able to understand the works of the great ones. For this, however, even seven hundred schools would not be too much. And what if it is precisely in the seven hundredth that a Haydn crops up?

Our remembrance of Haydn is, therefore, not meditation on the past: his example nourishes our faith and hope in our own artistic and scientific future.

(1959)

LETTER TO PABLO CASALS

Foreword to the Hungarian Edition of Corredor's Book on Casals

Dear Pau,

They've asked me to write a foreword to a book about you. The book is good, even in its Hungarian abridged version, but not enough to give any idea of your miraculous impact to those who have not heard your unforgettable concerts. Even the best records don't give any idea of this as they cannot recreate that atmosphere which surrounds you in the hall, or that life which you were able to breathe even into the simple bass notes of the Haydn Hungarian trio, not to mention greater works. This was free singing quite beyond the limits of the instrument. One was never aware of a single finger-change or string-change which is however often noticeable even with the best performers. Not even the best cellists could come near this in finger-sense.

There are virtuosos whose playing we listen to with bated breath as if we were watching someone walking on the ridge of the rooftop and were waiting in fear for him to tumble down. Or at the circus when alongside the most neck-breaking display the music stops. With you, the music never stopped. Your playing was not playing but life. An endless living song. The harmony of universal order could be heard in it. It was for this reason you were always most attracted to the one whose works reflect most clearly the indivisible unity and permanence of universal order. Beethoven said of him that his real name should not be Bach (brook) but Meer (sea). Even more than that—a whole world.

In the book we can read that even now you play his works every day, not only on the cello but for your own pleasure on the piano, too. (I do this myself as well, and am happy to think that this makes one more link between us. I hope that in time even my housekeeper will recognise the fugue themes.) You have made Bach's cello works understandable and enjoyable for people for whom they were previously like the Chinese language. But you were also able to play everyone else with an immediate effect: from Beethoven to Fauré, from Albéniz to Tovey. It has been proved once again that music does not belong merely to the initiated professionals: the general public also understands it when someone can genuinely bring the composer's thoughts to life before them. This was the secret of your effect.

And who can play Bach with such effect? Only someone in whom the harmony of universal order likewise lives and whose voice, for this reason, radiates physical and spiritual health. (In how many famous artists' playing lurks invisible disease!)

81

What the book discloses about your life bears witness to the fact that genius seeks the modest shelter of simple people and it is alongside life which is unostentatious that it lasts longest. Your life is that of a true man; just as no one can be a real artist who is not a true man.

Live in happiness, dear Pau, let your life be an example and edification to all of us. Even to those who have not had the chance to hear you.

(1960)

BÉLA BARTÓK'S FIRST OPERA

On the Occasion of the Première of "Bluebeard's Castle"

Today neither the public nor the critics see Bartók's music as the castle with seven locked doors which it appeared to be ten years ago, but even now there are few who have been able to follow him on the road from searching, based on older foundations, to his own discovery. Even his opponents to date reluctantly recognise the richness of his inventive capacity, the individual colour of his orchestra, the simultaneous birth of colour and thought, the strictly organic interrelationship between his ideas. No one has succeeded in categorising him into either of the branches of "modern music", neither into the motley style of the old-new mixture, nor into the anarchy-chaos of half-talents and pseudo-talents.

His completely individual combination of ancient primitiveness with the most developed culture makes his musical individuality stand quite apart. His music is a single-material, self-contained, unified organism, virtually without any trace of borrowing or imitation. He too has his ancestors, but the connection is not apparent in externals; the spirit of all great music of the past lives in him, all that is not bound to time, all that is permanently valid. But for average musical culture what is most difficult to approach in him is what developed from his connection with folk music.

More recently it has become customary to regard folk art as the incomplete survival of the older stages of art. Even if there is much of this among it, this does not wholly exhaust it. Its true value lies in what it has preserved from ancient music and that to which it gives an inspiring example—an expression of feeling which is free of all formal pattern, not limited by formal schemes, and for this reason of extreme intensity; it is the free, direct speech of the soul. Those who do not know this folk music—and how many do know it?—will not be able to recognise it in Bartók either; they will only feel some great peculiarity, for this is precisely what has no analogy either in art music or in Hungarian music so far.

The first musical efforts of the forties in the nineteenth century saw the bloodless song literature of the beginning of the century and gipsy dance music as their direct predecessors, and joined forces with them. Whatever got into this development here and there from below, from the more ancient layers, like sporadic rocks in a waste of rushes, led to freshly prospering Hungarian music which precisely through its more ancient and original side was able once again to grasp the broken thread of tradition.

I do not believe that this music is "felt" to be Hungarian by those who think the style of the few hundred songs written around 1850 to be the only Hungarian style. This semi-dilettante literature is not entirely worthless for what it is, but it shows such a superficial Hungarian quality and smells so much of the public house, and so many associations of the wind-and-gipsies atmosphere cling to it, that it had to remain outside the gates of higher art.

From the new Hungarian music flows the pure clean air of another Hungarian quality with deeper, everlasting roots, like that of the Székely pine forests where something was forced into hiding, something which remained of a life-current of monumental strength, something which had once embraced a whole country. The buds of this grew large, as with Bartók's music, providing volcanic work of a quite extraordinary creative strength developing into a spiritual language of infinite expressive force, but also having firm construction. Today we can search in vain for something comparable. This is no longer the sentimental revelry of the Bach-period* gentry, nor the rousing alarm of Kossuth, nor the sorrowing of the *kuruc* insurrectionists. In short it is not just one part of Hungary but everything together: a multilayered, deeply tragic world-Hungary containing within it the self-consciousness of the conquerors of the country and the wild energy of the will to live in the face of present wretchedness. This sort of music is really in its element when it is in association with drama. It was quite ready for it. It was only in the development of the vocal element that it proved necessary to tread an unbeaten track.

As until recently the great majority of our traditional operatic repertoire consisted of works translated from foreign languages, these developed a peculiar kind of musical declamation which even composers of original operas were latterly not very capable of avoiding. It became almost a general rule that in this declamation the stresses of language and music should always be at war with each other. Usually the music won, and for two generations the audience (mainly aristocracy and German-speaking bourgeoisie) put up with this murdering of the Hungarian language, their linguistic instinct making no protest against it. In the last few years some new artistic translations brought a considerable improvement. But even the best translation is still a translation. It can follow only imperfectly the melodic line born for another language. And possibly even the opera public of today does not fully appreciate that the Hungarian language is not only standing on its own two feet, but setting off under its own steam and even trying to fly.

Bartók set out to liberate the language, intensifying natural inflections into music, thus contributing a great deal to the evolution of a Hungarian recitative style. This is the first work on the Hungarian operatic stage in which the singing is consistent from beginning to end, speaking to us in an uninterrupted Hungarian way.

---

* This is the name given to the decade following the suppression of the 1848/49 Hungarian Revolution and War of Independence. It got its name from the leader of the government appointed, Alexander Bach (1813–1893), who was the personal symbol of the absolutist, oppressive politics of the Habsburgs.

This kind of composition, in which every word and phrase gains a cutting plasticity, illuminates even the tiniest linguistic unevennesses in the text. That such things might exist in Balázs's text would be a serious cause for complaint, but even strict critics do not mention it. Virtually unanimous condemnation of such unevenness—without any justification here, it is true—creates the impression that as far as opera libretti are concerned we are faced with very exacting demands. Nevertheless our writers do not consider the libretto to be a serious genre, forgetting that in the golden ages of opera even the text was always the work of a professional. For this reason it is a striking phenomenon when an opera text stems from a real writer or even a dramatist. For this reason special praise is due to Béla Balázs who did not grudge writing one of his most beautiful and poetic concepts in the form of an opera libretto, thus contributing to the birth of a magnificent work. His text "without events" is not indeed an integral part of any customary operatic scheme. But as the old tale is unfolded and the eternally unsolved man-woman problem is displayed before us, the listener is transfixed by tragic tension from the first word to the last. Its outline quality, the way the bringing to life of the contours is entrusted to the music, make it possible to weld it together organically with the music. Neither the drama nor the music is compelled to deny its own separate existence, and yet they are able to merge into a greater unity. This unity is not disturbed but rather enhanced by the symphonic construction in the music: the curve of the drama and the parallel curve of the music reinforce each other in a powerful double rainbow.

The constructive strength of the music asserts itself even better if we hear *The Wooden Prince* after it. This dance-play balances the disconsolate *adagio* of the opera with a playful, animated *allegro* contrast. The two together merge into one, like two movements of a giant symphony. And let those who consider atonality to be Bartók's principal achievement notice in the end that both of these works have a recapitulating basic key, like any Mozart opera.

The performance was one of the most beautiful in the whole season. Conductor Tango proved even last year that to understand the new Hungarian music it is not absolutely necessary to be twenty years old or Hungarian. To every new art talent, open receptivity and real technical knowledge provide a key. Last year, in the performance of the dance-play, it happened perhaps for the first time that an honest artist set about an honest work without the usual patronising attitude of conductors; and Bartók's music was heard perhaps for the first time as he had imagined it. Now this "miracle" has been repeated and on every occasion more and more people will probably discover that this music is not so incomprehensible after all.

In the singing roles Olga Haselbeck and Oszkár Kálmán carried out their responsibilities splendidly. We fully appreciate their work only when we reflect that they have themselves had to create a mode of performance for a new style which is without traditions.

(1918)

BÉLA BARTÓK

After a long decline the rebirth of the Hungarian spirit is linked with 1772, the year the French-influenced literary movement emerged. This trend paved the way for the two great generations that themselves laid the foundations of today's Hungarian culture.

The first, the 1790 generation—in which I include those born between 1780 and 1800—reached a pinacle in Mihály Vörösmarty in literature and in István Széchenyi, "the greatest Hungarian", in political life.

The second generation, that of 1820, of Petőfi, Arany and Jókai, perhaps even greater than the first, completed the gigantic work begun by their predecessors. In political life this was the era of Lajos Kossuth. Unfortunately, development was broken by the historic catastrophe of 1848–9, and the generation following it had too much to do to fill up the gaps in such a swift and uneven evolution. The work of the generation of 1850 was like an ebb after a powerful, swelling tide. After two such powerful outbreaks a rest was bound to come. In literature decadent successors followed after great poets and a cosmopolitan trend took the place of enfeebled patriotism.

It was with slow steps that music followed general development. For want of traditions the first period did not produce notable musicians. Only folk music, spread and distorted by the gipsies, managed to gain some fame—later increasing more and more—and provided the "raw material" for Europe. This is the origin of the music in the so-called "Hungarian manner", of which enough to fill a small library was produced by composers of different nations from Haydn to Glazunov.

It was only in the period that followed that the first great Hungarian composers appeared. Liszt, Erkel, Mosonyi and a considerable number of others were born between 1810 and 1830, their common ideal being the creation of a national music. This endeavour led to significant achievements. In the next period, however, development was broken by the strange division of musical life; the same phenomenon that made itself felt in political and literary life after 1849. On the one hand, a strong desire to raise Hungarian musical culture to a European level was manifested: an academy of music was established (1875) and an independent opera house built (1884). But in order to realise these intentions numerous foreign musicians were needed. These musicians banded together as a separate group and did not join the life of the nation; they did not even know its language. Nevertheless, they gave invaluable service, for they introduced a proficiency in the craft which, although almost completely built upon the German school, was able to provide a foundation for later development. The cosmopolitan trend of the period favoured the influx of foreign musicians.

On the other hand, the fostering of real Hungarian traditions remained the cause of gipsies and of such more or less dilettante composers who were not even able to put their melodies to paper correctly. Nevertheless, the whole country was reverberating to their original songs, as these suited the taste of the public.

It was the unfortunate outcome of the contrast between these two groups and of the exaggerated cult of the gipsies that a great part of Hungarian society, particularly in the country, felt lost when confronted with serious music, which accordingly could find audiences only in a few larger cities.

Trained musicians scorned the dilettante, despised the gipsies and denied even the possibility of creating artistic Hungarian music, particularly after the Wagner cult got into full swing. This was in spite of the fact that Wagner himself in one of his famous open letters recognised such a possibility and encouraged its pioneers.

And yet nobody succeeded in uniting the two isolated worlds. The generation of musicians making an appearance in the 1900s found on the one hand well-trained composers who nevertheless belonged to alien schools and on the other a new and vigorous flourishing of the songs said to be folk tunes but having no connection whatsoever with the ancient melodies of the Hungarian people. As yet Erkel's operas represented the highest level of Hungarian music, among them *Hunyadi,* already praised by Berlioz himself in 1846. Only a small group of music experts appreciated Liszt's symphonic works.

About 1900 a movement of tremendous force invigorated the country. The nationalist trend, oppressed since 1849, revived with new strength. In politics a separation of Austria and Hungary was discussed. The old Hungary started to come to life as a result of the enthusiastic work of scholars. The results of public education, more in a historic than in a scientific spirit, made themselves felt more and more. Old authors' works were published again and widely read; the patriotic songs of Rákóczi's time fired people with enthusiasm again. In all fields eminent talents emerged. The atmosphere was feverish: a portent either of great development or of great danger.

In 1904 the Budapest newspapers reported on an uncommon scandal. At an orchestral rehearsal an Austrian trumpet-player refused to play a parody of the Austrian national anthem as demanded by the score of a new composition. The Anthem *Gott erhalte* (written by Haydn and varied in his *String Quartet* in C major) was in Hungary the hated symbol of Austrian oppression, whereas the new work was Bartók's *Kossuth,* a programme symphony, its theme being the latest heroic effort of Hungary towards independence in 1848. The distorted anthem symbolised the Austrians' flight. (It is a well-known fact that only Russia's intervention turned the war in Austria's favour.) The composer, who wore Hungarian attire, had previously been known as an eminent pianist but now he became famous overnight. Although his work was too original to gain general appreciation it conquered the connoisseurs. It raised the question of national music so often discussed (this was a burning question in France as well), and it held out the promise of a solution in the near future.

Béla Bartók was born in 1881 at Nagyszentmiklós. After years spent in small provincial towns, in 1893 he settled down in Pozsony, famous for its musical life. There he came under the influence of another outstanding Hungarian musician, Ernő Dohnányi, whose talent was also unfolding at about the same time. Without any systematic guidance Bartók had been composing since he was nine years old and reached the stage at which he could write chamber music in the classical style, particularly in the manner of Brahms, who at that time often visited Hungary to present his new compositions. Between 1899 and 1903 Bartók, as a student at the Budapest Academy of Music, made rapid progress as a pianist, abandoning composing for two years. He seemed to be devoting himself to a promising career as a performing artist. What had been forced to become a subterranean stream by his studies at the Academy of Music (and perhaps by the oppressive memory of Wagner's and Liszt's work) merely awaited some inspiration for it to break through to the surface again. This inspiration came in the form of the Budapest première of *Zarathustra*. Bartók was fascinated by the new technique and electrified by reading Richard Strauss's scores; he dazzled the Viennese musicians by brilliantly playing on the piano the score of *Ein Heldenleben*. A fruitful period ensued: a sonata for violin and piano, *Kossuth* (1903), a *Piano Quintet*, a *Rhapsody* for piano and orchestra (1904), the *Suite No. 1* for symphony orchestra and a number of piano pieces. With its music, uneven but bursting with life and imbued with sunshine, this first period was a step of signal importance in the development of Hungarian music. For Erkel's art was built upon Italian elements, however much it availed itself of the possibilities of the Hungarian music of his own time, whereas Liszt merged the Hungarian elements with the new German style. The fascinating inventiveness of rhythm and melody alike burst forth in abundance from Bartók and although all the inventions of Strauss flashed up in his orchestra, and his inclination to unexpected turns and surprising resolutions and his harmonies revealed Liszt's influence, the predominant features of his works were more Hungarian than anything written before. His liking for larger forms, his aptitude for development—these were remarkable features of the efforts of his youth, too—his pleasure in richness of colour and decoration are characteristics of his valuable music "of many notes", sometimes not concise enough, yet fresh, youthful and full of *joie de vivre*. In Bartók's adagios the austere majesty of some of the melodies attributed to Rákóczi's period was revised, in his *allegros* the impetus of the famous Hungarian dances gained new life—and all this in the enchanting apparel of novelty.

However, while audiences were beginning to grow fond of his compositions (since *Kossuth,* which had been performed in Manchester under Richter's baton, very few works of his were played in Hungary—the première of the *Suite No. 1* took place in Vienna), he himself grew more and more dissatisfied with them. He began to feel

the limitations of the melodic style which, although he had widened it in a way un-known before, still bore far too much the stamp of nineteenth-century European music.

At this point he turned his attention to the songs that survived as rare harbingers of a more ancient tradition of tunes. He set out on travels, listened to the singing of peasants, wrote down melodies never recorded before and throughout many years collected a great many unknown or at least unusual sounding tunes. On the basis of his discoveries—and in this he was supported by the research of his collaborators—it became evident that the Hungarian peasantry had preserved such ancient traditions, untouched by any European influence, as had been long abandoned by educated classes. These ancient melodies emanated a captivating originality, proving a bene-ficial influence on Hungarian music, particularly that of Bartók. The *Suite No. 2* and *Two Portraits* already indicate the change. In the *Bagatelles* (Op. 6) this new style is quite mature and in the *First String Quartet* is transformed into chamber music of a purity and eminence on the level of Beethoven. In *Two Pictures* (Op. 10) it was enriched with orchestral colours for the first time. Finally, *Bluebeard's Castle* demon-strated that it was excellently suitable for dramatic media as well.

The new style roused a violent antagonism. It was accused of lacking melody, of an excess of dissonance, of a lack of form "bogged down in incomprehensibility", of in-coherence and obscurity—and finally even its Hungarian character was refuted.

Are not the same accusations voiced at the birth of every new art? What did old Griepenkerl say in his edition of Bach? "Does the assertion that Bach's works are allegedly incomprehensible depend only on the works and not on the narrow-minded prejudiced and uncomprehending audiences?" "Melody! The battle-cry of dilettanti!" (Schumann); every new melody had been attacked with this. True, in Bartók's works the well-known "Hungarian" clichés could not be found, nor the Italian–German melodic forms listeners had grown accustomed to over the centuries. And yet, if we are searching for a concise definition of Bartók's new style we must say that it is a renaissance of melody and rhythm.

In the fight between "vertical" and "horizontal" principles carried on since the sixteenth-century harmony became victorious. In the nineteenth century it gained such predominance in music that melody and rhythm became more and more impover-ished. In his often quoted saying Saint-Saëns foretold this process and experiments springing from the most differing efforts achieved similar results. What had been searched for by Saint-Saëns in the Far East and in the church modes and found by Debussy in Russian songs was discovered by Bartók in old Hungarian folksongs. The folksong inspired by the pentatonic system offered itself as a fruitful contrast to the harmonically predetermined world of melodies and to faded chromatics. It dis-played examples of fresher and more vigorous outlines and of more expressive and telling rhythms instead of the obsolete, typical formulae.

Encouraged by this example Bartók moulded an infinitely many-sided idiom; from the stabbing rhythm of the *Burlesques* to the most subtly shaded and most sensitive melodic lines. Perhaps these melodies do not always follow the course our ear—the slave of the past—expects. But if we have not completely lost our sensitivity we must after all recognise the singular melodic quality of these tunes, which, although strongly differing from classical formal practice, is nevertheless directed by more durable laws than the requirements of a style changing from century to century. Bartók does not "arrange" folk tunes thematically, but penetrates their spirit and transforms them as raw material into his own individual music. In all this he is guided by his sure sensibility and not by considerations of principles. Any attempt to find some special or contrived scale in his works proved to be fruitless. The pentatonic phrases themselves, which since the end of the century appeared more and more often, had emerged in his works long before he used them consciously.

Let us return to the dissonances. Bartók, who had pursued the development of modern harmony since *Tristan,* was an heir to Bach's harmonic world. Reger, too, in his opinion, professed that Bach still had a message for us, even after Wagner. The change in melodic style also inevitably influenced the harmonic world. The new connections between certain notes, which came about as a result of their "sequence" (their being played one after the other), also assumed a validity when they were sounded together. Chords that formerly we would have felt to be incomprehensible without their resolutions have now become satisfying.

But most of the condemned dissonances spring from the melodies. Frictions and coarser effects are brought about by the combination of two or more melodies. Bach's style is considered to have "not only passing notes but complete passing melodies and suspensions of not only a single note or chord but of complete melodic progressions".

This is the secret of Bartók's dissonances as well.

Since Bach we have lost the habit of being able to pursue two voices of equal importance; co-ordination has been replaced by subordination. We concentrate our attention upon notes sounded below one another and are immediately searching for triads if groups of notes are sounded simultaneously. But music, melodious in its essence, is not to be listened to in this way. If we succeed in surveying a larger area with our glance, that is to say, if we hear horizontally, the grating dissonance comes to an end at once. At such times sudden dissonances explode like cannon shots, but if they become separated into melodies they unswervingly proceed towards their goal. When two melodies meet, a stress is created that doubles the energy of movement and lends additional emphasis to one melody or to both. This renders Bartók's style particularly terse and implacably logical, creating a feeling of absolute inevitability.

We would be mistaken, however, if we considered him merely a master of polyphony. He has no "system". Side by side with his intricate pages we can find infinitely simple ones; the expression is dictated by the message. He even simplified his style, partly following the example of the French school with which he began to become familiar in 1907. Sometimes he completely abandons harmony. There are often unisons to be found, from the *Ninth Bagatelle* up to the most wonderful part of the

Second String Quartet (the Scherzo), which is aglow with colours despite its lack of harmony and an orchestra.

The charge of confusion and shapelessness is not even worth considering. Although there are verbose parts reminiscent of Schubert in works of his first period, where could one find a peer of the closed, epigrammatic structure of the *First String Quartet* among works composed since Beethoven? The unity of the movements ensured in the nineteenth century by all kinds of external means is here established in the manner of old masters: by dint of homogeneity in the musical material and something even above that: something we could call "psychological unity". The *First String Quartet* is an internal drama, a kind of *retour à la vie*: the return to life of a man who had reached the shores of nothingness.

The last argument of Bartók's opponents, namely that his music is not Hungarian, reminds us of a letter of Liszt, dated 1860, in which certain patriots are mentioned. "For them the *Rákóczi March* means more or less the same as the *Koran* meant for Omar—they would gladly commit... the whole of German music literature to flames on grounds of this fine argument: either it is contained in the *Rákóczi March* or it is absolutely worthless." Today, too, there are such patriots—admittedly, their Koran has been somewhat extended since 1860—and now they say: "It either reminds me of the *101 magyar népdal* (101 Hungarian Folksongs) I know, or it is not Hungarian at all."

Indeed the works of his first period are reminiscent of some well known songs. In his new style he built on unknown or almost unknown songs, sublimating them to such an extent that the listener no longer recognised in them fragments of tunes. Instead of a purely thematic Hungarian quality he bears witness to a different, a superior Hungarian-ness. For this music is Hungarian: a native of our countryside, of our education, our ideals and spiritual currents. The music is that of a man who had lived and suffered the whole range of the life and sufferings of his nation. And in the ancient tunes he recognised the long-forgotten mother-tongue because he found in them the force of nature and proud, human dignity—the force and greatness of ancient Hungary.

The *Two Pictures* testify to a radically transformed orchestral writing and to a superior mastery of the craft. As against the somewhat uneven and crowded orchestration of the early works there is manifested in them such a sure knowledge of tone colours and such an artistic sense of proportion that he does not fall behind the achievements of the French school in any way. The greatest masterpiece of this phase of his career was created at that time; with this he created a new era in Hungarian music. His one-act opera, *Bluebeard's Castle,* is as significant for us as is *Pelléas* for the French. If, in spite of the magnificent past of French opera, it could be declared that prior to Debussy there had been no musical diction suited to the spirit of the language, how much more is this valid for our own operatic literature! Since the first operas written to Hungarian texts (1822), the number of original works was insignificant; our programmes were overwhelmed with foreign works, their abominable translations being repeated outrages against the Hungarian language. Nor could the authors of original operas get rid of this "operatic dialect". Bartók was a pioneer in listening to the natural music of the Hungarian language in the recitatives and in following the guidance of the folksong in the more stylised sections.

At the same time, in *Bluebeard,* he created a powerful work, compelling throughout, surpassing all his earlier works in its expressive force.

The seven doors, opening one after the other, are the source of that number of musical pictures, pictures in which not the surface is depicted but the most profound feelings expressed. Only incorrigible theoreticians may meditate upon whether "this is an opera or not". It is not important. Call it a "symphony accompanied by pictures" or a "drama accompanied by a symphony"—it is sure that the two make an indivisible whole and that it is a masterpiece, a musical outburst lasting an hour, which arouses only one desire: to hear it again.

This was a great surprise. The man, considered before to be only a witty master of grotesque effects, was discovered to be a man of deep and passionate feelings. The young generation, harassed in spirit, tortured by the war but noble in intention and strong in will, recognised itself in his person. It was not a material success but a moral enrichment. By and by the last objections died down; Bartók had "arrived".

...But success was born only later. At first a jury rejected the opera, and the work, classified as unfit for performance, was produced on the stage only in 1918. The seven intervening years were the most bitter period. Resistance degenerated into persecution. "A great talent, gone astray and ending up in a *cul de sac*", "pathological efforts" were the remarks—that is to say, every nonsense that could be invented by alarmed philistines and malicious craftsmen. Finally, he was considered insane. Our dailies had more space at their disposal for criticism (or abuse) than those in France, and they thus echoed and varied these views *ad infinitum,* lacing them with affected witticism in the worst of taste.

So it was quite natural that the music society founded according to Bartók's ideas with the aims of studying new music and unknown old compositions failed after a concert or two. At these concerts Bartók devoted his extraordinary art as a pianist to presenting our audiences with new French music previously quite unknown in this country. After such disappointments he completely retired from public life and devoted all his energy to folk-music research. His interest in the music of other peoples living in Hungary had been awakened for some time and he collected thousands of Slovak and Rumanian folksongs—all of them unpublished apart from the small Rumanian collection brought out by the Academy of Bucharest—and, not to mention some easy and very interesting piano arrangements, he accumulated invaluable material for comparative studies of folk music. Slowly the scope of his interest expanded to embrace the music of all peoples. In 1913 he returned home from his tour of Algeria bringing with him Arab tunes from the region about Biskra. In 1914 he travelled to Paris but his efforts to find somebody interested in his collection were all in vain. He discussed some plans for concerts with Jules Écorcheville, but the war broke out... Only slowly was he able to find his way back to composing. Encouraged by the Budapest success of the Russian ballet Count Bánffy, Intendant of the Opera House, commissioned him as early as 1913 to compose the music to Béla Balázs's libretto for the ballet *The Wooden Prince*. It was only in 1916 that he completed it. The première was on May 12th, 1917. At the same time he wrote his two series of songs for voice and piano, the *Suite* for piano (Op. 14, 1916) and the *Second String Quartet* (Op. 17, 1915–17).

All these works reveal a new manner of composition. Isolation and incessant work had a similar effect on Bartók as the progress of deafness on Beethoven.

Alienated from the external world, turning inwards, he reached into the furthest depths of his soul. He came to know the suffering that inspires poets to immortal beauty while at the same time consuming their lives.

At that time, to some poems by Ady (1877–1919), the greatest Hungarian lyric poet since Petőfi, he wrote music worthy of such fine literature. He also depicted at this time the despair of the *Prince* with sounds that make the audience shudder. On account of this some critics considered the work unsuccessful, the music being too tragic for a fairy-tale. Finally it was in this period that he completed his *Second String Quartet*.

We cannot approach works of such cryptic meaning with technical analyses; they must be listened to and felt. What is the point of claiming that he had come closer to Bach than ever before? Is there any point in speaking about the influence of Stravinsky and Schoenberg, which, even if it exists, touches only the external form; for by the first composer he knew only piano arrangements of *Le Rossignol* and *Le Sacre du printemps* and by the latter virtually nothing apart from a few piano pieces that he himself first performed in Hungary. What is the point of analysing the suppleness and freedom of the rhythm, the expressive power of the melody? *"Wenn Ihr's nicht fühlt, Ihr werdet's nicht erjagen,"* said Goethe.

The première of *The Wooden Prince* was not without effect on Bartók's position in musical life. Thanks to the unflagging work of the conductor, Egisto Tango, the performance was perfect and the reviews—even though there were some reservations—changed their tone: they dared not attack any more. They recognised Bartók's genius "in his grotesque dances", particularly in that of the Wooden Puppet, but could not appreciate the more expressive scenes, which they considered cold. After this the Opera House summoned up all its courage and produced *Bluebeard*. The audience gave such an enthusiastic reception to the work that the reviewers, now retreating, gradually grew into a eulogistic chorus.

From 1918 onwards Bartók was disturbed in his work by never-ending difficulties. After the completion of *Etudes* (Op. 18), which might be termed "transcendental" (as Liszt had called his own Op. 1, and which came at the end of a long series of piano pieces worthy of special analysis), he completed in 1919 the sketches he had made for Melchior Lengyel's mime-play, *The Miraculous Mandarin*. It is the most outstanding work in the style he had used so far, but at the same time it also opens up new perspectives, particularly in the scenes expressing a hectic life. From that time onwards the internal conditions of the country offer sufficient explanation for his silence.

The artistic œuvre, the principal periods of which we have tried to outline here, is anything but a mere stringing together of national elements or contrived modernity with no lasting value. Upon a firm national foundation Bartók has built an edifice to which every great school has added something. Saturated with the music of his native land he first became the pupil of the great German masters. But he learned from them only as much as was for his own good; as an antidote to weightiness and pedantry he came under the influence of the Latin spirit. Both his birth and his culture set him between the Germanic North and the Latin South. His outstanding creative spirit stands for so significant an evolution in the world of universal music that international musical life can no longer do without him.

His innovations in style and technique are mentioned more often than necessary. Of these Bartók has as many as anyone else. What is more important than anything else is that he has poured glowing, throbbing life into them, that he knows all shades of life from tragic trembling to light playfulness; but he does not know sentimentality, caressing, "enchanting" softness. He was born with a soul essentially classical, but at the height of Romanticism, and was swept away by the rebellions against the obsolete practice of European music in the 1900s, by the last wave of the storm stirred up by Berlioz, Liszt and Wagner. But we can see that he stands out from the camp of those incessantly searching for something new, for he creates an ever purer, ever more plastic style in which the candour of the impressionist is disciplined by an iron will. He has inhaled the values of all great schools and reached the universality so seldom realised since the great Viennese masters, the wonderful unity springing from the marvellous balance between Germanic and Latin peoples' cultures. The music of the Viennese masters, too, radiated this perfect balance in elements, whereas later the individual elements were modified, developed, enriched, but always to the detriment of the others. Our age is still an era of tone colours but numerous signs point to the fact that the time of equilibrium is once more approaching. Bartók's music pursues this course.

(1921)

BARTÓK'S COMPOSITIONS
FOR CHILDREN

It is understandable that the ever increasing interest in Bartók's works is directed mainly at his greater compositions. However, it would be wrong to neglect certain of his smaller, more modest works because these too conceal a great many interesting and valuable points.

Such are the piano pieces he wrote for children. (*Ten Easy Piano Pieces,* 1908; *Gyermekeknek—Pro děti [For Children],* 1908/9; *Sonatina,* based on Rumanian folk tunes; *Rumanian Christmas Songs*; *Rumanian Folk Dances,* 1915. Of a kindred spirit, though more difficult to perform, are the *Fifteen Hungarian Peasant Songs,* 1914–17.)

His very first experiments in this genre were brilliantly successful, e.g. Nos. 5 and 10 of the *Ten Easy Piano Pieces,* which, although they are very easy, have become popular concert items. And yet, later on, whenever he wrote for children, he never again used his own themes, as though he would have preferred to get children's folk music closer to children.

Singing games and tunes give a send-off to children brought up in the country, which will all through their lives warm some small recess of their souls. Urban children do not know this treasure. In most cases their first musical impressions are worthless. This could be counteracted if the nursery rhymes and simplest songs of the Hungarian people could be engraved upon their memories. Primary schools do not yet provide for this sufficiently. But to young people playing the piano Bartók has given the possibility of making up for the experiences they have missed—at least in the field of music—in as much as this is possible.

Indeed, he went even further than that. In addition to the finest Hungarian folksongs and singing games he made use of the tunes, mostly collected by himself, of other peoples living in Hungary whose mother-tongue is not Hungarian. *Pro děti* contains Slovak folksongs and the works mentioned after that embrace themes of Rumanian folksongs.

These small sample collections evoke quite clearly and definitely—as much as is allowed by their brevity—the characteristics of each individual people. From them it is child's play to prepare a study of Hungary's folk music. And if through them interest is aroused, the next generation may put an end to the confusion reigning in this field at present.

This small and exceedingly valuable musical geography is enriched by a great deal of incentive belonging specifically to the sphere of music teaching.

What a lot is expected from a poor child learning music! I do not want to go into details about the infinite mass of worthlessness disguised by various pedagogical labels. No other field of music has offered such a vast sanctuary for bunglers and untalented people.

But in this genre even the works of greater or lesser masters seldom achieve the aim of becoming real music for children. The best of them are mostly played by adults and they do not always find their best audience among children. Other compositions again discourage children by approaching them as if they were strange little animals— in some adult way imitating the intonation and speech defects of children.

Bartók addresses them in a manner worthy of human beings and yet in a comprehensible way: he uses their own idiom. With Bartók, however, this is not a disguise, for it is his own language, too—one of the modes of expression he uses. He dresses old, traditional children's tunes in a tender piano tone, extraordinarily subtle in its emotions. Hungarian folk tunes in the past used to be harmonised in the widest variety of styles: sometimes being bungled in the manner of dilettanti, sometimes in a style classically correct, with virtuosic brilliance and finally even in Wagnerian fashion.

But Bartók seems to have found the right style prescribed by the melodies themselves. At first this style may sound strange—as do the tunes themselves, which educated people hardly know here in their own country. Children, however, will soon feel what is related to their own soul. They feel that somebody is approaching them without any hypocrisy and they will genuinely enjoy these pieces unless a punctilious pedagogue shuts them off from them. Old-fashioned teachers, who want to stick to their last, may be particularly apt to proceed in this way, because they have not yet recognised the practically unlimited possibilities and the necessity of a more profound rhythmical training. But those who have reached this level will prefer this living, ancient music for exercises of rhythm to any contrived exercise.

That is why these pieces are significant for children of other countries, too. Open-minded teachers have already pointed out that dealing with unusual phenomena is most fruitful in the teaching of music. (This has been done by Max Friedländer in the preface to his excellent little choral school.) In this respect the alien character is itself a particular advantage of Bartók's pieces for children. Let the children of more fortunate countries approach through this music their poorer East-European brothers.

(1921)

BÉLA BARTÓK THE MAN

The Trade Union may not know what a difficult task it assigned me when asking me to put Béla Bartók's life into words. Objectively, too, this is a hard task, but subjectively even harder, for in the course of forty years' joint work with another man one grows into a kind of bridge with two pillars, and if one of the pillars collapses, then the whole structure will stagger and it takes a long time for the balance to be restored. Besides, I have never been interested in artists' biographies. Even if I did read them I was usually disappointed because I did not learn anything about them that brought me nearer to understanding their works. A work can be understood without one's knowing its author but there is no understanding a man without his works, for this is where he has planted the best part of himself. Anyone who knows the language of sounds does not need what I can say about the man for he is in his music even more than in his handwriting, from which graphologists can decipher many a thing today. It would be much easier to pick up and select a bundle of his works and present him through those than to try to express in words what is really unutterable. The more comprehensibly I try to speak the cruder becomes the picture I am drawing of him.

Perhaps the poets, these genuine masters of words, could say something. Two of our poets have written about him: Lajos Kassák, whose poem is rendered excellent by the fact that it is not followed by any explanation, only by a demonstrative picture, which, however, has great perspective. The other one is Béla Balázs's poem. It is a more minute and meticulous description, thus bringing the details nearer to us. But at the end it gives an explanation, with which I do not agree. Here, too, the picture is good, but the explanation points to politics and this does not in any way suit him.

Possibly, precise people are not content with the impressionistic pictures offered by poets and they crave, first of all, for the positive facts of science. Let us see what we should write about him on the basis of the group divisions of Kretschmer's characterology. None of the *cyclothyme* traits refer to him. There are, however, features of the other, the *schizothyme* group, that fit him: fragile, fine, sensitive, cool, severe, withdrawn, cold, dull, indolent. (Grades from the uppermost extreme to the lowest.) Up to the attribute cold, all fitted him. The categories of psychic tension (beginning from the bottom): fanatical, pedantic, unyielding, persevering, systematic.

97

Only the upper extremes—capricious and confused—do not fit him, whilst the rest hit the nail right on the head. The agility aspect, speed in reactions to stimuli: inadequate, that is to say, reactions to stimuli quicker than customary. The subtitles of this heading are: restless, precipitate, hesitating, awkward, aristocratic, contrived, angular, rigid. With the exception of this last, all the rest more or less fit him. With respect to social relations: self-contained, reserved. Grades: idealist, reformer, revolutionary, systematic, organiser, self-willed, crotchety, dissatisfied, restrained, mistrustful, lonely, unsociable, misanthropical, brutal, anti-social. With the exception of the last three there is none that could not have been attributed to him with more or less reason. The categories of psychic tension: ingenious, lively, susceptible, energetic, inhibited. He could have been a typical example of the schizothyme mental form.

If we consider the more detailed characterisation we can distinguish three groups in each of the principal types as regards the differences in the degree of these qualities: an intermediate, a so called average degree, then one showing a more intensive agility and finally a duller one below the first. The average is cold, energetic, systematic, consistent, calm and aristocratic. The more agile: fragile, inwardly sensitive, nervous, idealistic. All these qualities fit him. Only the attributes of the level below the average: rigid, nervous, strange, crotchety—do not correspond, although there were occasionally times when many people considered him eccentric and strange—and not without reason.

This is what characterology says of him. It sounds fairly precise, though here, too, the conditions of life are such that science cannot catch up with life. For even if it is true that these qualities emerged at times, man is not so simple a phenomenon that his eternal secret can be solved by a label with a few lines on it. There are always times in life when certain qualities give way to others belonging to another group. A recent researcher has advanced the theory—much more reassuring than the former—that in the course of life a given basic type may not only change, but turn into its very opposite. According to Jung it is the psyche that matters: it is not the body's slave and strives to dominate it. Very few people achieve this, but the endeavour to become what will be appropriate to one's psychical features is to be found in everybody. Such phenomena could be perceived in Bartók's life, too, and to understand them we must cast a quick glance at the conditions of his life. What was it that produced these reactions in him? In what circumstances did Bartók live? After all, two absolutely identical seedlings will develop differently if one is in permanent sunshine and the other in the shade.

He became an orphan while he was still young. His father died early. His mother had an iron will, although as a schoolmistress she became so tired from her week's work that she usually spent Sunday in bed. And yet she lived to be almost ninety. In fact her fourth sister lived even longer. That is why we thought that Bartók would outlive us all.

His childhood was spent in his parents' solicitous care: frequent illness, spoiling and, accordingly, sensitivity and seclusion were its characteristic marks. Music chained him to his room even more. When he was about twenty he had a pulmonary condition. (During his stay at Meran, however, he had put on so much weight that characterology might well have classified him with the pycnic group.) He was afraid of people and did not warm easily. He longed for affection, for sunshine and a better fate. In addition to his own fate he worried over the fate of Hungary, too. For our generation the horrible memory of 1849 was still a living reality. Old gentlemen with Kossuth-beards, who had seen the War of Independence with their own eyes, were to be met with every day. Bartók, too, may have met such men. "The witness of great times"—thus the newspapers indicated in their obituaries the death of a warrior of 1848. I myself lived in a house with "cannon balls". When I was a secondary-school pupil a decree was issued that, instead of March 15th, April 11th was to be celebrated, that is to say, the day of the confirmation of the law. The young people marched to the Hungarian soldiers' monument at night, for daytime demonstration had been prohibited. At night Emil Ábrányi's poems for March 15th were recited. As far as I can remember, this happened all over the country. That was the soil the *Kossuth Symphony* had sprung from. Party allegiance cannot be expressed in music, but the dynamics of the War of Independence could. So this music signified a clear political stand. Otherwise Bartók never became involved in party politics and would certainly protest energetically against the political propaganda released in his name. It is a pity that the work did not turn out more successfully so that it might be performed today, too; its author considered only the funeral march to be worth printing.

Why did this work not turn out more successfully, we may ask. His artistic maturity was not proportionate to his will. He was prematurely swept away by the impatient wish to create something great; he had still not had the appropriate training. Nor was his orchestration good enough yet. In vain did he imitate the external elements of Strauss's scores; confidence was still lacking, the form was too naive. It is tragic that he uttered the appeal of Hungarian independence in the musical language of Germany. His difficult passages harassed particularly the wind players and later, too, parts can be found in his works which are virtually unplayable. At that time he still did not know how to achieve great effects by simple means. He felt he had been unable to do what he had wanted to. This feeling recurred a good many times. His first successes were veritable oases among unsuccessful works; for example the great success of the *Suite No. 1* in Vienna. (Though even with this the rehearsals meant a great deal of vexation. Only years later was the whole performed, though even then one or two sections were left out.) Later he regretted that he had striven for public recognition too soon. He himself had got himself a bad name, he said; those who had tried their hands at a less successful work of his often did not want to know the next. All this merely enhanced his misgivings. He was also concerned about his career as a pianist, which failed to get under way. It was in vain that he went to Paris to compete for the Rubinstein Prize; it was awarded to somebody else. This was a grave disappointment and rightly so, since later the winner did not prove to be worthy of it. Bartók was a phenomenal pianist, but he was not attractive enough to become very popular. When he was twenty-five the signs of despair were showing. In a letter he complained that although he was already twenty-five he was still "a beginner among beginners". Dohnányi, his paragon at that time, appeared like a meteor while he himself lagged behind. At that time Bartók was often ill, while Dohnányi's mother prided herself on her son never having had even a cold in the head. His unrequited love did nothing but aggravate his sorrow. But finally his will to work gained the upper hand—there is no better stimulus for artistic work than suffering—and he indefatigably and industriously put the notes to paper. Soon he produced such a masterpiece as the *First String Quartet*. From 1906 on he was supported by a new kind of work, too: the collecting of folksongs. In his own words: he had spent the happiest days of his life among country people. This means a lot if we consider his happy family life (he was married twice) and his talented children, who gave him a great deal of pleasure.

What was it he found in villages that he valued more highly than anything else? First of all, he found his own inspiration. An unknown world, the Magyar character, considered to have vanished long ago; and he found it flourishing. This was enough to renew his faith in the future of the Hungarian people. French music, too, contributed to the unfolding of his new style. This dual effect, the old Hungarian folk music and the Latin spirit delivered him from his early, one-sided German orientation. I should mention only the last phase of what he learned from Latin music: from 1925 onwards I often encouraged him to write choral works. For a long time he did not compose any; then (about ten years later) he presented a whole bunch. At that time he began perusing Palestrina's works and he was deeply captivated by this art. It is a great pity that this impulse was not more profoundly utilised.

To learn up to the day of his death—that was his passion. Although he was no linguist, his knowledge of Spanish, French, English, Slovakian and Rumanian developed to such a measure that he himself was able to translate what he had collected. His mania for collecting was so strong that, if it had been centred on money, he would have become a millionaire long before. He never borrowed books; if he could not afford to buy them, he copied them with his own hand (thus, for example, some of Lord Berners's compositions). Introversion was a basic trait of his character and so was a longing for experiencing unknown things. He spent one summer near the North Pole, another one in Africa. Had he not lived between two world wars he would certainly have travelled all over the globe. He often listened to the collection of folk music he had recorded on cylinders and discs. Most of his time was spent in writing down his own collections. He achieved a matchless precision in the collection of Slovak, Hungarian, Rumanian and Turkish folk music; he composed and played the piano, working more than anyone devoted to only one of the three pursuits. His willpower overcame the weakness of the body. We thought him practically indestructible and that is why the news of his death caught all of us unawares. By thirty-five Mozart had completely drained his physique. If he had lived longer he would hardly have written anything more. But in Bartók there was enough vital force and working ability to last for another decade. Indeed, his death is to be deemed a disaster and we can but deplore the fact that the mysterious disease, against which medicine is still powerless, has deprived us of him. He was not able to utter the last word, nor can it be uttered by anyone else in his stead. We marvel at his having fulfilled his mission even to such an extent.

I feel it would be mere verbosity to say anything else, since I could not tell you more. I turn to the poet; he could have written this poem about himself, and indeed he did so in music.

> *Neither gay forefather, nor successor*
> *Neither relative, nor acquaintance*
> *Am I for anyone*
> *Am I for anyone.*

He has gone. Happy are those who could help him in removing the barbed-wire fence he raised around himself in self-defence. It is up to those who have remained here to open up the way to his works. Let these works go where they were meant to go: to the hearts of the people.

(1946)

BARTÓK THE FOLKLORIST

"For my own part, all my life, in every sphere, always and in every way, I shall have one objective: the good of Hungary and the Hungarian nation."

Bartók, 1903

At the beginning of his career he would not even have dreamt that he would ever become a folklorist. Until the age of twenty-four he travelled the customary road of the professional musician in a double capacity: his first and main business was the piano, and alongside this was composition.

In his first compositional endeavours there is no trace of aspirations in the direction of a Hungarian style. He used the language of the Viennese classics, then that of Brahms. Even later he was not troubled by the problem of Hungarian-ness, but rather by the new western influences pouring in. His autobiography clearly states that after a lengthy break it was under the influence of Strauss's *Zarathustra* that he began to compose again. One reason for the long break can be looked for not so much in piano practice as in his teacher, Koessler. Koessler himself recommended him to drop composition for a time. Obviously he was unable to advise him well. They did not understand each other very well later on either. The symphony written in 1902 disappeared instead of being corrected: only the *Scherzo* remained. The undertaking was possibly beyond his technical ability at the time, but one thing is certain—he faltered in his development and in Koessler did not find a guide.

A somewhat petty one-sided argument went on between them later, too. In 1907, Bartók says in his notes on the B flat major Fugue from the second volume of the *Wohltemperiertes Klavier*: "The theme of the fugue definitely proves that a fugal theme can begin even on the highest note—in contrast with certain obsolete academic rules." In German (his own translation): *"im Gegensatz zu einer gewissen conservativen Schulweisheit."*

I advised him to omit this sentence since I had never seen any such rule in serious textbooks. But he insisted: "This was Koessler's teaching." This is how he summarised his opinion of Koessler's teaching. And the "definitely" bears witness to the agitated resistance which that teaching aroused in him.

It is strange that this resistance did not lead him to seek a Hungarian style even earlier. For it was Koessler's view that the Hungarian character could be used only within moderate limits in higher music, here and there as a patch of colour, as, for example, in the last movement of a Brahms piano quartet. Later he said of Debussy's *Pelléas*: *"Man kann nicht einen ganzen Abend im Dialekt sprechen."*

The creative fever which broke out as a result of *Zarathustra*, however, very soon presented Bartók with the problem of Hungarianism in music.

The wave of independence following the Millennium celebrations was then reaching its climax. Public opinion demanded things Hungarian in every sphere of life: Hungarian words of command and Hungarian insignia in the army, and a Hungarian anthem instead of *Gott erhalte*. The whole country echoed with the *kuruc* songs spread by Káldy and denigrating the Germans. Bartók, too, wanted everything to be Hungarian, from language to dress. For years he went about in the Hungarian-style clothes in fashion at the time, and that was what he wore on the concert platform as well. In letters he plagued his mother not to let German be the language spoken at home. He wanted to call Elza, his younger sister, Böske. Naturally in his music, too, he wanted to be Hungarian.

The *Kossuth Symphony*, the Op. 1 *Rhapsody* for piano and orchestra and the *Suite No. 1*, Op. 3, all border on the Erkel–Liszt kind of Hungarianism. But which way to go from there? In that direction there was no longer any room for development, nothing new to say. It was then that he began to become interested in the folksong.

In the musical atmosphere in Hungary at that time it was no easy task even to get at the folksong at all. The air was saturated with the crop of songs from the second half of the nineteenth century. This was the folksong of the more educated circles, but it was largely taken over by the people as well and anyone could make a mistake in the belief that *this* was the folksong. We can see what point Bartók had reached in 1903 in his knowledge of folksongs in a letter dated 1st April, in which he asks his sister for the text of a folksong. He was at that time occupied with the composed song beginning *"Az egri ménes mind sárga"* (The Eger horses are all yellow) then popular—several attempts at arrangement in his own hand have come down to us† he was especially taken up with the canon possibilities of the melody.

When he realised that this style could not be productive in higher genres, he tried vehemently to shake it off. But he lived within this and could not simply escape from it at the drop of a hat. Its traces stayed with him for a long time yet. This is indicated among other things by the *Four Songs* and the slow movement of the *Suite No. 2*. In our first folksong book, which came out in 1906, he included an Elemér Szentirmay song—the composer being unknown to him—on the basis of Béla Vikár's phonogramme collection (No. 5—but he omitted it from later editions). But the basic motif of this song, the repeated leap of a third, continued for a long time in his works (*Second String Quartet, Dance Suite*).

His first sporadic noting down of folksongs dates from 1904. A half-melody (No. 7 in the *Magyar népdalok* [Hungarian Folksongs] of 1906) which he heard from Lidi Dósa, a Székely servant of his, made him suspect the special quality of the music of the Székelys. But under the title "Székely Folksong" he published (*Magyar Lant*, 1905) a melodic fragment already familiar throughout the country, because he heard it from that same girl (No. 313 in *A magyar népdal* [The Hungarian Folksong]).

103

In 1905 he made a thorough study of my first collection which appeared in the periodical *Ethnographia* and then my 1906 study on the verse structure of the Hungarian folksong, and made penetrating enquiries concerning contact with the people and the collecting methods. He became acquainted with the phonograph.

His own systematic collecting began in 1906 in the Vésztő area, where he frequently spent the summer at his brother-in-law's, the overseer on the Wenckheim estate.

But Transylvania left him no peace of mind. He requested and obtained a scholarship (of 1,600 *koronas*) "for the study of Transylvanian folk music", and in the summer of 1907 he set off for Csík County.

He came back with such a pile of pentatonic melodies that, in conjunction with my own simultaneous findings in the north, the fundamental importance of this hitherto unnoticed scale suddenly became obvious. Yet we waited ten years, collecting and examining further data, before we considered it time to publish this discovery (1917).

From the outset he was perfectly aware that without knowledge of the neighbouring peoples' music it would not be possible to know that of the Hungarians really well. And since they had done little or no collecting, this work was also waiting for us to attend to. By the time he put away his Hungarian clothes, his earlier restricting nationalism, rooted in the atmosphere of the period, had opened out into a broader-minded internationalism without his Hungarianism suffering any damage whatsoever. When Rumanian composers displayed a desire to raise a memorial tablet at the house where he was born, he protested against being called a Rumanian composer in the inscription, arguing that Liszt did not become Spanish through writing a *Spanish Rhapsody*.

He began the collection of Slovakian songs as early as 1906. This also meant studying the Slovakian language. He was a great student of languages. He began English even as a student in the Academy of Music, French in Paris in 1905, and Spanish in 1906 when he toured the Iberian peninsula as Vecsey's accompanist.

It was in 1908 that he first noted down a Rumanian folksong. This soon captured his interest so much that he made a start on Rumanian on the basis of the Toussaint–Langenscheidt letters. His Bihar collection was published as early as 1913 by the Rumanian Academy.

Although he always had his publications read through by native Rumanians—György Alexits was of help to him in this respect and then, after his death, his son—it was not so much grammatical errors that they corrected as here and there some finer point which one is never sure about in a foreign language. They were further of help in the clarification of enigmatic dialect forms. (Oral information from György Alexits.) Even though he did not speak Rumanian fluently, he spoke and wrote the language quite well.

The attacks made on him from both sides on account of the Rumanian folksong are well known. It is true that his collections in Rumanian and other foreign languages are numerically superior to his Hungarian collection but for his comparative studies he required material and did not find enough in the collections then available. Apart from this, his interest was attracted by the novelty and unfamiliarity of the material. As in everything else, he was *novarum rerum cupidus* in this, too.

But there were two circumstances which contributed more than a little to the large-scale extension of his foreign-language collecting. One was that all these peoples opened their mouths much more easily than Hungarians, and also what they knew was virtually totally unfamiliar and consequently worth recording. He wrote of his first Transylvanian trip in a humorous letter to Stefi Geyer. It is a duet written almost in shorthand between the collector and a peasant woman, with excellent observation of the individual characteristics of the speech of the Székelys. The woman was reluctant for a long time, but eventually came up with some songs of the *"Kerek ez a zsemlye"* (This roll is round) type. At this time the joy of contact with the people was not sufficient compensation for futile labour. Yet later he confessed that the happiest hours of his life were spent in villages, among the people. Meanwhile this time-consuming searching and persuasion bored him, tired him and increased expenses. He kept precise records of his expenses. On one occasion he arrived listlessly from the Pécs area: he had found very little, and the expense turned out to be more than three *koronas* per song (then about three Swiss francs). Thus he soon arrived at the conviction that it was no longer worth collecting Hungarian.

And yet another circumstance facilitated to a great extent the collection of non-Hungarian material. The village intelligentsia of these peoples felt themselves much closer to the people and helped the collector much more gladly and effectively than the Hungarians. In the foreword to the Máramaros collection we can read that a Rumanian clergyman travelled with him, shared all the troubles of the journey and even helped in the writing down of the texts. In this way it was possible to collect enough material for a whole volume in twelve days.

He received an invitation from a Slovakian Lutheran minister in Hont County. In Egyház-Marót he sat in his room for several weeks beside the phonograph and from morning till night listened to the singers thus brought before him by the priest.

Or, having arrived in some Rumanian village, he settled into some suitable place and could say, "Now you can invite in anyone you like." For at that time "anyone you like" was still a likely source of folklore material.

In this way it was possible to collect a lot of material without a lot of trouble. In Hungarian territory he experienced co-operation of this sort precious seldom, and new material to be recorded also came up less frequently.

Around 1912, toying with the idea of a Chuvash–Tartar study-tour in Russia, he began learning the Russian language, once more by way of the Toussaint–Langenscheidt letters. Because of the threatening danger of war this tour did not take place. It can scarcely be imagined how much more we should know about the music of our eastern relatives today if he had actually succeeded in going there.

In 1913 he learned Arabic because of his Arabian collecting. And in 1938, on account of his collecting trip at the invitation of the Turkish government, he studied enough Turkish to be able to write down his recordings himself. Alongside such knowledge of languages and such exceptional musical ability, only the collector's passion was necessary to make a large-scale folklorist out of anyone. And that, too, was there: from early childhood Bartók loved to collect insects and butterflies (later bringing home some specimens from Africa). He often spent the summer in the Swiss Alps. On such occasions he conscientiously collected and pressed the mountain flowers and read the various plant-identifications. Besides this he collected folk embroidery, carvings, jugs, and plates, and studied their literature. Such widely diverging interests would have dissipated any other person's energy. It was Bartók's achievement that his various activities instead of obstructing each other, helped each other.

His creative and performing work was accomplished with the precision and fastidious care of the scientist. His scientific work, apart from the necessary precision and thoroughness, is brought to life by artistic intuition. The folklorist offered the artist knowledge of a rich musical life from outside the ramparts of art music. On the other hand, the folklorist received from the artist superior musical knowledge and perception. Apart from the two being an inseparable unit, in his work he was nevertheless able to separate them, unlike the majority of art-dabbling folklorists or artists who dip into ethnology. For he went all the way in both.

For the roots of science and of art are the same. Each, in its own way, reflects the world. The basic conditions: sharp powers of observation, precise expression of the life observed, and raising it to a higher synthesis. And the foundation of scientific and artistic greatness is also the same: just man, *vir justus*. And Bartók, who left Europe because he was unable to bear the injustice raging here any longer, followed Rousseau's slogan: *vitam impendere vero* (stake one's life on justice).

Thus it was possible, without any university studies, without scientific training, for someone who started out as a great artist to become a great scientist.

The man of justice can be recognised by the extraordinary sense of responsibility in his life and work. This was present in Bartók from the very beginning and merely increased in the whole course of his development.

In the works of his youth he sought an outlet for the ups and downs of life in the verbose, animated, though somewhat loose forms. Later his ever increasing concentration thrust out every superfluity, everything inessential.

Constantly he observed and studied; to the works of his contemporaries few active composers devoted so much attention. But he spent no less time on the earlier composers. Everywhere he sought his ancestors, his spiritual brothers.

He was stimulated by the knowledge of the loose and romantically incomplete composition training of his youth. In the end, having browsed through a borrowed copy of Jeppesen's counterpoint book one summer, he finally bought it in 1938. At the same time an occasional Palestrina volume came into view among the piles of music which covered his piano. He realised that here we can admire what is not to be experienced elsewhere—the highest level of responsibility. Who knows what he might have written once these later influences had matured in him, if cruel fate had not snatched the pen out of his hand so early?

A growing sense of responsibility is also evident in his noting down of folksongs.

Three stages can be observed. During the first period the writing is rough and sketchy, and even the detailed outline of the songs recorded on a phonograph is not given (published in *Ethnographia,* 1908). Later, in revising these on the basis of the phonograph, he gives everything in detail down to the tiniest ornamental notes. All his material was subjected to further revision from 1934 to 1940 when, in place of his teaching work, he was officially engaged for three afternoons per week in the preparation of the Academy of Sciences' great folksong collection. At this time he gained experience through the many complicated Rumanian, Arabian and other melodies, whilst the use of an earphone disclosed details until then concealed.

His written records represent the ultimate limit to be reached by the human ear without the aid of technical instruments. After this only sound photography can follow.

He was not concerned with sound measurements. It will be the business of the coming generations to make technical examinations of results obtained by the ear alone. It will become clear later whether there is any element in live music which disappears during the journey between the source of the sound and the ear, or whether it perhaps actually reaches the ear but remains subconscious. There can be no doubt that new light will be cast on many phenomena by sound-analysing instruments. But it is improbable that they will make any essential change in the basic features of the impression made on the ear.

Thus the best of Bartók's work is imperishable. It is the fate of science that each successive age produces new results and usually modifies or completely refutes the results obtained by the preceding age. Bartók was kept at a distance from every adventurous theory by his sense of realism. His main aim was complete faithfulness in the communication and interpretation of material. This, however, is not theory but life and enduring certainty even if the theories sometimes built on this basis do tumble down like ninepins.

He did have various ideas regarding interrelationships in music quite beyond matters of nationality, but he took great care in his elaboration of these ideas, thus emphasising that in this, too, truth can be reached only through unquestionable facts and whoever steps aside from this road becomes irrevocably lost in the mists of illusion.

We cannot at this stage appreciate the complete significance of his work as a folklorist. Apart from his book *The Hungarian Folksong,* so far only his Máramaros and Bihar Rumanian collections have been published. His other Rumanian, and his Serbo-Croat written notes remain unpublished to this day. He took the former away with him to America, since there was no hope of finding a publisher in any part of chauvinistic Europe. There he worked on the latter for years under commission

107

to Columbia University, but although it was ready for printing as early as 1944, indeed it was "astounding," he writes in one of his letters, "all the trouble they must have taken and the number of corrections they have made," and yet it is still unpublished to this very day.

When all this comes before the public it will become clear that the one who in his youth wanted no more than to serve the good of his homeland, represents with his work in this sphere, carried out as a second occupation, a milestone throughout the world.

(1950)

IN MEMORY OF BARTÓK

This year we are remembering the tenth anniversary of Béla Bartók's death. Throughout the world his work thrives more than ever. It is timely to ask how his legacy is being administered by his more immediate homeland, Hungary. Is it using him to raise its own culture, for its own nourishment? Is it taking as much from him as it might? To these questions we have even today to answer no.

What is the reason for this?

First, his individuality, and secondly the condition of our musical culture.

Bartók was the kind of man who, driven by permanent dissatisfaction, wants to alter everything, wants to make everything on earth better and more beautiful. From this type stem the great men of art and science, the great discoverers, inventors, the great revolutionaries in politics, the Columbuses, Galileos, Kossuths—who all left the world different from the way they found it.

Naturally there are many dissatisfied people who would like to change the world but they cannot. Bartók was able to. Because in his works there is present that mysterious living and life-giving force which is missing from many outwardly similar works.

For many have tried to write new music in the last half-century, thus the new spirit unfolding throughout the world broke out in many places into artistic expression; but very few were successful in giving this an enduring form.

Bartók belongs among these few, and for this reason is already today one of the most frequently played composers throughout the world, even though there are many all over the world who, holding on to the old, the familiar, do not gladly listen to the new voice. And every time a work of his is performed, people also think for a moment of Hungary; if for nothing else it cannot be such a worthless country when such a thing is produced there.

We can thank him for this as far as the outside world is concerned. Let us see what our own little world can thank him for.

It was not only in Ferenc Liszt's day but also at the start of our own careers that a Hungarian musician had to choose between two routes: whether he wanted to work here at home or abroad. Many chose the latter and today many of our finest musicians live abroad. Bartók, too, was haunted by the thought of success abroad; he prepared for it, and made attempts at it, but his strong patriotic feelings triumphed and when he

109

was only twenty-two, he wrote in one of his letters: "For my own part, all my life, in every sphere, always and in every way, I shall have one objective: the good of Hungary and the Hungarian nation."

He did not know at that time what a sacrifice that would mean. For the Hungarian composer could not, like composers of countries with a long cultural history, simply sit down in his room to write one work after the other. What should he write and for whom? After 1867, Hungarian efforts in art music turned away from the people; they did not at that time continue the magnificent impetus of the reform era which in any case had not yet arrived at a clearly formed Hungarian musical style. Musical life was nourished mainly on foreign works. At the turn of the century there lived in Hungary a very slender layer of musically cultured people, who were nevertheless completely estranged from Hungarians (to a large extent in their language as well). On the other hand here were the Hungarian masses, without any musical culture, their sole nourishment being gipsy music. It was obvious that from elements such as these it would be possible to create a public who desired and fed on a higher Hungarian music only if the cultured class could be made musically Hungarian and the Hungarian masses could be made musically cultured. This meant long and sacrificial work for many people; work for many years, assuming quiet years of peace. The events of the past half-century are sufficient explanation for this undertaking having had no success to this day and why we have had to start on it over and over again.

What gave and can still give us strength for this apparently almost impossible task?

Folk traditions. Profound study of the music of the people has shown that here there still lives an ancient, original and valuable musical culture, interrupted in its development; it can be lifted out from beneath the rubbish heaped on top of it, and a higher art can be built upon it.

Around 1900 it was necessary for the Hungarian composer first to collect folk-songs. Just like our writers a century earlier, even up to Petőfi and Arany.

To begin with we looked only for the lost ancient melodies. But seeing the village people and the great talent and fresh life being left to perish there, we gained a new idea of a cultured Hungary born of the people. We devoted our lives to bringing this about.

That Bartók, going far beyond the immediate necessities of the Hungarian composer, entered into large-scale collecting, extending his attentions to neighbouring and other more distant peoples, was due not only to his scientific leanings, tireless industry, and love of work, but also to his broad interests as a composer. He was attracted by the new, the unusual, what he had never heard before; he wanted to know man's every musical manifestation. These different kinds of music opened up more and more new perspectives and possibilities for him in his own creative work, too—the traces are to be found there in his works.

And this represents another feature sharply differentiating him from the western moderns. They in fact never acknowledged him as an innovator of equal rank simply because he stands on the ground of folk traditions. They write and concoct their works freely, throwing out all tradition, whereas even in Bartók's most daringly experimental works the firm ground of tradition is to be felt. Even when he flies away to the stratosphere, he does not break all bonds with Earth. Even if he did take some inspiration from them occasionally—and of course he did, the very man who was so interested in the music of every people of the world—it is still much more a case of the influence of his originality being apparent in every corner of western composition.

The question remains: what must we do so that Hungary, too, can partake of the life-giving, constructive strength of his rich legacy?

Nowadays one can find here and there an occasional teacher even in a village school, who, by using the new educational methods, can with absolute assurance direct his pupils towards the ability to read and write music.

If these teachers could be increased to the requisite number (and this cannot be recommended too strongly to our educational directors), musical illiteracy could be made to disappear within the foreseeable future just as in the case of linguistic illiteracy. Then the road towards higher music would lie open for the widest range of people.

For the village child, struggling with the elements of solmisation, the next stage of his music education will not be *Bluebeard* or the six string quartets. We do not offer Tokaj wine to a child, but for all that we do not pour away the Tokaj just because it is not for children.

It is a matter of pedagogical tact: what do we offer of Bartók's work, to whom, and where?

There is plenty for children, for beginners, and for the advanced. There are, however, works by him, as is the case with any great master, the untrodden or even untreadable paths of which can be followed only by the initiated, and not without some difficulty even by them. Too enthusiastic advocates merely do harm when they try to introduce that kind of work to the uninitiated masses. His work is one and indivisible but it can be appreciated in all its details only with wide musical knowledge.

The precondition of Bartók's triumphant and final homecoming is a musically educated country. To bring this about all the various factors must unite.

Once his art reaches those from whom it originates—the working people—and once they understand it, then there will be a Hungarian music culture, then the people will be truly happy.

(1955)

ON BÉLA BARTÓK

Presidential Opening Address
at the Commemorative Session of the
Bartók Memorial Committee

That we have assembled here today in Bartók's name goes far beyond the customary commemoration of anniversaries of someone's death. The name of Bartók—quite independently of anniversaries—is a symbol of great thoughts. The first such thought is the search for absolute truth equally in art and in science, the one prerequisite for this being moral seriousness elevated above all human weaknesses. The other concept is lack of prejudice concerning the individual peculiarities of different races and peoples, the result of which being mutual understanding leading to friendship among the peoples. Bartók's name furthermore stands for the principle of and the demand for regeneration stemming from the people, both in art and in politics. And finally it stands for the spreading of the blessing of music to the widest possible range of people.

It is in the spirit of these great concepts that we seek unity and co-operation with the best of all peoples. We use Bartók's name as a banner since we cannot find any collective name in the recent past which might be suitable for the expression of these manifold aspirations.

There is need for unity, for serious music is threatened by danger. Its significance is diminishing throughout the world because it is not keeping up with the spread of general education. It is not spreading to the same degree.

Even if we do not share the extreme pessimism of our recently departed colleague, Honegger (see his book *Je suis compositeur*), we cannot nevertheless deny that interest in music is pushed into the background all over the world by sport and technology.

I should like to believe that this represents the teething troubles of the development of culture. If we think back to Greek culture we can imagine that once more there will come a time when physical and spiritual culture will again merge into a harmonious whole.

Even technology cannot be a permanent enemy of music, for its inventions in connection with music have given us unimagined means towards the spreading of music. It is merely a question of time and training for all these aids to be used in the service of true and valuable art.

Good music therefore has to be fought for, and this fight cannot be fought with any success by one country alone within its own boundaries.

The age of musical world literature is approaching, and is partly here already. (*"Nationalliteratur will jetzt nicht viel sagen, die Epoche der Weltliteratur ist an der Zeit, und jeder muss jetzt dazu wirken, diese Epoche zu beschleunigen"*—said Goethe to Eckermann on 31st January, 1827.) According to Schumann, the world's music is like a great fugue in which the various nations sound alternately. Bartók continues this world-fugue with a new theme and in every direction this theme's counterpoints and accompanying voices are being heard.

I will end with another saying of Schumann's. "In all ages there is some secret connection between related spirits. Close the circle more tightly that the truth of art may shine ever more purely, shedding joy and blessing in all directions."

(1956)

OPENING ADDRESS

*From the Series of Lectures Held on the Occasion
of the Eightieth Anniversary of Bartók's Birth*

Eighty years is not a long time in the eyes of contemporary medicine. Bartók was not allowed even that much, though I always hoped that the characteristics of his mother, who lived for more than ninety years, would triumph in him. But not even a hundred years would have been enough for him to live to see the fruits of his work.

For what would he see if he had lived to this very day? True, it would give him some satisfaction that from among his contemporaries he is the composer most often played all the world over. But he would not be content with the state of the work to which he had sacrificed half of his life—indeed, more than half of it.

The Turkish collection, the large-scale Rumanian collection, left behind ready to be printed, are not claimed by anybody even today. Although his Slovak collection is being published—it is not what he would have wished it to be. His only joy would be the increasing *Corpus,* which is in preparation, because our group works as though he were still living among us. Alas, it is only his marble image that is with us. But whoever passes before this portrait feels that he is struck by a living, radiating effect and all his omissions and carelessness will immediately receive their punishment. Every one endeavours to avoid this.

That is how his spirit lives among us and ensures the further impetus of our work.

(1961)

LISZT AND BARTÓK

*Opening Address at the Second International Conference
of Musicology in Budapest*

The two artists in whose name we have gathered together today are not connected by
the coincidence of anniversaries. They belong together in the most profound way.

All through his life Bartók, both as a performing artist and as a writer, fought for
Liszt. In his student days he already attracted attention by his performance of the
B minor *Sonata* and throughout his career as a concert pianist Liszt's works were included in his programmes, particularly the less well-known compositions. In his
writings, too, he dealt several times with Liszt, to whom his inaugural address at
the Academy of Sciences was also devoted.

But, most of all, he is connected with Liszt by his own works. At first as his direct
follower, then by the unfolding of his own originality he, as it were, realised the intui-
tions of Liszt.

Such a close connection is a sign of spiritual affinity; recently attempts have been
made to explain it by pointing out a relationship in the type of genes, which can exist
even in the case of polar opposites. And, there are, indeed, such apparent contrasts
between the two.

Liszt's relationship to his country was centripetal, Bartók's was centrifugal. Liszt
grew up in foreign countries, in foreign metropolises but always longed for Hungary,
which he felt was his motherland. It was due to his close foreign connections on the
one hand, and to the historical events in Hungary on the other, that only towards the
end of his life could he work, at least partly, here.

Bartók, son of the Hungarian countryside, always yearned for the west, until
he emigrated for good. There he sought the appreciation and affection he had not
been given at home. His over-sensitive constitution was not armed with the *aes triplica
circa pectus* (the triple armour round his heart) that would have enabled him to
endure the last years of his life at home.

He was allowed a much shorter life than Liszt, but their destiny is also similar in
that it was only long after their deaths that their work gained full understanding and
appreciation.

This conference also indicates that in the work of both there is still a great deal to be
discovered and explained. One part of the task falls within easy reach of Hungarian
researchers. But the widespread international relations of the two men demand the

participation of scholars from all the countries visited by them. Only close inter-national collaboration can offer the promise of success.

If we can get but a little nearer to understanding the miracle that the work of every great artist means, none of the efforts made at this Conference will have been in vain.

In this hope I welcome the participants in the Conference, and wish them good and successful work.

(1961)

III
ON MUSIC EDUCATION

CHILDREN'S CHOIRS

Anyone who is concerned about what will take place here musically in a generation or two cannot pass a school indifferently when he can hear singing coming from it.

What does this singing say? Mostly this: "For us this is good enough! There is little time and little pay; the headmaster does not like choral singing. I have no ambitions, I am happy to keep body and soul together..."

This is not the text of the song, and yet this is what is heard from it louder than anything else. What they sing does not even approach art. The way they are singing is far below the level of talented naturalism.

If we look into the curriculum we can see that those who planned it were far away from the Greek ideal of education which cast music in a central role. And in most cases practice is unable to realise even the prescribed minimum.

Children brought up in this way will scarcely come in contact with music as an art in their whole lives. At most they can get as far as singing circles, where they can find an edition of "school singing" for adults. Of more refined music all they know is that it is a kind of head-splitting task, and flee from it with the cry "I have no ear for music!"

That is why even in our educated circles ignorance in music is often quite painfully apparent. Musical infantilism goes hand in hand with a highly developed culture in literature and the visual arts; and those who fight for what is good with their right hand, sponsor trashy literature in music with their left.

Hungarian society, which can very well distinguish between inferior and vintage wines, drinks inferior wine in music.

No wonder that at most five thousand people go to the Opera House and a thousand or two to concerts. Or that the more valuable the programme the emptier the concert hall.

Because of the higher requirements of an insignificant minority the state must maintain musical institutions at the cost of great sacrifices.

Millions are condemned to musical illiteracy, falling prey to the poorest of music.

For what do children hear outside their schools if they do not belong to the minority that practises good music at home, too?

The children of Pest, poor things, pick up the refuse of street music.

And rural children? The other day I listened to the singing of a group of girls on an excursion in the Buda Hills. What do they choose when they sing for their own pleasure? True, there was not a single "school song" among the pieces. But I heard "Snájder Fáni"—along with other equally worthy songs.

They were pupils of a Budapest teachers' training college, children of provincial middle-class families, the future mothers and teachers of Hungary.

Village children are closest to art. What they hear outside their schools comes mostly from the old and noble material of folk music. What is bad is driven towards them by the gramophone and radio from cities.

They are said to be hard to teach. I have not yet heard of anybody who seriously tried.

Bad taste spreads by leaps and bounds. In art this is not so innocent a thing as in, say, clothes. Someone who dresses in bad taste does not endanger his health, but bad taste in art is a veritable sickness of the soul. It seals the soul off from contact with masterpieces and from the life-giving nourishment emanating from them without which the soul wastes away or becomes stunted, and the whole character of the man is branded with a peculiar mark.

In grown-ups this sickness is in most cases incurable. Only prevention can help. It should be the task of the school to administer immunisation.

Instead of doing this, today's school itself spreads the corruption. The debasement of the language spreading from schools has recently been pointed out pertinently by the articles of Zsigmond Móricz and Count Kunó Klebelsberg. Something similar is taking place in music, but it has a deeper effect and there are even fewer antidotes against this than against linguistic debasement. Artistically deprived, contemporary life with its unhinged culture does not contribute anything good to the improving of taste. The Greeks, when they stepped out of their homes, inhaled culture even in the market place. We, today, must protect ourselves from the art-destroying germs, floating in publicity, in the very air. There might be people happy even without art. *Ignoti nulla cupido.* Let us not envy them. Let us try to develop in the young masses the noble organ that has become atrophied in those people. Powerful sources of spiritual enrichment spring from music. We must spare no effort to have them opened for as many people as possible.

What is to be done? Teach music and singing at school in such a way that it is not a torture but a joy for the pupil; instil a thirst for finer music in him, a thirst which will last for a lifetime. Music must not be approached from its intellectual, rational side, nor should it be conveyed to the child as a system of algebraic symbols, or as the secret writing of a language with which he has no connection. The way should be paved for direct intuition. If the child is not filled at least once by the life-giving stream of music during the most susceptible period—between his sixth and sixteenth years—it will hardly be of any use to him later on. Often a single experience will open the young soul to music for a whole lifetime. This experience cannot be left to chance, it is the duty of the school to provide it.

I do not mean that the school can offer this in its present framework, but I consider it self-evident that the framework will undergo substantial transformation. The teaching of singing must cover at least the same distance as has been covered by gymnastics, until the old "gym master" has grown into a teacher of physical culture.

I do not in the least consider what has been done in recent years in the field of physical culture to be too much. Indeed, I find it too little. We cannot speak of physical culture until children can wash themselves from top to toe in the crystal clear basin of the school after their daily gymnastics.

But do not let us forget the soul either. Why, sooner or later the school must face the sport madness that considers the cutting of the record by one-tenth of a second an event of world importance, and the champion of boxing the very summit of mankind.

A vast area of Hungarian children's souls, a region that can only be cultivated by music, is wasteland today.

But we cannot wait till the framework is expanded. Even today we can do a lot for preparing a better future.

Today singing is the Cinderella among school subjects. But this is in vain: the Prince will come to fetch her; the shoe will fit only her foot.

No other subject can serve the child's welfare—physical and spiritual—as well as music.

With us it is scarcely every twentieth person who uses his speech and breathing organs correctly. This, too, should be learned during the singing lesson. The discipline of rhythm, the training of throat and lungs set singing right beside gymnastics. Both of them, no less than food, are needed daily.

Is there anything more demonstrative of social solidarity than a choir? Many people unite to do something that cannot be done by a single person alone however talented he or she may be; there the work of everyone is equally important and the mistake of a single person can spoil everything. I do not want to declare that the peerless solidarity of British society and the discipline of the British individual have been created by choirs. But there may be some connection between them and the six-hundred-year-old choral culture. In the same way as one of the reasons for the difference between British and Hungarian workmen is that the former sing and know Bach's *B Minor Mass,* too.

That Hungarians do not like to unite is a fatal national error which we should struggle to correct by every possible means.

Choral singing is the most rewarding subject, because it gives the greatest rewards for the effort expended on it. The school produces in scientific yardsticks. This needs greater maturity and a longer period of study.

On the other hand, the choir of any school can reach the level at which it becomes suitable for an educational role within the school. And one step further: it can be of significant value in public musical life as well.

It is not technique that is the essence of art, but the soul. As soon as the soul can communicate freely, without obstacles, a complete musical effect is created. Technique sufficient for a free manifestation of the child's soul can easily be mastered under a good leader in any school.

Taken separately, the boys of Wesselényi Street certainly cannot sing as Gigli can. On the other hand, Gigli alone cannot create the same kind of effect as they can when a hundred of them sing together.

Pure enthusiasm and naive instinct—rare gifts with grown-up artists—are to be found in every healthy child. With a few years' technical preparation children can achieve results measurable by the most exacting of absolute artistic standards.

Below the age of fifteen everybody is more talented than above it; only exceptional geniuses continue to develop. It is a crime to miss that talented age. If we do not organise children's choirs properly, our adult choirs will increase neither in number nor in quality. A grown-up person will in any case sing differently if he has the opportunity to preserve the fervent enthusiasm of singing from his childhood. And the child will remember and understand that without conscientious work there are no results.

Let us stop the teachers' superstition according to which only some diluted art-substitute is suitable for teaching purposes. A child is the most susceptible and the most enthusiastic audience for pure art; for in every great artist the child is alive—and this is something felt by youth's congenial spirit.

Conversely, only art of intrinsic value is suitable for children! Everything else is harmful. After all, food is more carefully chosen for an infant than for an adult. Musical nourishment which is "rich in vitamins" is essential for children. Without it the chronic and by now almost incurable musical "avitaminosis" of the whole of Hungarian society will never come to an end.

An endless number of suitable masterpieces is at the disposal of schools.

Every type of school can find music suitable for it. Catholic secondary schools could be beacons of a revival in Hungarian musical culture if in the course of the service they used the masterpieces of church music with Latin texts from Palestrina up to our own times. They offer an inexhaustible choice of pieces which are fairly easy to sing. Even the smallest Hungarian town could acquire a programme—from Allegri's *Miserere* to Haydn's *Tenebrae*—which would not only help towards the religious edification and general spiritual elevation of youth, but would perhaps have some effect on the spoiled taste of grown-ups, too.

By performing the choral transcripts of French psalms and the masterpieces of German and English motet literature, Protestant schools could work similar wonders. Luther's frequently quoted words on polyphonic singing have not so far elicited much response from Hungarian Protestant churches.

Modern language schools could find plenty of excellent material for singing in the languages in question. To sing in the language of the people concerned and to get to know their character from their music, too, is an indispensable aid in learning a language.

Of course, every school should deal with Hungarian folk music as thoroughly as with the mother-tongue itself. Only then can the pupil reach a proper understanding of foreign music.

If school orchestras were to give up insipid light music and make their choice from the range of irreproachable masterpieces only, sooner or later such a musical atmosphere would be created in schools that the souls of the young people leaving them would be immune to the swamp fever of Hungarian musical culture.

Provided the formal framework of teaching can in the meantime be extended so that it is worthy of the subject and the purpose (tuition by qualified teachers in every school, in the country, too, up to the final class in the secondary school), our present Potemkin musical culture would be filled with content in a generation or two; new masses longing for good music would fill the concert halls now gaping empty and a network of choral societies founded with serious artistic ends would thread our social life together, which today is split in a thousand parts and has no cohesion whatsoever.

In many people's view the playing of instruments is the only course leading to results.

We must lead great masses to music. An instrumental culture can never become a culture of masses. Instruments have become expensive and the number of pupils learning to play instruments has fallen. Many of my young friends, pupils between eleven and fourteen, have their share of the struggle with life; there are quite a few wage-earners among them. However, delivering the milk or the newspaper in the morning and such like does not yield enough for violin or other music lessons. Should they be, for this reason, deprived of the blessings of music for a lifetime? Why, is it only through tormenting the violin, through strumming on the piano that the path leads to the holy mountain of music? Indeed, it often rather leads away from it.

What is the violin or piano to you? You have an instrument in your throat, with a more beautiful tone than any violin in the world, if you will only use it. With this instrument you will come invigoratingly near to the greatest geniuses of music—if there is only somebody to lead you on!

Some statistics: among the 100 members of the choir of the Attila Street boys' elementary school 5 are learning to play an instrument; of the 67 boys of Markó Street school, 27; of the 79 of Hernád Street, 14; of the 110 of Rottenbiller Street, 18; of the 117 of Wesselényi Street, 15; of the 200 girls in the Erzsébet Szilágyi secondary school, 170. From the total of 673, 249 are learning to play an instrument.

The programme that the above schools have recently performed so brilliantly is much more difficult than the usual choral singing in schools. And yet: no special musical training was needed for it.

Indeed, the voices and sense of music of our young people are so excellent that they can perform to artistic perfection anything that fits their physical and spiritual development, however difficult the task may be. Everything depends on the leader.

And this is where urgent reforms are required.

The qualification demanded today from music teachers in higher elementary and secondary schools represents such primitive musical knowledge that nobody can do the work prescribed even in today's curriculum unless he has voluntarily learned a great deal more.

The situation is only aggravated by the fact that in appointing teachers it is not the best that are chosen; "influential friends" are decisive.

Thus it is natural that absolutely unsuitable people hold important posts and to have the right man in the right place is virtually a chance phenomenon. And yet today only personal eminence could make up for the deficiencies in the curriculum and qualifications.

It is much more important who the singing master at Kisvárda is than who the director of the Opera House is, because a poor director will fail. (Often even a good one.) But a bad teacher may kill off the love of music for thirty years from thirty classes of pupils.

And yet, I look at the question of teachers with certain optimistic expectations. True, those who brought about the "Evening of Children's Choirs" belong to the élite of singing teachers in the capital. But there might be some undiscovered aptitude concealed in those more modestly trained.

Indeed, suppressed ambitions might come to life in many of them if they saw that better work meant better advancement and more appreciation for them, and that the scales were not always weighed down by omnipotent contacts.

During the transitory period before a new higher qualification can be enforced, considerable support could be given to the most talented teachers, and to those who have fallen behind through no fault of their own, by means of extension courses.

New singing teachers should be ensured positions equal in every respect to those of the other teachers. For today it is of no avail to direct better trained young musicians to this profession. There is no use telling them that they cannot find a more exalted calling, a vocation contributing more to the building of the nation. They have one look at how much the salary of a singing master is and they go straight off and play the piano in a cinema because by starving they cannot build the nation.

And what about choral literature? In Latin and foreign languages it is so rich that it makes selection difficult. Nor is the choice easy in the Hungarian field. But here it is hard to discover what is good.

About 1870 the whole country resounded with the German singing circle's "So weit die deutsche Zunge reicht", and a network of the "Schulverein" was operating everywhere.

Jenő Rákosi had an easy job in fighting against them in his "Reform". He and his companions fought against visible enemies.

Since then the texts of the German *Liedertafel* have been translated; but a number of Hungarian composers have written new melodies in the same spirit. Up to this very day this style is in the forefront in Hungarian schools. And this is the better side of the matter. Because what is not in the style of the German *Liedertafel* is, as a rule, blatant dilettantism.

If the German publicist writes today that "German Lieder can be heard ringing in the Buda Hills, in the woods of the Bakony Mountains, on Lake Fertő and the banks of the Danube and the Tisza just as they can in the forests of Thuringia, in the Oden-wald, along the Neckar and the Rhine" (quoted from the *Frankfurter Zeitung* in *Pesti Napló* on 13th May, 1928), he is much more right than he himself would believe.

Because he does not know that on the lips of the Tisza region *Hungarian* children, even the songs with a *Hungarian* text ring in the spirit of the German *Liedertafel*!

Nor does he know that in the course of the nineteenth century our eminent poets became so submerged in forms of verses borrowed from alien sources that a great many Hungarian poems, otherwise valuable, can be sung only to tunes with an alien lilt.

And the poor Hungarian boy has the vague idea that music of a higher level is where Hungarian words shift uneasily in a declamation going against their grain, as if they were wearing a borrowed festive attire. He learns to look down upon the natu-ral Hungarian lilt, in which the words breathe freely in a workaday manner, "peasant-like". And since he is taught only the poorer part which floats on the surface of ancient folk music—if he is taught it at all—he looks up devoutly to foreign music, which he thinks is more distinguished. And when it is from this outwardly more cultured but inwardly emptier music that he receives the spiritual nourishment he has been craving for, he loses his faith in better music and remains in this state of musical infantilism for the rest of his life.

So by communicating only inferior music both in foreign and in Hungarian works, the schools cut off the way to a higher development of the musical sense. In the name of good taste and of the Hungarian spirit alike school literature generally used today must be protested against.

I include in this the greater part of unison school songs, too. Some writers of text-books consider Hungarian children practically idiotic by torturing them with such little verses and songs as could be improvised much better by any sound child given the chance.

Of foreign music: only masterpieces! There are plenty of them. It is up to Hungarian composers to create literature in the Hungarian idiom.

So far they have not dealt with it over much. When my mother wanted me to sing something other than the songs of the servant-girls and gipsies and tried to find some artistic Hungarian songs, she could find only the songs of the meek Ignác Bognár. She inoculated me with "Náczika", but the rest simply did not work. Strangely enough, children learn what is good much more easily than what is bad. This, too, is a crite-rion, Masters!

Had Ferenc Erkel written even one or two little choruses for children, more people would listen to his operas today. Nobody is too great to write for the little ones; indeed, he must do his best to be great enough for them.

Original works are to be written, compositions starting from the child's soul, from the child's voice in text, tune and colour alike. Let us show singing, ringing Hungary to urban children! They hardly know that they live here. Let them feel that the "motherland" is not the few, inane platitudes they are made to sing but buoyant life, healing warmth, a colourful virgin forest to which they can cling with a thousand feelers. Then they will be really at home. What rural children have preserved of ancient traditions should be the urban children's encouragement and model. As we have seen, they can find themselves in this element at once. On the lips of Budapest children Hungarian songs resound with the same victorious assurance as in villages. This is one of the most valuable and hopeful lessons learned from the recent concerts of children's choirs.

It is the custom with us to recommend a single physic for the healing of every disease: the state should give money.

I have pointed out a few things that would greatly advance the musical education in schools, things that would not cost the state or anyone else a single penny.

It only needs some singing teachers who, at the chime of the mid-day bell, do not throw the mortar back into the mortar-trough: for whom, even if it is not their official duty, a little additional work is a spiritual need, which can provide the stimulus and is the soul and significance of the teacher's task.

Luckily, there are teachers like this, too.

The additional work refers only to the teacher; for the pupil it should not mean an additional burden but refreshment and joy. Only thus will he profit from it.

A systematic building up of teaching will then be the job of the state, a job that cannot be shirked any longer. The state maintains opera houses and concert halls in vain if nobody goes to them. Audiences for whom high-level music is a necessity must be reared. Hungarian audiences are to be raised up from their unexacting demands in music. And this can only be commended by work in the schools.

That the economic crisis is the cause of everything? Everything will be set right as soon as the economy is in order? I do not think so. Penury may hamper development but wealth does not always promote it either. Money does not produce ideas. Anyhow, there would be sufficient money here if only it were always spent on what is needed. However, the most valuable things cannot be bought with money. The greatest trouble is not the emptiness of the purse but the emptiness of the soul. And of this we have got more than our share.

The recent development of music in Hungary is a straight refutation of the economic view of history. Now, too, a new crop is sprouting: it will have a thorough transforming effect on Hungary's musical life when it is fully grown. And who have sown the seeds? Singing teachers, who have to cope with the worries of everyday life; Budapest pupils, who deliver the milk and newspapers at dawn. It is unthinkable that there should be no blessing on their work.

(1929)

MUSIC IN THE KINDERGARTEN

The greatest deficiency in our culture is that it is built from above. When, after centuries of constraint in national life, freedom was achieved in this respect as well, we wanted to make up too hastily for what we had lost. There are no leaps in nature. Culture is the result of slow growth. To accelerate it, to change the order of evolution is impossible.

We put up the fancy spires first. When we saw that the whole edifice was shaky, we set to building the walls. We have still to make a cellar. This has been the situation, particularly in our musical culture.

If in 1875 instead of establishing the Academy of Music, we had laid the foundations for the teaching of singing in schools, today's musical culture would be greater and more general. I am not saying that without the Academy of Music we should have achieved the present degree of professional musical teaching and of individual technique. I only say that it came too early and that its operation was ineffective for many years. For want of suitable pupils Hubay and Popper—happy times!—played billiards in the Műcsarnok Café, across the street. They would have carried out their duties and would have guided the pupils needing higher training—but such pupils were not to be found, at least not in the beginning, because no measures had been taken to provide for elementary and intermediate teaching. As though a university were founded in a country that had not even any primary schools.

When the Academy of Music, after its initial fruitless years, took up elementary and intermediate tuition as well, it gradually reared excellent professional musicians. Then it turned out that they were not needed at home. They played excellently, but there was nobody to play to. We had forgotten to see to this. We thought the country would develop on its own to reach the level of the Academy of Music. It was in vain that we waited for this. We produced musicians, and even music—but there were no consumers. It was only abroad that most of them found a livelihood for body and soul; the poor Hungarian state trained musicians at its own cost for rich foreign countries. In our circumstances it was only the primary school that could have reared audiences. It is enough to cast a glance at the role of music in schools at present to understand why they were unable to fulfil that task.

First of all, they did not even have time for it. Only since 1868 has singing been a normal subject in our elementary schools—on paper. In reality this meant in the best schools one hour of singing by ear per week. In many of them the pupils just learned a few religious songs, in others nothing at all. True, the curriculum mentioned the reading of music, but no one was ever seen who had learned to read notes in the elementary school. Since special tuition has been introduced in the capital one or two clever teachers may succeed in achieving it, but hardly before the fourth class. This is taken into account by the curriculum, too, for it resumes it in the secondary school; since 1926 (!) it has been resumed and continued for two years (so as not actually to complete anything), and finally, it is begun for the third time again in teachers' training colleges, but only very few pupils learn to read fluently even there. Germany's great musical culture would never have reached its present level without the teaching of singing having been systematically carried out in schools for centuries.

In utilising the educational power of music not only the Germans are far ahead of us, but even our southern and eastern neighbours have stolen a march on us.

No doubt, neglect on the part of our professional musicians is one of the reasons why our schools have become such music-less deserts.

Some strange professional haughtiness is not rare among musicians. The fewer the people who are proficient in the craft, the more valuable they feel. They despise those who do not understand it, but are unwilling to do anything to increase the number of those who do understand it. They consider it particularly beneath their dignity to be interested in schools. This is the heritage of Romanticism: the artist defends himself with haughtiness against a society of philistines who despise but do not understand him. Doubtless there are philistines even today. Why, we rear them ourselves. Nothing but philistines can come from the musical education provided by our schools. For what is a philistine if not an unfeeling dolt, failing to look for the value of life in the very place where it begins for the man of the spirit.

The haughty, anti-social artist will never become a prophet. He lives in his ivory tower waiting for times to change for the better. He thinks that some popular concerts will do the job of "musical mass education". However, it is not only among the people but also in our educated society that musical illiteracy prevails, and this ill can hardly be cured by efforts to popularise high-grade symphonic music. Anyone who has not been prepared for it will not understand much of it, nor will the belletristic pseudo-professional literature, so fashionable with us now, take him nearer to it.

To this end a gradual conditioning to the elementary phenomena of music, beginning in childhood, is needed together with their practice over many years; a systematic education in listening to music, which can only be based upon tuition at the primary and secondary school.

The start must be made as early as in the kindergarten, because there the child can learn in play what would be too late to learn in the elementary school. Particularly now children only over six can be admitted to the primary school, the significance of the kindergarten has increased. Or rather, it would have increased if every child attended it, or could attend it. For out of 700,000 children between three and six years of age only 125,000 can attend it, because we have no more than 1,160 kindergartens.

This is why I have heard that it is not worthwhile dealing with kindergartens; it does not matter what is being done there for it will not have any effect on the majority of the nation anyway.

Unless one is convinced that this cannot go on in this way, one cannot believe in the future of Hungary. It is absurd that the education of six-sevenths of Hungarian children should be left to chance when they are at their most important age.

Recent psychology has set forth convincingly that the years between three and seven are educationally much more important than the later ones. What is spoiled or omitted at this age cannot be put right later on. In these years man's future is decided practically for his whole lifetime.

> *For like a tree, the child, unless he's cared for,*
> *Will grow ugly; the mistakes of a tender age*
> *Can never, or only with difficulty, be*
> *put right in years to come.*
>
> *(Dávid B. Szabó)*

If the soul is left uncultivated up to the age of nearly seven, it will then not yield anything that can be grown in it only by earlier cultivation.

Not only from the point of view of individual education but from that of the nation, the work of the kindergarten is indispensable. Not even the most careful education in the family can supply what the kindergarten offers: adjustment to the human community. It does not belong to this topic, so I am only going to point out briefly that innumerable absurdities of Hungarian life spring directly from a lack of community education. A Hungarian child will learn only late—if ever—that we do not live for ourselves but for one another. In brief, the task of the kindergarten in rearing the nation is to provide a good and Hungarian education in early childhood for the whole nation. In places where there is good early education it is usually not Hungarian enough. But the overwhelming majority have no early childhood education at all.

In music, too, the work of the kindergarten is irreplaceable. But seldom do parents care in good time about a development of a sense of music, and even the most careful and wealthy parents, however good the teaching they supply for their children, are unable to provide them with a collective education, which, at the initial stages of music, is a tremendous help. Most children have no opportunity to make use of their natural sense of music in time. And for want of development this sense becomes stunted and the majority of people proceed through life without music; indeed, they are better off if they have no idea of what they have lost. But they usually realise it when it is too late. This is the root of the grotesque or hopeless musical studies of many an adult, or their bitterness over the omissions of their youth (see, for example, the *Reminiscences* of Vidor Kassai, Budapest, 1940, p. 345).

It is at the kindergarten with us (in the first years of the primary school for most children) that the first laying of foundations, the collecting of the first, decisive musical experiences begins. What the child learns here, he will never forget: it becomes his

129

flesh and blood. But it will not become merely his own individual possession. "What the child receives at the kindergarten becomes, at the same time, a component part of the public spirit" (Sándor Imre). It will affect the public taste of the whole country. This very idea warns us that the first songs are to be chosen with special care.

But there is something else here, too. In music we possess a means not only for a general development of the human soul but also for an education towards becoming Hungarians, a means that cannot be replaced by any other subject. The frightening lack of music in our curriculum, indeed the definite anti-music tendency, is gravely detrimental to the education of the nation, too.

The curriculum and instructions (as we should term them) for British schools declare on the role of music in education: "By now the value of music in school life is so well recognised that it is superfluous to dwell at length upon it."

What a long way we are from this! We, indeed, have still to set forth in great detail the importance of music from every point of view.

Taken separately, too, the elements of music are precious instruments in education. Rhythm develops attention, concentration, determination and the ability to condition oneself. Melody opens up the world of emotions. Dynamic variation and tone colour sharpen our hearing. Singing, finally, is such a many-sided physical activity that its effect in physical education is immeasurable—if there is perhaps anyone to whom the education of the spirit does not matter. Its beneficial effect in health is well known; special books have been written on this.

But let us examine its role in educating the nation. By this I do not mean some stupid irredentist songs, complete with banner-waving, dressed up in sham-Hungarian mummery. At the kindergarten age the implantation of subconscious elements of being Hungarian and then their gradual development are our duties. It is here, as it were, that the subterranean foundations of the edifice of our Hungarian character are to be laid. The deeper these foundations are built the firmer the building will be.

Language is the first subconscious keystone of Hungarian-ness. The more unfavourable the linguistic surroundings the child has so far lived in, the greater is the task of the kindergarten. Thus in cities the work of the kindergartens is generally greater. Only by a much deeper and more firmly rooted knowledge of the Hungarian language can the kindergarten teachers counterbalance up to a point the degeneration of the urban population's language.

The other subconscious keystone of Hungarian-ness is music. In the kindergarten it is perhaps even more important than language. It is not principally to the intellect that it appeals, although its possibilities in developing the intellect are also highly valuable. It is a natural manifestation of the small child that he hums to himself; his speech is half singing. From the human and Hungarian points of view alike what he should sing is a question of vital importance.

There are opinions, according to which he should only sing songs improvised by himself. This view has particularly many adherents in America. This is the same as though the child were not taught any language but was allowed to create it by himself.

Indeed, he would do so but in all probability nobody apart from the people closest to him would understand it. In the same way, he cannot be left to his own resources in forming his concept of music.

Folk traditions, first of all with their singing games and children's songs, are the best foundations for subconscious national features. There are among them some that we share with other peoples of Europe, but there are also differences. We can see the difference if we see on spring days in public parks how a foreign-born governess hammers into Hungarian children's heads the subconscious elements of her own language and music. Such children will have changed souls and will be unable all through their lives to speak and feel Hungarian. When they have grown up and are appointed, thanks to their family, to some leading position, they will not understand either the language or the soul of Hungarians. There is nobody to enlighten such parents as to what they are doing to their children: they are excluding them from the national community. The basic layer of the soul cannot be made from two different substances. A person can have only one mother-tongue—musically, too. Anyone who has been brought up on two will never know either. Anyone who has learned a foreign language at an age under ten will only mix up the different structures of the two languages, their different ways of shaping images. Everybody may have experienced that languages learned under ten will melt like the first snow; they will later have to be started anew; only the wounds inflicted on the Hungarian language will remain in their place. There are innumerable examples of people who started learning foreign languages at the age of ten or over and learned several of them better than those with whom the legacy of the foreign governess was nothing but inexterminable, faulty usages. And today this madness is no longer restricted to wealthy classes; in the foreign-language nursery schools which are springing up like mushrooms it has become available for people with modest incomes as well.

But do Hungarian kindergartens meet the requirements in every respect in relation to their importance? As a matter of fact, it looks as if they were meant merely to be substitute foreign governesses for the poor. The other day, walking across a square, I heard the pupils of a day-school singing the game beginning "The farmer ploughs the field". This is not the only singing game we have taken from foreign sources and translated badly. If a rich child learns something like this in a foreign language he will, at least, not believe for a moment that it is Hungarian. But a poor child grows up with the conviction that this, too, is a Hungarian song!

Our song-books used to abound with these; through kindergartens or schools one or two found their way to the people, too. But they could not do any great harm there: they vanished in the wealth of folk traditions. There is no antidote against them with urban children, and where bigger doses were administered, the children's sense of the Hungarian language and music indeed became stunted.

The folk tunes, nursery rhymes, jingles and singing games, which have a principal role in the initial stages of education with all cultured peoples, found their way to our kindergartens very late, or, have actually not arrived there to this very day.

Theresa Brunswick opened the "Angels' Garden" in Buda in 1828. There the children sang in German. Where, what and when they started singing in Hungarian has not yet been discovered. The first Hungarian song-book with music was published in 1840: *Flóri könyve* (Flori's Book), by Amália Bezerédj. She did not see it in print, having died in 1837 at the age of thirty-three. This extraordinary woman, who, in the spirit of her distinguished education, wrote romantic short stories in German and knew German better than Hungarian, for all that reared her little daughter on Hungarian poems and songs. Out of these the book came into being; it grew when she founded a school for peasant children in her village, Hidjapuszta in Tolna County, and taught them herself. Among the twenty-five tunes in the book only four have some connection with Hungarian traditions; the rhythm of at least five is Hungarian in style. The rest are all alien, feeble melodies (their sources are unknown), and with the exception of one—the French–German *"Ah, vous dirais-je, maman"*—they have all sunk into oblivion.

We should be surprised that they are not *all* foreign ones. For it was scarcely a century before (1825) that Kölcsey had declared "the spark of genuine national poetry is to be sought for in the songs of the common people", and a long time had to pass before this was recognised with regard to music, as well. Then it was believed that culture could only come from above and from outside. Amália Bezerédj may have thought that if she set up a school for the children in her village they should be taught there something better, something other than what they knew in any case, what they were chirruping by themselves. We should be surprised at not finding a single iambic melody in her book from a time when poetry in iambics was flourishing. Only one trochaic one, too, and one tune in $\frac{3}{4}$ time in a rhythm that had been fairly well acclimatised by Faludi's poem "On Fortune's carriage you safely should sit".

In vain should we look for folk traditions in Flori's Book: their significance had not been recognised yet by that period. Nor do we hear for a long time yet of their use in schools. For decades on end our song-books for schools contained mostly German school-songs, with translated texts or "original" songs written in the same spirit. The endeavours of the Bach era to Germanise Hungary are reflected in Peter Schmidt's book: *Dallamok az Ausztria-birodalombeli kath. magyar elemi tanodák számára írt Első nyelvgyakorló és olvasókönyvben foglalt versekhez* (Melodies for the Verses in the First Language and Reading Book of the Catholic Hungarian Elementary Schools in the Austrian Empire), Pécs, 1859.

The first traces of folk traditions being directed towards schools are to be found in the publication of Szini–Győrffy: *Ötven magyar népdal és dallam* (Fifty Hungarian Folksongs and Tunes), published in 1871 (melodies selected from Károly Szini's collection, which was published in 1865). We do not know how successful this experiment was from the point of view of the schools: no further editions of the book were brought out. The history of singing in Hungarian schools has not yet found a researcher.

The alien spirit lived on in our school-songs, although Kohányi, and later Bartalus more and more frequently interspersed them with new composed songs in the pop-

132

ular Hungarian style. The texts of these songs were mostly replaced with words produced specially for schools. Even where the original texts were retained "lover" was always substituted by "mother", etc.

It was in the Fröbel period that the inanity of the texts reached its summit; and yet we have to consider it fortunate that these texts were linked with popular melodies in the Hungarian manner and did not introduce foreign tunes. Here is an example from István Tóth's collection:

24

Allegro moderato

Pa - pir négyzet   és hosz négyzet, mind a   ket - tő.

Kel - le - me- sen   mu - lat - ta - tó   s el - me - fej - tő.

Nyolcz da - rab- bal   szép i - do - mo - kat   rak - ha - tunk

És   a - zok- ból   szá - mo - lást is   ta - nul - ha - tunk.

(A paper square and an alongated square, both of them / Delightfully amusing and mind-stretching. / With eight pieces we can make beautiful figures / And from these we can also learn to count.)

Fortunately, the Fröbel fashion did not last long. But it was only Áron Kiss in 1883 who called attention more emphatically to the use of folk traditions. At the beginning of *Magyar Gyermekjáték gyűjtemény* (A Collection of Hungarian Children's Games) 1891, we can read: "As a result of my proposition the 1883 National Assembly of Teachers accepted the following propositions:

"1. The games and the tunes that may go with them are to be used in Hungarian national education and for this reason the Hungarian character of the games is to be preserved.

2. Children's games and their tunes are to be collected in all regions of the country."

The book, every one of the 518 pages of which radiates Hungarian children's fresh vigour, humour and originality, and the pure air of folk poetry, is the fruit of collecting under his guidance. Having immersed themselves in the atmosphere of this collection, children who have come to the towns and had their Hungarian characteristics worn off may regain them, and newcomers, if they want to become Hungarians, can gain access to the world of Hungary.

One would have expected that teachers of every kind would have grasped at it. But what happened instead? In 1893 a *Daloskönyv* (Song-Book) was published, edited

133

jointly by Áron Kiss, Sándor Péterfy, Lajos Pósa and Ágost Tihanyi. Over half of the texts were from Áron Kiss's collection; but none of the 137 tunes!

Why not?—We can read the foreword: "We have *not* included in our book actual, already existing folksongs—by this we mean tunes and texts alike. We could not have included them, particularly not at this initial stage. On the one hand on account of the texts, which, in the folksongs, are almost without exception full of erotic references; on the other hand, because of the range, which—with only a few exceptions—go beyond the range in which the voice of a child between three and six can move... *Let the genuine folksong in its unmutilated completeness belong to the vigorous people or even to more mature youth; for tiny tots songs should be supplied which, being formed from the motifs of folksongs, suit the mood of children, both in music and text, and which are suitable to develop them in the right direction."* (italics in the original).

Although the foreword does not say so, the songs reveal that a range of five to six notes is considered to suit children's voices. Out of the 137 tunes 65 range from the first degree of the scale to the sixth; 42 from the first to the fifth, and 5 from the fifth to the third. This circumstance alone represents an immense monotony, incessant hexachord melodies and T–D–S functions. It is not true that this range is so very rare among folksongs: even among the folksongs published up to 1893 there would have been hundreds of this kind. Thus the range would not have been an obstacle. But the foreword expounds that "the emotional world and the contents of the texts are very remote from the children's world". The emotional world of folksongs of a compass of six notes cannot be so remote from the world of Hungarian children, for such tunes are sung all over the country, indeed, *horribile dictu*: even some of a compass of eight notes. Just as numerous "actual folksongs" found their way into Áron Kiss's collection.

But why did the editors omit the music, too, of "proper children's songs"? Of this the foreword does not say anything. It is surprising that over eighty of the *texts* of Áron Kiss's collection were found suitable, but the *melodies of all of them were omitted*. Even, that is, of those that have tunes—since, unfortunately, even in Kiss's collection the tunes of numerous texts, obviously meant to be sung, were missing. That they wished to replace these was understandable, although it would have been quite possible to collect the melodies subsequently to the newly collected texts which Kiss assessed as being worthy of publication. The material had been collected by teachers all over the country and many schoolmasters were certainly unable to write down the tune and so they submitted only the texts. By the mobilisation of a few people able to write music, this deficiency could easily have been corrected. But to sever *existing* melodies from their texts and replace them with new ones is only permissible for someone who knows better tunes than the original ones. Let us just compare some "new" tunes with the original traditional ones. Underneath the folk tunes (a) to be found in Áron Kiss's collection are the new, contrived ones (b):

25

Süss fő nap, Szent György nap. Kertek a- latt a lu-da-im megfagy - nak.

Süss fel nap. fé- nyes nap. Ker-tek alatt tyukok vannak, megfagy- nak, meg- fagy - nak.

(a) Warm up, sun; St. George sun. / Down there in the garden my poor / Geese are cold /
(b) Shine forth, sun; radiant sun. / There is poultry in the garden. / They are cold; they are cold.)

26

Kis Ko - má- rom, Nagy Ko-má - rom, De szép kis - lány ez a há - rom!

Kis Komá - rom, Nagy Komá - rom. De szép kis - lány ez a há - rom!

(a) and b) Small Komárom; Big Komárom. / These are lovely little girls three! / I would love just one of them / The loveliest of all of them. / Small Komárom, Big Komárom.)

27

El - vesź-tet - tem zseb-ken-dő- met, Meg-ver a- nyám ér - te,

El - vesz-tet - tem zseb-ken- dő- met, Meg- szid á-nyám ér - te,

Ha va- la- ki .meg-ta - lál - ja, csó-kold meg majd ér - te.

Egy kis le-ány meg - ta- lál - ta, csó- kot ki-ván ér - te.

(a) I have lost my handkerchief, oh / Mum will thrash me for this / But if someone comes across it / Kiss her later for it. /
(b) I have lost my handkerchief, oh / Mum will scold me for this / But a little girlie found it / She'd like a kiss for this.)

The first two reveal fairly well the effort of somebody wanting something different and yet following the model in a servile way. I should not have mentioned the third if I had not discovered that it is being taught even today. This book, over fifty years old, has appeared in several editions and is in the hands of practically every kindergarten teacher up to this very day. In the following one of the chief mannerisms of the book, the sequence of seconds, is easily seen. This renders the melodic line un-Hungarian even if the first couple of notes do present a genuine folk motif:

28

Er - dő mel - lett nem jó lak - ni, Mert sok fát kell ha - so - gat - ni.

Ti-zen-há-rom ö - let meg egy fe - let, Ö-lel-jen meg en - gem a - ki sze - ret.

(No use living near the forest — / Too much wood is to be cut there / Thirteen cords and one half over. / May the one who loves me hold me closer.)

Its parallel in folk music is so well known that it is perhaps superfluous to publish it. In Kiss's collection (p. 178) it appears in four variants.

The principles of the foreword are given the lie by those melodies which are more complex than any to be found in Kiss's collection. Thus the tune of *"Szedem szép rózsáját"* (I pick its pretty roses) is twice as long as that to be found on p. 412 in Kiss. The melody of *"Mély kútba tekintek"* (I look into a deep well) is also simpler and more beautiful with Kiss (p. 435). The same refers to the melody of *"Mit visztek, mit visztek selyem sátor alatt"* (What are you carrying under this silken tent!) (pp. 363 and 368). In Kiss it has a simple, beautiful melody of twenty-four syllables. In the song-book two stanzas of each are "re-composed", and a more difficult and intricate structure of forty-eight syllables ensues; its tune cannot be compared with the beauty of the one in Kiss. The sickly melody of *"Kicsiny vagyok én"* (Little am I still) is dwarfed by the folk tune well known since Színi (1865). Its third line is reminiscent of the characteristic third line of a Catholic hymn Endre Zsasskovszky: *"Égből szállott szent kenyér"* (Holy bread descends from Heaven).

The collection meant to offer something better in place of the well known tunes of *"Gólya, gólya, gilice"* (Storkie, storkie, turtle-dove) and of *"Katalinka"* (pp. 33, 40; pp. 12–13. in Kiss). A new tune was given to *"Kis kacsa fürdik"* (The duckling is bathing) (p. 78), although in the Kiss collection there were thirteen variants available. The children's plebiscite has already decided that these folk tunes are suitable for a child's mentality and voice-range, for it was on the basis of their singing that the Kiss collection came into being. And we have seen above that the new melodies are not easier, indeed in many cases they are more difficult than the folk tunes. Mention should be made of the chromatic semitone steps occurring a few times, which cause difficulty even in secondary schools.

"Independent" melodies, which cannot be compared with the folk tunes, also expose a total lack of invention. Alongside awkwardly put together composed-song clichés (No. 135) the imitation of *"Érik a, érik a búzakalász"* (Now ripen, now ripen the ears of corn), fragments of folksongs crop up here and there. However angry the foreword was with folksongs it could not get rid of the memories of them. Of course, it is only fragments of the most common, un-Hungarian "urban folksongs" that appear: *"Ez a pohár bujdosik"* (This cup is now wandering) (p. 11); the first five bars and the whole structure of *"Este későn ne járj hozzám"* (Do not come to see me too late) (Bartalus II, No. 114, p. 4). *"Fáj, fáj, fáj, fáj"* (Pain, pain, pain, pain) (No. 129, p. 97) and others (pp. 24, 26, 47, 65, 89 and 93).

We have already mentioned the foreign melodic line of some songs. It easily happens with anyone who has not lived deep enough in musical traditions that he will write— as did the author of song No. 84 (p. 59)—an alien, upbeat melody. The real rhythm of this tune becomes apparent if we shift the bar line forward by a crotchet.

Thus the book took a step backwards rather than forwards.

Formerly contrived, bad texts were sung to folksong tunes. Now, in most cases, texts drawn from folk traditions were put below contrived, bad and un-Hungarian melodies, ousting the traditional, and often beautiful, original tunes.

The book does not reveal the perpetrators. It could not have been Áron Kiss and Pósa; thus only Péterfy and Tihanyi could have been responsible for the melodies. According to the verbal information of the late Béla Sztankó, Péterfy was the author of the tunes. To my question how any sober person could commit such things to paper Sztankó could only answer that it was the author's own vanity that must have dazzled him. In the guise of the pedagogue he indulged his creative desires. Nobody can be forbidden to compose melodies—if he keeps them to himself. But what about someone who uses the authority of his official position to spread his worthless rubbish?

The foreword fulminates thus:

"In our opinion those who get immature children to sing our vigorous, beautiful folksongs with texts changed with good intentions—but usually bad results—commit not only reprehensible tastelessness and an offence against literature but, at the same time, pedagogical tactlessness. We deem the time to be ripe today, when laws foster the cause of public education from the lowest grade, at least to point out this preposterous and intolerable situation."

If the word "texts" were replaced by "music" could not these words be applied equally justifiably to this book?

Forty thousand secret dramatists are said to exist in this country. What might be the number of secret composers of songs? A good many of them have been turned loose on the kindergarten, too. Péterfy had numerous predecessors and successors. It is not advisable to peruse their collections. At first one laughs, then one becomes annoyed and finally one despairs and cannot imagine that in a country where such things are printed and even sung aloud, there may still be room for anything better.

137

It is understandable that our better musicians turn their backs on all schools, live their separate lives in the secluded groves of higher music and offer no more than a gesture of resignation at endeavours to open paths from the one extreme area to the other.

But no! This lifeless rubbish cannot be consumed by sound children, nor can all kindergarten teachers be so inhuman as to torture their pupils with them.

Let us put aside the books and look around at life. What's new in the kindergartens? What do they actually sing there? This is how I arrived back there after fifty years. I thought it was either in the kindergarten or at school that I had learned all the bad songs I knew. Must this remain like this for ever?

But let us be just. All was not that bad. Not even the contrived texts put below the well known melodies. Even today I can still hear good old "Auntie" enthusiastically singing Pál Lukács's verse at the kindergarten in Galánta:

> Eljött a szép karácson
> Aranyozott kis szánon,
> Hozott diót magyarót,
> Jó gyermekeknek valót.

> (Christmas tide has come our way
> With his shining golden sleigh:
> Walnuts, hazelnuts he brings,
> And for children all good things.)

She pronounced the word *"mogyoró"* (hazelnut) *"magyaró"*, because she was Transylvanian. Only later did I discover that through this I had learned the tune of *"Mégis huncut a német"* (Crafty are the Germans all) and Auntie enthusiastically explained to us that in her youth, during the Bach era, this had been a forbidden song... And I met old acquaintances again when I later came across *"Attila, Lehel, Árpád"*, the *Chlopiczky Song* and the Liszt *Rhapsody*.

True, it was also Auntie who taught me the song *"Kismadár, hangja száll, Visszazengi a határ"* (Birdie mine, singing fine, By no frontier is confined). She had no idea that this was a German song, nor would I have found this out if I had not perused German collections. And how many kindergarten teachers will actually think about what they are teaching? They have learned it so they pass it on. Thus a number of foreign tunes have become a matter of common knowledge in Hungary and the more Hungarians grew susceptible to Indo-Germanic music the more they became alienated from Hungarian music; because not sufficient Hungarian music was taught to counterbalance it. And all kinds of schools have played a big part in Hungarian music deteriorating to such an extent, or not even developing at all.

My visits to kindergartens confirmed this, too. No other consciousness of music could possibly have come out of the musical material prevailing there. Áron Kiss's book, even in its abbreviated edition, is not to be found even in the best equipped kindergartens. They do not even know it. Various tunes are sung, including folksongs. Last spring it was mostly soldiers' songs that were sung. Often the kindergarten teachers did not know them themselves: the tunes had been brought by the children. In one case it turned out that they had learned it from their elder sisters or brothers who attended schools. Lo and behold: if it is not from high above, then it is from below that the new spirit of schools has infiltrated into the kindergartens. Children do not care much about the theoretical restrictions of the compass. If they are able to, they will sing even the "National Anthem" or the "Appeal", with a range of eleven notes. Some small five-year-old songstresses score successes with new urban songs with a compass of ten notes, songs they have learned at home. But in some places the kindergarten teachers themselves teach composed songs full of false sentimentality, with texts admittedly suited to the kindergarten, but with tunes of a ten-note compass, with augmented seconds and chromatic notes. Do they perhaps mean to prepare children for Hungarian life by these songs?

A child will learn anything... I tried to see how quickly, when I invited four or five little girls, pupils from the fourth form of the elementary school, to visit the kindergarten. They all knew the folk tune *"Ciróka"* (Dee-dum hush), published here. They all joined hands in a circle and sang. On the third or fourth repetition their singing was joined by the humming voices of the kindergarten pupils, who, by the time they had heard it six or seven times, knew it by heart. It is interesting that wherever they experimented with this tune in elementary schools, it had to be repeated more often, ten or even twenty times before the pupils had learned it. A lot depends on the teacher, too, because it also happened that the tune had to be repeated more often in the third form than in the second. It is also possible that a song demonstrated by children of the same age, or just a little older, sticks more easily than that sung by the teacher. I should not be surprised—on the basis of frequent experiments of this kind—if it turned out that the perception of kindergarten pupils is quicker.

29

(Dee-dum hush, dee-dum hush. / What've you cooked? Gru-el. / Where've you put it? 'Neath the bench — / It's been eaten by the cat.)

It would seem that just as the old gipsy forgets a song every day, the young child would learn a new one.

The question has arisen: how much does a child learn of what he has heard at the kindergarten? I have succeeded in getting reliable data on the store of songs a child has acquired at the kindergarten. In the course of a year and a half, up to the spring of 1937, he had learned fifty-four songs, that is to say, almost one a week. And yet, by fifty-four well-chosen songs the chief basic phenomena of music could be implanted in the child's soul and, at the same time, a whole miniature Hungary! Now let us see what this child has received in this lot: seven folksongs—two of them lively soldiers' songs, the rest rather worn-out school-songs (they are not worn out because they got to schools, but presumably got to schools because they were worn out). Then there are four composed songs; among them the *"Kőrösi lány"* (Girl from Kőrös), *"Három a tánc"* (Three times you dance) by Simonffy—with different words, of course. There are a couple of German songs, "A grey haired old man's standing in the woods". The other forty-four are contrived school-songs. Two of them have survived from Péterfy's book, but have become simplified in an interesting way, perhaps even improved (see its original form published above, No. 27):

30

(I have lost my handkerchief, oh / Mum will spank me for this / I have lost my handkerchief, oh / Mum will scold me for this.)

In the others Péterfy's spirit lives on. Here and there some folk motifs provide the beginning, but the continuations are "independent"—a thankless enough task.

31

(Left, right, left; / Left, right, left; / La-la-la. . . . . / Fine flowery field and it's there that we're going. / Our little army can then have a rest there.)

This is nothing but the well known children's song beginning *"Méz, méz, méz"* (Honey, honey, honey).

At other times the structure of new folksongs, the AA⁵BA formula, is used with non-folk motifs.

The range is broader: there are 22 songs with an octave compass, 10 of nine notes, 1 of ten and 1 of eleven notes as against 4 with a compass of five notes, 12 of six notes and 4 of seven notes.

Here, too, we can find "improved" folk texts, which have much finer traditional tunes, even as many as three, by Áron Kiss:

32

(I have lost my partner / Dear little companion. / Come back, my partner, / Dear little companion.)

For fifty years Áron Kiss's collection has been lying around. A dead treasure, because two generations passed it by uncomprehendingly and because all kinds of people replaced the beautiful original tunes rooted in tradition by their own clumsy, ungainly melodies! I did not investigate who these people were, nor am I interested in their persons; it is a question of principles.

Finally, a study in *prosody:* (Music example)

33

(High let the flag fly away up high. / Loud let the drum roll and bang out loud. / Quickly the children do march in time / Just like a big real army band.)

If we accustom children to such things, how can they learn by the time they grow up what a good Hungarian poem is like?

This reminds me of the case mentioned by Miklós Misztótfalusi Kis in his *Mentség* (Plea, p. 77), which is edifying for every Hungarian intellectual. His opponents hated him because he wanted to correct every mistake. "One should not struggle with such details," they said, "even if the *loci* and suchlike were bad the child would learn from them; why, when he grows up he will notice that this or that is not so and he will then learn it correctly." To this Misztótfalusi answered: "This is the same as if one were to teach the child that swans are black and ravens white; why, when he grows up he will notice that this is not so and will learn it correctly. But in my view, right things should be implanted in tender minds, for these things remain; as they say: *Quod nova testa capit, inveterata sapit.*"

Maxima debetur puero reverentia. The pure soul of the child must be considered sacred; what we implant there must stand every test, and if we plant anything bad, we poison his soul for life. I doubt whether anybody would dare assert that the above

141

and similar things are good enough for nourishing children. How could so many bad songs find their way into the kindergarten? There appears to be no authority to judge from an artistic point of view the songs that are to be taught. But whatever "lessons" are contained in music which is worthless from an artistic point of view, these works are harmful from the pedagogical aspect, too.

The harmful effect of such nourishment may be overcome by someone who gets the right musical education in good time to counterbalance it, or if he at least gets the antidote in good Hungarian songs. But what about the masses for whom this remains their only music? Can we be surprised if, by the time they grow up, they cannot get further than the music of the trashiest hit?

But let us have confidence in the future! Let us glance into the latest publication. (*Óvodai foglalkozások*—Kindergarten Activities—Vol. II. Ed. by vitéz Antal Rozsnoky; edition of *Kisdednevelés,* Budapest, 1939.) It may point to a better future. In Chapter Five of the new book *Dalok, dalosjátékok* (Songs, Singing Games), it strikes the eye immediately that there is only one single traditional text. They are all new, even the Christmas carols, with the exception of one shepherd's song. This is right and necessary if it has been ensured that the children have already become acquainted with all the traditional songs of any value to them. But, as we know and have seen, we are a long way from this, the kindergarten teachers do not know the traditions themselves and have no collections to hand from which they could learn them, so we must consider such a rich crop of individual poetry a bit premature. But even if it comes early, what is good never comes too soon, and it will find the place it deserves.

I cannot deal with the texts in the detail they deserve. Nevertheless, I cannot forego one remark. It seems to me that the rationalism, the educational, moralising or politically patriotic inclination of most of the texts is completely alien to the emotional world and way of thinking of children in the three to six age group.

The texts do not start from the soul of the child and his view of the world but impose upon him the author's own "self", and this self is not a poetic individuality (the only one allowed to influence others), but a kindergarten "Auntie", a pedagogue, with the dusty conventions of the school, with its empty truisms and papery feelings. They view the child from without, describe what the child is doing and make him sing it while performing it. All this may be very reasonable and edifying—but it is neither poetic nor childlike. Although the two are more or less identical.

The child delights in the play of musical forms at a stage when he does not care about the meaning of the text. That is why the adults' songs he acquires by chance get distorted into meaninglessness. A small child will often hum senseless words (senseless, that is, for us), and enjoy the purely musical kaleidoscope, as if it were a handful of coloured pebbles. That is why he loves meaningless refrains. The ninety-three tunes of the book do not afford a single occasion for such joy. But if Mozart—a genius—enjoyed at the age of three or four a song with a meaningless text he had invented himself, why should we deprive the three–four year olds who will not become Mozarts of this pleasure?

142

34

O - ra - gna fi - ga ta - xa fa ma - ri - na ga - mi - na fa.

O - ra - gna fi - ga ta - xa fa ma - ri - na ga - mi - na fa.

By this I do not mean that the child should sing only meaningless words. But let us give some scope to this purely musical element of poetry in the kindergarten, too, at least as much as is given to it by the songs of all peoples of the world, indeed by the greatest of poets.

The versification of the texts is infinitely monotonous and, consequently, so is the rhythm of the melodies. And yet, rhythm should be the real empire of the kindergarten. By the time the singing voice has evolved every child could be developed into a veritable virtuoso of rhythm without any great effort, by means of polyrhythmic games (blacksmith's forge, etc.) and with simple percussion instruments. Before learning to write letters English children learn to write down the rhythm. Every child likes to doodle, to draw. With some guidance he could doodle to some purpose instead of pursuing an inane pastime.

In his successors and imitators the ringing variety of Pósa's verses became faded. Not that all of his poems were masterpieces. But he was a writer, all the same, and was rooted in traditions. Once István Turi Mészáros strictly rebuked him for the following two lines:

> *Sülülü, bülülü*
> *Csiba te, nagyfejű,*

calling them "Chinese–Hungarian nonsense". (*Kisdednevelés*, 1894, p. 708.) But István Turi Mészáros evidently did not know that the word "Sülülü" originated from a traditional song well-known in Gömör County and that Pósa had certainly taken it from there (*Ó te vén sülülülü…*)

We shall not achieve much with small children with the tyranny of reason. And he who has been trained from the age of three to understand every word, may perhaps never get to the real meaning of words and to Hamlet:

> *There are more things in heaven and earth,*
> *Horatio,*
> *Than are dreamt of in your philosophy.*

I do not know whether the text of this book has undergone expert literary revision, but I can definitely declare that its music has not undergone revision. I must say that to overwhelm unsuspecting kindergarten teachers with so many poor tunes, people who can hardly form an opinion themselves, and to render these melodies compulsory

143

by an official exterior, as it were, has been injurious heedlessness. I rely on the kindergarten teachers' better judgment and hope they will not teach most of them.

A third of the tunes are dilettante works—indeed, the work of bunglers. They were written by people who have no idea that this craft can be learned and even mastered. They are rough and fumbling improvisations. There is not a single note that could not have been safely substituted by another one: the character of the tune—or rather its lack of character—would not change a jot. Their musical substance originates from fragments of old school-songs and international singing games.

Another group of so-called "Hungarian" character has been produced with Péterfy's method from motifs of "Hungarian national folksongs". The difference is that there the "folksongs proper" which Péterfy had omitted are included more often and so are the hackneyed shavings of composed songs. Nor is the compass restricted to six notes: there are 53 tunes with a range of five—six notes and 40 of seven—nine.

Traces of composed folksongs are to be found: *"Hejretyutyutyu"*, pp. 8, 35; *"Hajtogassuk a kancsókat"* (Let us empty all the tankards), p. 30; *"Kinek nincsen kutyája"* (He who has no dog), p. 68; *"Haragszik a pusztabíró"* (Wrathful is the Bailiff), for one line or the other taken from them haunts the songs in as many as four to five places. (Vol. I. pp. 18, 30, 74, 78–79.) It is typical of botchwork that in the same tune heterogeneous elements are mixed, one line from here, another line from there. One line of Count István Fáy's "Counter Csárdás" gets on quite well with a line taken from a folksong (p. 46). A similar *"quodlibet"* can be found on pp. 40–41, too.

If we tear off the petals of a flower and then put them together again in another way, we shall not get a living flower again.

The "paraphrase" of folksongs is so obvious in some places that by changing a few notes the original folksong can be restored (pp. 3, 5, 27, 33, 40, 41, 59, 62, 63). Whether the change is intentional or only spontaneous memory at work, the original is always more beautiful. In other cases the melody is absolutely identical with a folksong recorded in writing forty years earlier (bottom of p. 5). The gentleman professing to be the author may not have known that this is a folksong and quite naively felt it to be his own.

Here is a characteristic example of a folksong transcription (p. 80):

35

144

(a) Snow white lily flower stem / Gently bow yourself down / Bow down to the Tisza. / In the cool Tisza you / Wash clean white and fair and / Comb your smooth white forehead. / In the golden sun ray / In your lovely clean dress / Walk with me now in the / Chariot of Breezes. /

(b) Snow white lily flower stem / Snow white lily flower stem / Hi, jump into the Danube, / Hi, jump into the Danube.)

We do not quite understand why this had to be "transcribed for kindergarten pupils", for the original (Áron Kiss, p. 310), would hardly exceed their comprehension either. Of course, musically the transcription brought about an unnatural rhythm and wrong accents (see the beginning of the original). The next has completely lost its childlike and Hungarian aspect, its very bloom. It has become a genteel, precious, urban idiom. Whether the children's imagination will climb into the "chariot of breezes", must be left to itself.

Quite exceptionally there are some pieces in the book which reveal the trained musician's touch. But training is not inspiration and it must be stated that the authors of these pieces have not overstrained themselves. Their melodies are not fresh: they are dry—and difficult into the bargain. At this stage a modulating tune is rather out of place.

The kindergarten is not the place for music with an alien rhythm or an alien melodic line, just as it is no place for a foreign language either. There is plenty of time left for demonstrating the *mazurka* rhythm after we have introduced the child to the many forms of Hungarian rhythm. And even then it should be demonstrated on original Polish examples rather than on pale imitations. And we should say where they have come from. Do not let us steal other peoples' songs, we have plenty of our own; let us use them rather to get to know other peoples better. The children should sing *"Fuchs du hast die Gans gestohlen"* (pp. 37, 39) in its original language, when they are learning German. There it will be of valuable service; here, disguised into Hungarian, it only does harm.

But nothing is as harmful as a distorted Hungarian folksong. The child will become bored, in fact he will come to loathe the hackneyed outward trappings of the superficial Hungarian character before he comes to know the genuine one. It is the greatest crime to fill the child's soul with that sort of thing instead of the traditional songs. Not even the most excellent individual creation can be a substitute for traditions. To write a folksong is as much beyond the bounds of possibility as to write a proverb. Just as proverbs condense centuries of popular wisdom and observation, so, in traditional songs, the emotions of centuries are immortalised in a form polished to perfection. The more of them we implant into young souls the more closely we link them to the nation. No masterpiece can replace traditions. Far less can cheap imitations or distorting transcriptions. What would we say if teachers of Hungarian or of any other language were to fill young people entrusted to them with self-made wise maxims instead of proverbs, and with stylistic exercises fabricated by themselves instead of folk tales?

However poor imitations of folk embroidery may sometimes be, they at least have the justification that the real thing is rare and perishable, there are not enough for all those who would like them. But songs can belong to millions at the same time and never run out; wear and tear do not show on them. Here cheap imitation has no justification at all.

I could increase the number of examples. But perhaps this much will suffice to support my statement that the songs taught in the kindergarten are not satisfactory from the point of view of education, be it general or national.

1. They exclude tradition and do not supply the only possible foundation for an awareness of Hungarian music to be developed later on.

2. By their alien elements they disturb the creation of pure musical concepts and lead to a foreign musicality.

3. By their numerous rubbishy melodies they do not lead to good music but to cheap trash.

4. They do not develop the power of musical comprehension to the highest possible degree.

What has been promised ever since 1868 by every curriculum, namely that the musical education of Hungarian children must be founded on Hungarian music, should be put into effect at long last. For a decade or two now the ancient tree of tradition has spread its branches over schools with visible results. True, as early as 1889 Béla Sztankó based the first school-book he published on such foundations. But there was great opposition; the books of alien spirit, and those with songs composed by the authors themselves, hindered the spread of his books. Only when musical public opinion started paying attention to more recent collecting did the ears of schools start opening up, too. Strangely enough, the kindergartens did not take any notice of this: they went on living their own lives in the hermetically sealed world of edifying songs, turning their backs upon the other schools. This stubbornness is the aftermath of old crimes. There were occasional voices crying in the wilderness against them—but all in vain. At random I open a book at a complaint voiced forty-three years before my own (*Kisdednevelés*, 1897, p. 14).

"Which nation has a richer and more beautiful store of singing games than our own? And for decades this mine of rich treasures has lain unexploited. Our kindergarten teachers may occasionally have some memory of the sweet tune of *"Kiskacsa fürdik"* (The duckling is bathing), but which of them thought of introducing it into the kindergarten? Not one. Instead they collected and translated the games used in German kindergartens and, with these as models, nearly every kindergarten teacher manufactured (this is the expression I consider most suitable for them) games and songs that spoiled taste and twisted the tongue..." They observed folk games and endeavoured to utilise the way they were played, but "Heaven preserve us" from the text and the melody. Instead of "The duckling" in their opinion "A lady's walking now in front" was more suitable. They needed gymnastic games. There is *"Fehér liliomszál"* (Lily, pretty, snow-white), but did anybody find it? Not on your life!

For "My thumb I'm showing now to you" and "Now let us sing together, On our tiptoes jump and leap" (Ida Gegus) were more beautiful.

First Áron Kiss's collection *Gyermekjáték* (Child Games) should become public property, but now together with the tunes. Then the most suitable songs should be chosen from the more recent range of folksongs now used in schools. The pentatonic ones are particularly suited to the kindergarten. It is through them that children can achieve correct intonation soonest, for they do not have to bother with semitones. Even for children of eight–nine years of age, semitones and the diatonic scale are difficult, not to mention the chromatic semitone. This latter is difficult even at the secondary school. And yet, they are to be found in every kindergarten song-book.

Traditional folksongs offer so lavish a choice that for the time being, hardly anything else is needed; there are more of them than can be taught in three years. If, nevertheless, something new is needed, let it be written by talented and qualified composers—there are plenty of them. We do not make shoes for our children ourselves; there are craftsmen who understand the job. Texts, too, should be written by talented authors and not by dilettanti. There are always verses for children in recent literature; they have merely to be borne in mind. With regard to the songs, it is easier to adjust the words to the tune if they are written to a ready-made tune than to do things in the usual way. But both have to stand up to the strictest criticism before we can allow them to be sung by children.

Kindergarten teachers must be enlightened as to their enormous responsibility, and the extent to which they harm the child in his human and Hungarian character if they nurture him on poor songs. And though they can be forgiven if they are not aware of what they are doing, they must be urgently taught how to distinguish between good and bad. By a couple of short extension courses the ability to judge independently cannot be imparted. Continuous post-graduate teaching of every kindergarten teacher should be institutionally ensured and kept up until it naturally becomes constant self-education. They must be made to understand it is not only a question of prettiness that the songs they teach the children are better: it is a matter of survival. It is of vital importance chiefly for the middle class to absorb folk traditions and to establish closer links with the ancient culture of the Magyars. To sink roots in the Hungarian soil and not to toss with a feeling of not belonging anywhere!

Our little world should become Hungarian not only in external trappings, in banner waving, but to the very depths of our soul, because only in this way will it become really our own. And the depths of the soul are particularly the realm of music. In vain do we wave flags and scream irredentist songs... to foreign tunes; if that realm is under a foreign overlord, we are lost.

And this rebirth must be started at the bottom. The finest curricula and the wisest regulations issued from above are of no value if there is nobody to put them into practice with conviction and enthusiasm. Souls cannot be reshaped by administration. But souls reshaped by beauty and knowledge are easy to administer.

True, for this, public opinion must also change.

Hungarian public opinion does not take schools seriously enough. It believes that school and life are different things. But school, and even the kindergarten, stands for real, full-blooded life. Anyone who is hurt there, may not recover from the hurt till the day of his death. And if we sow a good seed in him it will flourish all his life. A three-year-old human being is nonetheless a human being. The earlier we enclose him in an imaginary world the more difficult will it be for him to find his bearings in the real one later on.

Let us take our children seriously! Everything else follows from this. True, in theory we profess: only the best is good enough for a child. But in practice this is mostly reduced to: "anything is good enough for a child; he will play even with a button."

In a busy street in London I once saw two children, a rosy-cheeked boy and girl of about four or five, wanting to cross the road. The policeman stopped the traffic, two dozen motorcars stopped on either side and waited patiently until the policeman, bending down to the children and talking merrily to them, escorted them to the other side. By no means is it due to chance that it is in England that the teaching of singing in kindergartens and schools is most highly developed.

I dare say, recently a lot has been done for children with us, too. But it is no use sending them for summer holidays if we do not care about what they are singing. If we had given them food of the same quality as the songs we teach them, they would have perished long ago. But the lack of spiritual vitamins does not show in such tangible phenomena.

A split in Hungarian culture is often discussed nowadays. Every thinker finds the remedy in a meeting of all kinds of culture on the soil of folk tradition; that is where they should try to become a single unit. With its trashy and un-Hungarian songs the kindergarten has so far helped the split. No greater effort would be needed for it to help towards unification, indeed it could even create it in its own, small circle.

Folk traditions are knocking on the locked door of the kindergartens, which they want to bring back to Hungary. To let them come in would mean a better future. In the courtyard of a kindergarten in Budapest I saw a big, grey hill of sand. I thought it had some new purpose in physical education; perhaps to get the children of Pest, the inhabitants of the plain, accustomed to hilly ground. But the kindergarten teachers told me that it was just dirty sand waiting to be taken away; they could not move because of it, but there was not sufficient transport available.

This hill has become a symbol of the music in kindergartens. There it lies unmovable and gives no space for fresh sand; it catches all the air, the light, the sky. Who is going to take it away? There is no transport! Indeed, every person is needed here, who does not grudge lifting his finger for it. We have a song about this:

I'll cart that hill within my four cornered hanky fine
But you will be mine, my sweet dove, you'll be mine.

148

Postscript in 1957

Public opinion has asked for a new edition of my "pitiful lament", voiced sixteen years ago. Then I related what was going on and what was not in the field of music in kindergartens and how our children's taste, their sense of Hungarian music was being spoiled at their most tender age, instead of being developed.

Up to 1945 no substantial changes could be expected. But now, after so many years, it may be worthwhile looking around to see whether the situation has improved. It would be desirable to have somebody make a survey of what kindergarten pupils are singing today throughout the country. To see whether they do not still learn many a thing that would be better left unlearned. *(Quod fuerit melius non didicisse.)*

At that time, about 1942, a grandfather proudly told me that his grandchild, a kindergarten pupil, had learned the "Transylvanian March". I listened to it. Of the music, with a range of twelve notes and written to a worthless text, nothing survived but some memory of rhythm and senseless cacophony. Incoherent choral speaking instead of singing. And yet, even the youngest can sing correctly what is suitable for them. Are there such crazy kindergarten teachers even today? Or have enough of those found their way to the increased number of kindergartens who are aware that they have been entrusted with the education of human beings, and so also with the laying of the foundations for music education? There is no sense in raising the number of music schools if children of seven arrive there with an empty or already poisoned musical consciousness: between three and seven their fates have already been decided. That is where intervention is required. *Principiis obsta.* (Resist at the very beginning!) I do hope that today nobody uses the books criticised in 1941. Quite a few have appeared since then that deserve similar criticism. We should investigate what the few books that have appeared beside the poor ones have been able to transfer from paper into life. I hear that the farmer still goes to the field, to ask long-legged storkie there whether little birdie has flown away. And when will it get back? When will Hungarian children find their way home at last? And when will all Hungarian children have kindergartens? (According to official information, out of 620,260 children of kindergarten age 161,220 attended kindergartens with places for a total of 140,000.) So there is still work to be done here.

First of all in the training of kindergarten teachers. True, many of the kindergarten teachers coming from rural parts and trained in short courses have proved competent in practice, even in singing, for they have brought with them a healthy nature and unspoiled taste. Nevertheless the high-level, intricate work of a kindergarten teacher needs several years of study in many fields and a cultured taste. Wherever there is a person like this, she can work wonders with the little ones, even in music. A child will learn anything if there is somebody who knows how to teach him. What is a miracle today must in time become quite natural.

On the basis of more than fifty years' observation I claim that there is no tone-deaf Hungarian child. I remember a single school-mate of mine who had no sense of pitch at all so that everybody burst out laughing if he sang. His name was Gedeon Schirkhuber and at fifteen it was impossible for him to learn what at five he might have been able to learn.

As regards rhythm we excel over our neighbours. Already in the common army of the Austro-Hungarian Monarchy it was asserted that it was the Hungarian soldiers who would learn rhythmic marching soonest.

Our seventieth "music primary school" is being launched now. The unbelievers are amazed at what can be got out of six-year-olds by competent teachers with some expert knowledge in six singing lessons a week. One could likewise be amazed by our kindergartens, too, if those in charge knew their job and there were singing every day.

To give an example of nationwide effect would be a job for the Radio. It has, indeed, already taken half a step towards this end. It is no good raking over the mistakes of the past twelve years. But it might do no harm to cast a backward glance upon them to avoid a relapse and to facilitate the taking of the second half-step.

1. The teaching of songs. Not to mention that they wanted to teach a lot of worthless songs (did the children learn them?) the Radio did it by means of time-consuming dictation of texts, and primitive parroting instead of teaching by example songs which were unknown to them and which were new to the children singing, too! In this way the Radio would have given valuable guidance as regards method to singing teachers throughout the country. Once, one of the speakers wanted to bring the listeners musically closer to the song he was teaching like this: "And now the melodic line rises in the same way as the standard of living..."

2. In the half hour for kindergarten pupils a Russian folksong was sung with some Volapük text: "Why fa Ther winter you Are late", etc. but there was no announcement that it was a Russian song. The same mistake I have been rebuking for sixteen years in connection with German.

3. Then the kindergarten teachers said: "And now let us play a folk game." So, at other times, what are we to play, games of the gentry or what? What is the opposite of "folk"? Are we not striving to be a homogeneous people, at least up to the eighth form of the primary school? Here and there we descend to the people? We don't have to descend to the people but rise to it.

4. In some of the Radio's programmes for kindergarten pupils the piano is such a non-folk (anti-folk?) element. Moreover, it is anti-style and anti-pedagogy. At the very beginning it is nonsensical. It begins its very signature tune, a song with words, by strumming it on the piano with clumsy chords and without its text. Is this how they want to put children in the mood for singing? If a kindergarten teacher in the country hears this, she will heave a sigh of relief: of course, it is easier like this! But she is mistaken! Continual piano accompaniment (1) deprives the child of the pleasure and profit in independent singing. Anyone who always walks with crutches will never be able to walk without them. (2) Nor does it follow the inevitable drop in pitch in the singing of children. I once heard a children's choir accompanied by a piano finish two–three tones lower, while the piano stayed where it was. (3) A tempered

piano, even if it is tuned daily (though it is practically always out of tune), cannot lead to correct singing. (4) Even in a room children's songs must create the illusion of open space. This is totally hindered by the piano. (5) No less superfluous is incessant piano playing while a tale is being told. It is a caricature of programme-music. Anyone who gets accustomed to looking for the representation of external processes in music, will never understand music itself. A tale, unless it includes a song organically belonging to it, does not need musical accompaniment; indeed it abhors it. It has its own particular music and rhythm; the piano, by trying to rock us into it, actually chases us away from it.

Here I dispute a statement (on page 51) of a manual, otherwise excellent, which has just been published *Ének-zene az óvodában* (Singing–Music in the Kindergarten). "By tastefully accompanying the songs the kindergarten teacher can give the children a great deal of pleasure and amusement." She might—if she plays an accompaniment by a good composer, for given the present degree of her training the kindergarten teacher is unable to improvise it. But it is an even greater "pleasure and amusement" for children if they accompany themselves on their instruments.

Besides, if we incessantly accompany singing, the sense of the beauty of pure, unison melodies, which ought to be developed above all, will not develop. And then: in how many kindergartens is there a piano? Not as if there should be one! If kindergarten teachers are not to be discouraged by examples which are for them unattainable the only instruments played in radio broadcasts should be those found in every kindergarten. It would not do any harm if the proper use of the violin were demonstrated. The xylophone is not so bad either. I shall never forget the charming sight and sound in Nagyvárad in 1942 of forty children playing the xylophone simultaneously. In introductions of "folk games for children" we saw pathetic examples of piano accompaniment. These introductions, however heartening the development they signify may be, give rise to another observation. Obviously, the little ones were happiest when their joy in playing could assert itself freely, when they did not bother whether they were being watched or not. They were less happy during the production they had been drilled to, items of the programme designed for effect. Indeed, it would be better to hold such things in the open air, on dust-free lawns and not on dusty stages, so that the children should not play for the public but for themselves, or, at most, for one another, in alternating groups. It is more important for them to see and hear one another than for the public to see them. That is how the homogeneous society of the future may gradually come into being.

And I would advise my young colleagues, the composers of symphonies, to drop in sometimes at the kindergarten, too. It is there that it is decided whether there will be anybody to understand their works in twenty years' time.

(1941, 1957)

HUNGARIAN MUSIC EDUCATION

(Lecture held in Pécs)

There might be some people who suspect chauvinism in the title of my lecture. Because art is international, and music is particularly so. Two times two is four everywhere and the C major scale is identical in all parts of the world. Nor can the fingering of the piano or violin be different with different nations. What may a separate Hungarian music education be and what is its purpose?

Well, it is not quite like that. First of all, a great many peoples of the world have their own special tonal system. But even in the so-called civilised world, wherever the identically tuned piano is found, different things are played on it in every country and in different ways. And if we examine the works played in every civilised country we have to state that every one of them has strong national roots. It is the same in literature and the visual arts, too. From Homer to Verdi, from Shakespeare to Petőfi, from Greek sculpture to Rembrandt and Raphael, it is the works expressing most strongly the artist's own national characteristics which have the greatest world-wide appeal. Since these very same works also represent the zenith of the individual's creative power, it is clear that individual originality can be rooted only in a national originality.

And this holds good not only for creative artists but for performers as well. The characteristic features of his or her nation can be found in every great performing artist. It is not how a Hungarian performer plays Bach or Beethoven that is of principal interest to foreign audiences but how he can bring them nearer to the Hungarian psyche, so mysterious for them. From the performer, too, they expect above all the key to his own people.

We have observed in many cases that when our performing artists have gone abroad they have soon become lost in the sea of peoples and are absorbed by the host country *because the foundations of their national culture* were not deep enough. Quite different from them is, for example, an Italian musician who has emigrated. He remains an Italian everywhere, not only because he propagates the art of his own people but also because in performing even foreign works he asserts his own special national character, sharply distinguishing him from all others. This is already enough to make it clear that something is missing in Hungarian music training.

As far as our audiences are concerned, the connoisseurs among them have been reared on purely foreign music; they have no sense at all of the Hungarian character

which to them is often even repulsive. On the other hand, the group which feels Hungarian music to be its very own is musically absolutely uneducated and is, therefore, unable to comprehend a more demanding composition. So the two seem to exclude each other; the Hungarian character and a musical culture seem not to agree with each other. Thus culture is tantamount to what is foreign, and "Magyarism" to lack of culture. There are grave historic reasons for this and the chapter of Hungary's cultural history that can report on the amalgamation of these two contrasting groups will be one of the most important. When this will happen we cannot tell in advance. But one thing is certain: the three words *Hungarian musical culture* represent a programme for many decades, perhaps for centuries.

To bring this programme into effect a start is to be made at the same time on two separate, though parallel, courses. Up to the age of seven–eight the two courses advance on the same lines.

Frequently and for a long time I have professed how the soul of the child should be nursed on the mother's milk of the ancient Magyar musical phenomenon; how the Hungarian way of musical thinking could be built and strengthened in it. For the time being *only* that. In the same way as a child should not be allowed to learn any other language apart from his mother-tongue until he has consciously mastered this latter, that is to say, not before the age of ten. Finally, a multilingual child will not know any language really well. A child nurtured on mixed music will not feel musically at home anywhere, Hungarian music being the most alien of all to him.

The past course of our music education has been identical with the whole of our public education and this latter we know—and have complained enough about it for decades without achieving any essential improvement—to be of an alien spirit; it stamped the souls of Hungarian pupils into a foreign mould, thus helping to prepare the deplorable events of the recent past.

In music we have tried to help. For about twenty years the real voice of the Hungarian people has been banging on the doors of schools. Sometimes it managed to get in, sometimes it did not, but only seldom did it succeed with official support. The pupils, however, took up its cause with great enthusiasm; recognising themselves in it they evidently felt that the life throbbing in it was their own life, too, whereas the school music forced upon them was mostly worthless paperwork.

After two decades the official forum, the Education Council, considered the time ripe to approve what had been achieved, and recognising that pupils could learn the elements of music more easily from songs they liked to sing they published an *Iskolai Énekgyűjtemény* (Collection of Songs for Schools), edited by myself.

It will take years, perhaps decades, for the contents of this book to become general knowledge. When this has come about music education will have prepared a foundation on which to build further. But until then, if we do not want to rear children into aliens, we can do nothing else but teach these tunes, introducing the pupils through them to reading and writing and then building the study of an instrument on this foundation.

This has been done by other nations for a long time. I myself learned from German piano and violin manuals full of German folksongs and could play *"Brüderlein fein"* on the violin before any Hungarian folksong. Up to this very day there are no Hungarian piano or violin tutoring manuals built systematically upon our ancient traditions.

This is understandable when we consider that until very recently the training of professional musicians was in the hands of foreigners who did not know Hungarian and lived here as aristocratic foreigners, on an island, as it were, having no connection whatever with Hungarian life and culture. Even among their pupils only a few could struggle upwards to Hungarian music, which will become the natural mother-tongue only of the third or fourth generation of musicians. Until then a great many professional musicians must pursue their careers, people born here and speaking Hungarian but with a culture absolutely foreign. There will be many a struggle before the Hungarian string vibrates in the soul of our musicians reared mostly on foreign music. Its soft tone is suppressed by the blaring of world music even in the souls of those of purely Magyar origin.

And this is where it becomes clear that the C major scale, although it is identical everywhere, does not have the same significance everywhere. With the Germans it is fundamental, with us it is of secondary importance. Anyone whose education starts out from this system, that is to say, follows the German curriculum, will remain insensitive to the peculiar characteristics of Hungarian music. But would it not be simpler to educate children to it? Then everyone would reach it in a natural way.

The road from Hungarian music to the understanding of international music is easy, but in the opposite direction the road is difficult, or non-existent.

Thus we need a Hungarian musical education, both from a Hungarian and from an international point of view. The more Hungarian we are the more can we expect an international interest. And this is the only way in which we can achieve a Hungarian musical culture; without it all our music teaching is nothing but finding lodgings for foreign art.

When all is said and done, we must make the choice: shall we continue to be a colony or shall we become an independent country not only politically but culturally, in asserting our own personality, too?

If this is what we want we must find the roads that lead to the freest and fullest possible expansion of our musical individuality.

Schools have already set out on the right course; if they pursue it consistently, success is sure to follow. The Hungarian method of instrumental teaching has not yet been elaborated to the same extent. *Children's Dances,* to be performed here, is a modest attempt in this direction.

By presenting these pieces in a provincial town before they have been performed in the capital, I want to express my conviction that in putting Hungarian music education into effect such a town can play a great part; it can take the initiative which may set an example even to the capital.

154

Already efforts are being made here, the like of which are not to be found in the capital, and which may be of decisive importance for the whole of our music education. By this I mean the initial course of the music school meant to teach music before teaching an instrument, and besides this the extra-mural singing lessons of selected primary school pupils. I am looking forward to the results with great expectation, and ask everybody able to do so to support the venture with might and main. This is sowing the seeds of the Hungarian musical culture of the future.

At this point democracy means two things: one is to make the means of musical education available to everybody, and the other a full assertion of national characteristics.

The pioneering work of Pécs promotes them both.

(1945)

THE NATIONAL IMPORTANCE
OF THE WORKERS' CHORUS

For a long time I have been observing the singing activities of the working and farming people. In every country the source of physical and spiritual regeneration—for which there is always need—is the people, and so care of the people is strictly speaking the main guarantee for the survival of the nation. This is becoming increasingly obvious in Hungary in particular, and especially in the sphere of music. When the development of our individual culture was soon to be suppressed by the foreign culture brought in from abroad, it was the folksong which showed the way by which we can achieve the independence of our literature and music and by which we can preserve our originality.

The position is similar in the field of performing art. In singing we went according to foreign examples—our main ambition was to sing Verdi in as Italian a way as possible, Wagner in as German a way as possible. There appeared to be no necessity at the highest level of music education for a separate Hungarian singing style. What there was of it in the bud was to be found in the singing of the people and the musically uneducated intelligentsia: it remained on the level of dilettantism.

Very occasionally there appeared an outstanding singer who instinctively gave a flashing vision of the outlines of the Hungarian singing style of the future. But it created no regular school, or tradition. Mihály Takács was able to sing even the very worst opera translation so that it did not offend the Hungarian ear. Otherwise the ear even of that small number who did originally have a good feeling for the Hungarian language became dulled by the many bad opera translations. Even our original operas sounded much like the translations. The audience were under the impression that this was how things should be, that it was refined and distinguished if the Hungarian stresses were broken to pieces. This was reflected on the periphery of musical life, in our choral societies, as well, only affecting much wider circles. There, too, whatever went against the natural Hungarian stress was considered more high-class. Some of our choral societies sang in German or in German as well. The singing flowing from the Hungarian language's own nature was left to the despised folksong or at most became stuck in the dilettantism of the popular songs of the gentry.

The opera, even if in distorted Hungarian, did at least do something to familiarise musical masterpieces. The programmes of the choral societies were not Hungarian and for the most part not artistic either.

Yet this state of affairs, in spite of two wars and a thousand obstacles, has slowly made a start in the direction of change. With the raising up of the folksong, the possibility of a higher Hungarian singing style has begun to dawn on many. The stress has begun to land in the places demanded by the language. Higher music has begun to become more Hungarian and at the same time more artistic.

Marvellous! Moving nearer to the people has not lowered but raised the standard.

There were special reasons for the workers' choral societies not having been able to take part in this development to the desired extent.

At the start of industrialisation in Hungary it was possible to find qualified skilled men by bringing them in only from abroad. Their knowledge of the Hungarian language and their feeling for Hungarian music could not have been other than inadequate even in the second or third generation. The village people stuck to their agricultural work right up to the present and did not rush in such crowds among the industrial workers as to sweep them into a more fundamental awareness of Hungarian. Along with this went the inevitable social isolation of the Hungarian workers.

So at the beginning the workers' choral societies' repertoire was largely limited to foreign workers' movement songs and in this way represented even more markedly the direction of taste in our choral societies.

Workers' singing groups began with workers' movement songs abroad as well. But there they developed relatively quickly towards art of more general validity. For example, the Dutch workers' choral societies celebrated the thirtieth anniversary of their existence with the *Ninth Symphony* and the *Buda Castle Te Deum*. In England development was nourished on an even older choral culture, so that in the twenties one could hear such difficult works being performed by workers' choirs as Handel oratorios and Bach's great *Mass*.

But we don't have to go so far afield: in neighbouring Austria it was the printers' choral circle in Vienna who gave the first performance of the *Psalmus Hungaricus* in 1927, under the baton of Anton von Webern, my deeply respected colleague and fellow-composer who died such a tragic death not long ago.

After my more intensive work with children's choirs in schools it became quite clear to me that the reason for our backwardness is not to be sought in the abilities of the singers but in their leaders. The repertoire and standard of the Dutch workers' choirs improved in leaps and bounds as soon they chose as their leaders highly qualified musicians with good taste. I myself made a few experiments. When I heard of the efforts of the Erzsébethely Choral Circle in Békéscsaba, I went there and became thoroughly convinced of how quick they were in the uptake. They learned the soprano and tenor parts of the *Székely keserves* (Transylvanian Lament) in a single two-hour rehearsal, without any instrument, simply by singing it after me. (If they could read, they would get the same result in ten minutes.)

I began to encourage my pupils to spend some time with workers' choirs. Until then it was a rare thing to see a qualified musician in front of a workers' choral group. Anyone who had gone through the music academy considered this beneath his dignity. But even so it was not all that easy for a better musician to break into the circles controlling the workers' choirs.

When a few of them managed to do this, I learned of two further obstacles to development. The workers were not willing to sing folksongs. "We are not peasants." It was only gradually that they came to realise that by singing folksongs they were not descending to the level of the peasants but raising themselves into a wider and richer national community composed of the people. The second point was that they refused to have anything to do with any piece with religious reference, and in this way they discarded the greatest masterpieces of world literature. This was a Hungarian speciality: we have seen that organised workers abroad have not put up with such limitations for a long time now.

Progress was greatly impeded by the inability to read music. The pioneering efforts in this direction by József Ujj did not gain many followers. I was always amazed at how an intelligent adult was willing without the slightest protest to let himself be treated like a parrot. A choir which has even half an idea of reading will in a given period of time learn ten times as many works and its perspectives will become ten times as broad as one which repeats like a parrot by ear.

It is to be hoped that once the new primary school curriculum is put into practice, there will be very few adults who will be unable to read music. But we have to realise quite clearly that decades will pass before the new curriculum will bear its fruit all along the line. Until then, to be sure, there still remain a few things for adults to see to.

Once the last obstacle has been removed, a great mission awaits the workers' choirs, and they can achieve great significance from the aspect of the whole nation's culture. *First,* as choirs. In the present-day condition of society in Hungary only the farming people and the workers form the sort of larger homogeneous group, united in thought and feeling, without which choral singing cannot flourish. It is only once our singing masses begin to feel the culture which is necessary for choral singing on a higher level that they will have a fruitful effect on the whole country. For culture is much like knowledge: to get it and keep it at a high standard is difficult; to lose it is easy. We must not be too pleased with ourselves because of one or two successes abroad—won at the expense of tremendous effort. We can only speak of culture once the standard which has been achieved as an exception and for a short time becomes lasting and general. Then it will be a serious factor in Hungarian musical culture.

Secondly: folk and workers' choruses can greatly contribute to the development of a Hungarian singing style. This style can evolve only from the singing of people who can speak and sing only in their mother-tongue, but, within that, with superior assurance. Some sort of foreign quality always gets mixed into the Hungarian singing of our trained singers: the aftermath of foreign-language studies and repertoirs. He's a rare man who can make this sharp distinction, so that for the time being, in the question of Hungarian stress and pronunciation, a simple Hungarian who knows no other language is a greater authority than the cultured townsman who knows several.

But the systematic musical education of the farming and working people may be of significance in yet a *third* way. It is common knowledge that the greatest vocal talents have usually stemmed from the very poorest classes all over the world. A whole list of singers of the most modest origins can be made from Maria Wilt to Shaliapin, and in Hungary from Mihály Füredi to Béla Környey. It is understandable: in the classes striving upwards the tension and energy are much greater and this makes their every manifestation more intense, more direct, more free, while the brake of education and "good upbringing" is inclined rather to dull everything and make it grey from generation to generation. Apart from this, the physical preconditions of the singing voice and biological superiority, a good constitution, strength and perseverance are more likely to be produced in the hard life than in the enervation of prosperity.

If we succeed in carrying out systematic music education in the schools and choirs, then from that time on it will not be by accident or by chance that a vocal talent will appear from among the people and it will be possible to deal with training at the proper time and thus prevent waste.

From all this it is clear that the nurturing of singing among the workers and farming people is a long-range matter, above and beyond the interests of individual classes, promising results of importance to the culture of the whole nation. The Orosháza singing festival represents a great step on the route by which the workers may progress further towards and eventually reach the area of general national music culture. From there the route leads on towards the masterpieces of world literature. Familiarity with these and frequent singing of them brings to everyone the very spiritual elevation which increases the value of living.

Bearing this ultimate aim in mind, the workers must not become satisfied with half-solutions. They can only travel further along this road if they make gradually increasing demands on themselves and on their leaders.

Nowadays all sorts of potted courses are the order of the day, where choir leaders are trained for the factory choruses. But I have not yet heard of "Workers' doctors" being trained in abbreviated courses for the National Institute for Social Insurance. Here it is a question of life. But music is life, too. It is possible that exceptional aptitude, a bit of practice and a little study will produce an acceptable leader for an intermediate period. But serious tasks can only be undertaken by seriously qualified experts. The workers must insist that only the very best choir leader will be good enough for them. It is only in this way that they can achieve ends for which it is worth fighting.

(1947)

A HUNDRED YEAR PLAN

The aim: Hungarian musical culture.

The means: making the reading and writing of music general, through the schools. At the same time the awakening of a Hungarian musical approach in the training of both artist and audience. The raising of Hungarian public taste in music and a continual progress towards what is better and more Hungarian.

To make the masterpieces of world literature public property, to convey them to people of every kind and rank. The total of all these will yield the Hungarian musical culture which is glimmering before us in the distant future.

It began some time about the turn of the century. Anyone who had only attended secondary school in the provinces could be made to believe that our culture was in good order. But after a year or two at the university, in the capital, by the age of twenty, those who had not been born blind began to see clearly. It was easy to see that here nothing was what it pretended to be. A Potemkin culture. Mirages chasing each other instead of reality.

The thin layer of educated people fed on a foreign culture and did not develop. Nobody bothered with the culture of the Hungarian masses. All the efforts of great individuals failed, they were swallowed up by quicksand and could not merge into a homogeneous national culture.

It was in 1680 that Miklós Misztótfalusi Kis had the idea that every Hungarian should learn to read. It took 250 years for it to come true.

With music reading, we shall, perhaps, achieve it in a shorter time. But what curse is upon us that always makes us do things wrongly at first?! Why is it always the incompetent people that force their way to the scene of action, spoiling things to such an extent that twice as much work is needed to put things right again than would have been required to do them well at the first go!

All right, but instead of meditating let us get down to brass tacks. What has happened until now?

1906. We recognised the basic layer of our folk music, the rock upon which a culture can be built.

In 1913 the first basic collection of songs could have been published if the Kisfaludy Society had recognised its duty. But it did not; as it had not in 1846 either. Even at that early date it could have published a collection of music on the standard of the period. Since this was never done, the work had to be started over and over again.

1914–18 and later: war numbness and a stumbling continuation. There was much to be reaped but the reapers were few.

1925: *The Straw Guy. See, the Gipsy Munching Cheese*... A final recognition of the fact that the future can be shaped only through children. Only by children becoming better musicians and better Hungarians can a Hungary spring forth that loves and creates better and more Hungarian music.

1929: *Whitsuntide*, etc. A slow progress towards "knowing yourself". Response in children accelerates, the watchfires of Singing Youth flare up all over the country; the opposition of the old and of official circles slowly gives way.

1936: Bartók choruses for children. "Singing Youth" on Margaret Island. *Énekes Ábécé* (Singing Alphabet), the pioneer of the new spirit in many schools.

1940: War again, more horrible and damaging than the previous one. And yet: an official commission for the *Iskolai Énekgyűjtemény* (Collection of Songs for Schools). The first part was published in 1943, the second at the end of 1944, in the midst of the bombing.

1945–6: A new curriculum; singing and music are introduced to the higher forms of the secondary school, too. The principle of expert tuition is declared. In theory great progress, but how far away is the complete fulfilment? When shall we have enough well-trained professional teachers? Day after day we can see how difficult it is for a nation to change the false image it has formed of itself into a real one.

Even after so many years of expounding, explaining and demonstrating we have not yet managed to instil the right view on the character and significance of pentatony into the public consciousness. Not long ago professors of the Academy of Music whispered their suspicion that the whole thing had been invented by Bartók and myself, our collections being forgeries. In 1942 a singing master in Transylvania (where pentatony flourishes most) doubted the very existence of pentatony. "They are amazed at its ancient presence," and struggle on even against recognised truth.

In his policy speech delivered last spring the highest guard of our culture said the following: "With the whole weight of my responsibility I must point out here how regrettable it is for me to see in certain phases of our musical training a striving for the exclusive domination of pentatony, which is only a section, a segment even of Hungarian music, however valuable it is."

And before this: "If, namely, only pentatony were the basis and content of our musical training we could not deal with Mozart, Bach, Beethoven and the whole of western music."

In spite of his being an ethnographer, he was taken in by those who misled him malevolently. Nobody wants to stop at pentatony. But, indeed, the beginnings must be made there; on the one hand, in this way the child's biogenetical development is natural and, on the other, this is what is demanded by a rational pedagogical sequence. Only in this way are we able to create in the child an impression of it which will last for a lifetime. This is all the more necessary as pentatony is not only "a segment" of the treasury of Hungarian folksongs but its very centre: it is the core of the Hungarian approach to music. Everything else is placed around it in more or less concentric circles, more and more distant from the centre. It was just before its discovery that we were tossed about on various segments, failing to feel where the centre was.

In music, as in language, it is only by a Hungarian-centred start that we can begin a rational education. Otherwise we shall get, as we have done so far, a multilingual generation, that is to say one that has no language at all. As a child taught several languages prematurely will finally know none really well, a musical attitude will also become confused if its foundations are not laid by a single, closed system. On this one the rest can easily be built. Finally, pentatony is an introduction to world literature: it is the key to many foreign musical literatures, from the ancient Gregorian chant, through China to Debussy.

We cannot prophesy, but if the principle of expert tuition comes to be realised in practice by 1968, that is to say a hundred years after the birth of the primary education act, it may well be hoped that by the time we reach the year 2,000 every child that has attended the primary school will be able to read music fluently. Not a tremendous achievement. This, however, will only be an external sign of what will surely have developed by then and will rightly bear the name of Hungarian musical culture.

(1947)

AFTER THE FIRST SOLFÈGE COMPETITION

This year we have had a closer look for the first time at the results of the fight begun three years ago against the inability to read—illiteracy.

It does sound strange. Are there also illiterates in the Music Academy? They are not only in it—they have been receiving diplomas from it for decades.

The historical explanation: the institution was built from above and only very slowly extended downwards to the laying of foundations. Secondly, it was built completely on the German model, and the Germans have always neglected *technique générale*.

The systematic teaching of this is now only in its third year in Hungary. The last link in the chain, the elementary, has been working only for one year. Anyone who has seen this can imagine how much better musicians those people will be who already know when they are eight or ten what the students of the old system did not know even when they were fifteen or twenty. But not even those should lose heart: with untiring industry they may still be able to right the wrongs of their misguided training.

A five-year plan should be fixed for the complete extermination of illiteracy. In five years it would be possible to achieve a situation where everyone could read, at a level appropriate to his age. For today this does not exist. This is shown by the reading competitions. What has been displayed by the best here as exceptional knowledge ought to be known by everyone; we ought to reach a situation where this would be the norm.

Understand once and for all what this is all about: the psychological procedure of our whole music-making is faulty—it must be inverted.

So far it is the fingers that have run ahead, with the head and the heart hobbling after them. The way of the true musician is the opposite: he starts with the head and the heart and from there directs the fingers, the larynx, or whatever instrument. It is because they do not go about it in this way that so many of our pianists play mechanically. When someone is twenty or thirty they announce that he has no talent. But perhaps if he had tried to make music with his voice when he was six years old, he might have come closer to the soul of music and his piano playing might have been more musical as a result.

For all that, I must say we have progressed a bit in three years—in this area perhaps more than in the preceding thirty years. But we are still far from the goal. There is still need for mutual and devoted work by teacher and pupil.

We must not believe in a teacher who only wants to teach what he has learned, who does not want to eliminate in his pupils the mistakes of his own education, who does not proclaim—study, child, be wiser than your father.

The teacher, on the other hand, must dismiss the student who is incapable of progressing properly, or does not even want to.

Increased production of quality is what the aim must be here. To rear better and better musicians: this is in the interests of the community, of culture, of our country, and the duty of everyone. But it is at the same time in the interests of youth, too. Anyone who puts in extra work is repaid a hundredfold by life. Anyone who puts things off will bitterly bring about his own undoing in his career.

It is between the ages of six and sixteen that the fate of the musician is decided. Everyone must strive to make good use of the time.

So let's get at it! Illiteracy to disappear in the next five years!

Once everyone knows what today only the exceptional people knew, the winners of the competition, once we have to search with a lamp for anyone who does not know such things, who gets the downward fourth wrong, then we really will be an academy, then we really will be building the Hungarian future as the country expects of us, then we really will be the educators of the widest range of people in the nation towards the happiness of music.

(1949)

ANCIENT TRADITIONS—TODAY'S MUSICAL LIFE

(Lecture given at the Institute of Popular Education)

(As an introduction the audience sings the folksong "Peacock" at the lecturer's request. The lecturer points out that the tune is of the type with an answer at the fifth, the second half being one-fifth lower, though not exactly, but with a so-called tonal answer. The same phenomenon is to be found not only in folksongs but in fugues as well.)

Someone who has graduated at the Academy and knows twenty-five fugues by heart may be liable to think that this phenomenon can be found exclusively in polyphonic fugues. On the other hand, we can see that it has nothing to do with polyphony; it was not polyphony that created it; it was not polyphony that gave birth to it. It is a principle in the construction of music in one voice and can be demonstrated in various musical literatures—in the Far East and all over the world—that never knew polyphony. Thus it cannot originate from polyphony. It is a principle that wants to maintain melodic unity by, among other things, not jumping with a jolt out of the initial key but by linking smoothly and cautiously the first notes of the tune with those following it and thus creating a closer connection between them.

This phenomenon can be found in many of our folksongs. If we inspect all the songs in which there is a fifth relationship—by the second section being either lower or higher—we shall find such "tonal" symptoms at every turn, that is to say divergences from the strict, crude fifth transposition by the use of a fourth here and there, and by the first phrase not exceeding the octave. The octave of the phrases forces this because it is the octave we want to hear. If we go beyond it, the effect offends our ear in certain respects. But there also are exceptions; there are continuations of the tune where the crude fifth transposition asserts itself so rigidly that we are obliged to leap nine notes right after the final note of the first phrase or section. One of these, for example, is the song about the "Lads of this place or the other"—in every village they sing it differently—"who had stolen geese, poor things". *(They sing it.)*

If the ear has become accustomed to a tonal continuation it cannot help finding this sudden jump of a ninth jarring, or, at least, sharp. It poses a problem from the singing point of view, too, and it is not impossible that in the development of the ancient tonal custom the fact that tonal answers are generally easier to sing may have played a role. (Anyway, we have to acknowledge that there are ones like this, too, and that we call them real, as opposed to tonal answers—initial themes transposed literally, in their complete reality.)

The same can be found in the field of the fugue, too. There, too, certain composers in certain periods preferred the real continuation to the tonal one. By and large it can be stated that one difference between Bach and Handel is that Bach was drawn rather towards tonal answers and Handel towards real ones. It occurs more frequently with Handel that the second voice is precisely a fifth higher, whereas with Bach this is less frequently the case. In Bach's works we can observe all varieties of this tonal answer, as well as its more concealed characteristics. At present we are not concerned with these, we have only to note that such things are to be found in our folksongs, too; but, of course, not only in ours but in all that are related to them and accordingly, similar phenomena can be observed in them.

I assume that at least some of you know in which peoples we can look for this relationship. In the peoples who still live in the parts where Hungarians lived 1500 years ago. The Magyars wandered away from there, the others stayed—faithful to their territory. But, as we can see, their migration did not make the Magyars unfaithful to these songs, because, however unbelievable this may sound, it is an undeniable fact that the songs survived with all their characteristics and regularities, indeed in some places with variations tallying letter by letter, although, according to the assessment of linguists at least 1500 years have passed since the Hungarians became separated from the peoples who still live there today. History proves that throughout this time no further contact, connection, visiting or migration has taken place in either direction.

These facts are particularly noteworthy, because everyone's first thought is that the most ancient elements of Hungarian folk music are those which are held in common with the music of these peoples, elements that are to be found both here and there. Both here and there we can find a lot of songs that cannot be found anywhere else. These, of course, are the results of later development. Both groups evolved in their own separate ways, absorbing many new effects, making many new types their own, either taking them from their neighbours or developing them themselves. But the basic capital, which can be proved to be common, may presumably have existed 1500 years ago. This is one of the rare cases when a folksong can be dated (since in general it cannot be stated when a folksong came into being). It may be a hundred years old or two hundred or it may be fifty or even ten years old. But here it is almost certain that these songs have at least 1500 years behind them.

There are very different degrees of identity or similarity between Hungarian, Cheremiss and Chuvash songs, for the Chuvash, too, have a number of songs identical to ours. Of course, different modifications are different in their weight as proof. There are some that are identical note for note. And here we should revert to the second characteristic that makes this "Peacock" song such a rare treasure, a feature which it does not share with any other song. Namely, that it exists, almost note for note with the Cheremissians, too, and the most important thing is that the tonal *mi* answer, the second part, is to be found there as well. It would be easy to imagine that in the course of 1500 years this song might have undergone a change, the tonal

166

answer being forgotten and slipping into a real answer, since the majority of our newer songs in particular prefer the real answer. But, marvel of marvels, the tonal form exists in the Hungarian song, too. Let us sing the song once more, thinking of the *re* and making conscious what is so remarkable in this. Let us sing it in sol-fa! *(They sing it.)*

There is something we have not said yet. What do we find in the second section? The beginning is tonal: *mi-re-do,* then, in the last phrase, it is real. This is particularly remarkable, for it sometimes happens that whenever the phrase of the melody occurs the answer remains tonal, but it also happens—and this again leads us to fugues, for it happens there, too—that a fugue beginning with a tonal answer will later take up the real form in the dominant or any other suitable key. If the demand of the tonal answer—whose secret and supposedly unconscious purpose, as I have said, is to make the connection with the antecedent closer by avoiding an interval that is striking or jarring and produce one that smoothly flows from the preceding one—well, if this demand has been satisfied by the lower or higher motif appearing first in the tonal form, the melody is no longer bound by anything and can take up a real form in the continuation. This is a subtle difference. How deep the law regulating this lies is proved by the existence of this dual play in the Cheremissian form as well: there, too, the first answer is tonal, the fourth line real. This can be observed in melodies where the same phrase is produced four times. It cannot be observed so well with tunes in which the second phrase is different, for example A–B–A–B.

The only difference between the two tunes is in the rhythm. But even the rhythm shows some similarity, as you will hear yourselves, if there is somebody kind enough to sing it. *(Singing.)*

You have heard the stressed notes; in Hungarian these are the peak notes. This may be only a slight difference, which perhaps originates from the language, which we do not know, because we do not know these languages well enough yet. But we may also doubt whether the rigid $\frac{6}{8}$ time, in which you have just heard it, exists in this form in reality.

The collection of tunes of related peoples is still in its very beginnings. It was in 1924 that we first got written down Cheremissian tunes from the Soviet Union. They were put into writing in a dilettante, primitive manner so that neither the rhythm nor the pitch could be discerned with any certainty from the recordings. But particularly not the rhythm. More competent experts have only recently started to deal with this. We have already learned that since the songs have been collected by collectors of their own nations, who know the language well, the rhythm lies differently. At first they were collected by Russian collectors, who knew only their own up beat idiom. We know that there is a great difference in Russian between stressed and unstressed syllables and that West-European languages, Indo-Germanic just like Russian, have no short stressed syllables. They perceived them all as up-beats. Russian collectors wrote all these tunes down as if the first note was unstressed, although it was actually short and stressed, as it is in Hungarian.

167

No collection has yet been published that indicates this quite exactly. We are looking forward to it for we have heard that a new Cheremissian collection is now being prepared. It has been produced with the collaboration of Cheremissians, who know the stresses of their language and apply them in the right place. There are a great many rhythms where the stressed note is the short one.

Having mentioned the Soviet Union I am going to make a little detour in this connection concerning the age and unchangeable quality of language and music.

No doubt several of you read Stalin's articles last year on linguistics and the debates connected with them. These articles were most reassuring for those who had been convinced before that things were the way Stalin said they were and who had not been dazzled by the theories of the linguists he attacked, or we might say, reprimanded. From the whole argument we can see that there are still a great many cranky people in the Soviet Union, too, who are willing, by means of a purely mechanical and theoretical way of thinking, to make the phenomena of life geometric, to force them into boxes and keep them there. Opposed to these, Stalin's articles give voice to common sense. They make it extraordinarily easy for us to adhere to our conviction that in language and folk music alike there are phenomena which do not change, which are independent of any kind of social transformation. If there were no other proof, the fact that 1500 years could not change certain melodies, would be enough evidence, although who could count the number of social transformations both peoples have undergone during this period. Even someone who can see only this much must understand that there are elements in music, and especially in folk music, which should be judged from the same angle as the unchangeable parts of language, pointed out by Stalin, parts that can be and are to be sharply distinguished from the changing ones.

This again leads us to the question what the choir leader is to do with folksongs. As I did not know that dancers would also attend this course this was the chief point I meant to develop here: of what use are folksongs to choir leaders, what are they to do with them? First of all, the work to be done must be divided into two parts: one is the *notio,* the cognisance, the other is the *practicum,* the usefulness. The chapter on cognisance is not short, and not exactly easy either. It is not settled by somebody browsing through a few short popular publications or even learning them. Because, there is an important job to be done here: to distinguish the folksong from the composed song. Why is this difficult? Because these songs have been going around by the ton for a hundred years. The first collection was published in 1834 and since then shorter or longer collections have been brought out at shorter or longer intervals, under such titles as *100 magyar népdal* (100 Hungarian Folksongs) and *101 magyar népdal* (101 Hungarian Folksongs). In them, from the very beginning up to most recent times, ancient folksongs and more or less old songs have always appeared intermingled with the latest composed songs. That is why it is difficult to find one's bearings, and if he wants to be absolutely clear on the matter, it requires a little time and some fairly profound study from the choir leader.

How can one reach one's goal here? The start is to be made from the composed songs whose authors we know beyond any doubt, songs published under their composers' names. I must tell you that even this is not an easy job because the songs were often published anonymously in the collections. Thus we must go back to the original publications which indicate the names. When one turns their pages for a time, for a year, two years or even ten, one will recognise which are the composed songs among the anonymous ones. Anyway, there are quite a few songs whose authors we shall, perhaps, never be able to discover, for they have never been published with names, always only anonymously. Another tricky problem arises if the same song has been published under two or three different names, for this also has happened.

The host of lawsuits about songs was a Hungarian speciality fifty to sixty years ago. Not only did the same song appear under several different names, but several persons were willing to take an oath that they had been the author, and the court was quite frequently unable to dispense justice in a satisfactory way. The suit of "Blue forget-me-nots", for example, has remained undecided and up to this very day it could not be ascertained who the author was.

By now these cases have become less thorny because in most cases those songs have vanished, they have been worn out. These are the superstructure—in Stalin's meaning of the term—if there is such a thing in lyrical poetry and songs: they are the products of a passing, or rather of an already terminated period; they are closely connected to it and have mostly gone out of fashion by now. Nobody knows them and therefore dealing with them belongs to the area of historic studies. This very feature separates them sharply from the songs that belong to the stratum of 1,500 years ago, songs that have not changed and are independent of any superstructure.

The best way is to start from well-known, renowned authors, such as Simonffy, Szentirmay, Egressy. Their songs have some common stylistic features, but, after more lengthy study, one may discover their individual characteristics. Then even if one encounters them without the authors' names, one will not consider them folksongs, because one has formed an idea of the phrases and relationships between notes which characterise each of them.

Here we may stop at the question of tonality. There are never any modulations in folksongs. They remain in the same key from beginning to end. But there may be some in composed songs here and there. This can also be a criterion. You certainly know Simonffy's song *"Árpád apánk"* (Our father Árpád). *(They sing it.)* I do not know whom I shall surprise by declaring that this was never written like this by Simonffy. It has become simplified to its present form through being used, being sung by the people, because the original had some little modulation. The second line of the original is different; it has a digression brought about by a rather complicated harmonic process. *(He whistles the original version with the modulation.)*

In this form the people felt the song too complex and did not use it, so that the simpler variant has completely ousted the original, which can be found only in old editions, in libraries.

169

If one likes to potter around with old songs one can discover with amazement that the printed form is sometimes quite different from what one knows, or the version that has become well known later on. Why does this happen? Chiefly, because these authors were not trained musicians but fumbling dilettanti, who hit upon a good melody and then rounded it off as well as they were able to. But they did not always succeed in giving their tunes a final and unchangeable form and when the songs came to be sung by the people they became changed quite freely. Indeed some authors —even Simonffy himself, for example—sometimes adopted the variant created by the people in singing the tune, and had it printed in later editions. A good example of this is the song "This is my dear sweetheart", also by him. Here we can find a bifurcation at the end of the third line. Some people sang a high *la,* others a *ri.* This latter is the printed, chromatic note, the high one had perhaps come into being in the form sung by the people. But the original form of this song has completely disappeared both in its popular use and in the later editions. Its second line, namely, did not end on a fifth. Anyone can convince himself of this by looking it up in an old edition, that of 1853 or 1855. There it ends on a fourth. But the people, having been accustomed to an emphatic stop on the fifth in the second line, did not take any notice of the fourth and shifted it to a fifth.

For those who deal with these songs another interesting study is offered by the glimpse they may get into the workshop—or witches' kitchen—of the melody changes, since, needless to say, it is not only composed songs that change in use, by being sung by the people, but folksongs too. That is why there are seventy-seven versions of one folksong in different parts of the country, versions which differ considerably from each other, not only in pitch but also in rhythm and in every other respect. But material consisting only of folksongs does not offer enough of a foothold for such observations, as nobody can say which one the original was. With composed songs, however, the first printed edition is available in most cases. If we take a look at these we can observe through the various versions how it has changed.

In such cases we have the original as a model with which we can compare the changes. There is no such model for folksongs, for who could tell what the original form of a folksong with fifty versions was if there were no regularities in folksongs— the answer at the fifth, for example.

In such cases one is quite justified in assuming that the original form of the folksong was a pure fifth-answer. This can be observed in innumerable songs which have a fifth-answer even today. But in some instances it becomes blurred and faded; notes other than those expected may appear. At the beginning of the third line—that is at the beginning of the second part, the whole song being divided into two parts— changes are to be found, and it is rather towards the end that it jolts again into the fifth-answer. This can be seen in songs in which the fifth-answer can hardly be recognised now but the cadences at the end of the lines demonstrate them clearly. A good example of this is the song "Rivers Tisza, Danube flow". Let us sing it! *(They sing it.)* So everybody can hear that the two descending fourths at the very

170

end are absolutely identical, with the distance of a fifth between them. By using a magnifying glass we can find a fifth-answer in the remainder of the tune—and a tonal one at that.

Where is the tonal phenomenon here? In the first section there is a *mi. (He whistles it.)* Thus it jumps from the fifth to the octave, whereas in the second section it goes like this: *(he whistles it).* Here there is a fourth jump, whereas in the first there is a fifth jump. This is nothing but a tonal phenomenon; it fits in with it exactly. In certain other details it does not correspond exactly with it, but at the end the cadence still points accurately to the fifth-answer. We have many songs in which the fifth-answer appears only in details. It can rightly be supposed that originally these songs once had the pure form of the fifth-answer. Having been subjected to many more foreign influences and pressures, Hungarian songs have undergone more changes than the Cheremiss or Chuvash ones, that is to say Hungarian songs have retained fewer of the old fifth-answer tunes in their original form. Those peoples have hundreds of songs in which from beginning to end the regular fifth-answer still exists. There it is a rare occurrence for a few notes to have changed. There are some, but side by side with such a mass of regular and exact songs there can be no doubt that these latter are the genuine ones. This great mass serves as evidence that this was once the situation with us, too. With a number of songs which today show only traces of the fifth-answer, it can be assumed that they, too, were pure fifth-answers once. Of course, we must adhere to reality: we have no right to "put these songs right" into the way they may have sounded. We must take them as they are. But we should know that they used to belong here once.

I think that choir leaders should expend some effort in distinguishing as clearly as possible between folksongs and composed songs. I do not mean by this that all composed songs are without exception poor, that they are to be persecuted and of no use. Not at all! There are ingenious, original and viable melodies among them too, which is indicated by their very survival. Though most of them have become worn out and can hardly be heard today even in the country, many of them are still alive and may be kept alive further. Choir leaders can make good use of them, particularly from a practical, tactical point of view, when they are faced with a choir that knows these composed songs and likes singing them. It would not do to scare them by saying "leave them alone; it's worthless rubbish, don't have anything to do with them, sing only these". By this we should get the opposite result, sometimes the choir singers might even go wild and become alienated from folksongs before even growing fond of them.

The relationship between choral singing and the folksong can take a great variety of forms. Those who are inclined to copy mechanically everything originating in the Soviet Union forget that different circumstances bring about different results. Russian workmen are, *eo ipso,* descendants of Russian peasants, for they cannot be anything else. Fifty-sixty years ago Hungarian workmen's choirs used to sing in German, the members did not even know Hungarian.

When industrialisation began in Hungary there was a shortage of skilled labour and a great many skilled workers had to be imported from abroad. They arrived here and retained their language; nobody forced them to learn Hungarian. Naturally they did not know any Hungarian songs. When they felt like singing they sang what they knew: partly their own songs, those they had brought along, partly the songs of the labour movement of the times, that is to say, songs that were internationally known. Only by and by did the second or third generation begin to learn Hungarian in a way, and along with the Hungarian language they came to know Hungarian songs, too. It would have been difficult to coerce them into singing Hungarian songs. And what is more, even today it is only with a great deal of tact and caution that their descendants, the second and third generation, can be made to sing Hungarian songs, which must be taught to them like a foreign language.

It was about twenty to thirty years ago that I first started guiding my pupils towards conducting workers' choirs. Up to then it had not been fashionable for a musician with a diploma from the Academy to conduct a workmen's chorus. They had their own, mostly dilettante, choir leaders, to whom they were accustomed, and trained musicians could not establish any contact with them. And when such musicians as felt like it went to the workers trying to get them to sing folksongs, they at once met with the strongest resistance. This was an idiom quite alien to them; they had never heard it before; heart and soul they turned their backs upon it. If they were forced—as may happen with young and enthusiastic people—they simply went on strike and refused to sing. These times are over; today the majority of workers are more Hungarian but there are still such remains, and choir leaders need a lot of tact and caution lest, by forcing the Hungarian folksong upon members of their choir, they should merely make them hate it. In many places it had to be administered by the drop, like a medicine. One must wait for the psychological moment when they find out what its taste is and demand it themselves. They should not be given injections of it, nor should folksongs be imposed upon them by force; this would lead to no good.

When a choir leader has progressed so far in the *notio,* i.e. in getting to know the material, that he is able to discriminate with certainty, he may begin to think of what is to be done as far as its practical use is concerned. First of all, I should like to dispel a misunderstanding here. Many choir leaders think that singing folksongs in unison is not choral singing, and that it is not worthy work for a choir leader. This is a great mistake because to sing a folksong in unison is a big artistic task and it is but rarely that we hear a perfect performance in this field. Here I do not have in mind stuffing it with subtle nuances and rendering it more interesting by sophisticated dynamics and tempi. No. Often it is the simplest performance of a song that causes the greatest difficulty, because there is a tendency, more or less conscious, to try to make the performance interesting; and this tendency is to be subdued, to be dampened down. Most of our folksongs are of a monumental character, the singers are to be guided towards simple and grandiose singing. This is by no means a trifling matter and the choir leader who succeeds in achieving it has good reason to be content.

This, of course, does not mean that it is forbidden to make nuances and to change the tempo. The golden mean must be found through good taste. This is particularly permissible with tunes of several stanzas, where the expression of the text by itself gives the justification for singing more loudly or softly, more quickly or slowly; this, however, must never degenerate into distorting the outlines of the melody or making them unrecognisable.

It would be a great help if choir leaders were to include in their concert programmes quite a few folksongs to be performed in unison, with the very purpose of introducing them to those who are still a bit remote from them, and getting these people to grow fond of them. This unison singing is a more suitable means towards this than singing in several parts, for in the latter one has to pay attention to the other parts and these often more or less overshadow the principal part, whereas one can fully enter the spirit of a unison folksong.

Needless to say very great care is to be taken with clarity in pronunciation because a folksong is lost unless every word is comprehensible.

As far as transcriptions for several parts are concerned, they have given rise to numerous arguments and many different views. The fact is that it is impossible to provide a rule here. Every type of transcription may be good and may be bad. There is only one rule: the melody must always be understandable and audible. The transcription that blurs the tune to such an extent that it can only be followed on paper and not by the ear is not good.

Debates have been entered into whether folksongs should be sung and transcribed one by one or gathered in groups. This argument, too, is quite pointless, because one is as good as the other. There are short songs which are not suitable for being performed alone. They must be coupled with other songs, contrasting or related ones. On the other hand there are tunes on larger lines which are very effective if sung in unison, too, particularly if they have several stanzas, in which all kinds of different nuances can be used.

The question to be decided is how much of the programme should be taken up by folksongs. It is difficult to give a general rule for this, because I can imagine cases when the whole evening's programme would consist of nothing but folksongs. For some reason or the other, a situation might arise where this would be the most suitable, or indeed the only solution. On the other hand, there may also be programmes in which not a single folksong is included. The choice is to be adapted to the requirements of the moment and the given circumstances. At rehearsals (so far I have been thinking of performances) folksongs are never to be omitted in study for practice— if for no other reason, for maintaining continuity, for keeping alive (or developing it, if it has not yet been awakened) the sense of the relationship between language and music. For, after all, the most perfect relationship between language and music is to be found in the folksong. Because of the numerous translations this sense has been considerably blunted in Hungarian singers. Translations, particularly from Indo-Germanic languages, always give a wrong stress in Hungarian. This cannot be helped;

even the most sophisticated, most skilful translators are unable to get over this obstacle fully. Thus choirs that sing a lot of translations easily lose their sense of what sounds good in Hungarian in the same way as the Hungarian middle class, indeed precisely its musically more cultured section, has lost this sense owing to the century-old operatic cult. Opera libretti are also translated from foreign originals. If we have a look at an old opera translation it sounds horrible to the modern ear, even to the most insensitive ear. For this very reason translations of operas were revised from time to time; they were reshaped and the new translator always thought: well, now I have hit the nail on the head and solved the problem. The new text was scarcely sung for ten years when the writers appeared and declared that it was intolerable, it must be translated again, such deplorable, strained stresses could not be put up with. Accordingly, all the better known operas were translated three or four times, but never successfully. The triumph of the translations lasted only a few years, then it was realised that they, too, were bad. Translating poses insoluble problems; only a compromise can be achieved. This, however, had the lamentable result that audiences grew accustomed to the wrong stresses, they did not mind them and thought they were right. It was the beauty of the arias and the voices they paid attention to mainly; the language was pushed into the background. The fact that some of the singers never knew Hungarian well enough contributed to this, and even those who knew the language did not care a pin about pronouncing the text comprehensibly. You see, it had become a household word that the text of operatic singing could not be understood. All the better that we do not understand it, was the general opinion, because at least we do not get annoyed at these distorted accents.

We must take care that the working class do not fare as badly now as the middle class did over a hundred years by losing its sense of good Hungarian as a result of translations with wrong stresses. The labour movement songs we have heard in the past few years are all marred by such poor translations and it is to be feared that the number of those stopping in the street because their ears are hurt by the crucifixion of the Hungarian language will be fewer and fewer. The writers can work as hard as they like, there is no perfect solution to be found here, unless they take hold of the tunes more boldly, too, and double a note here and there, which, in my view, they might well do, since the melody is not altered much through the repetition of a note and from dividing a note into smaller parts. In this way the Hungarian accent could often be saved.

Workers should be protected from having their ears blunted by translations. The singing of folksongs is the best remedy and that is why I say that one or two are to be sung at every rehearsal, so that the Hungarian ear may be kept awake by them.

I think I have said everything I considered necessary. But if anyone has any questions or is interested in any matter I have not touched upon, I shall gladly answer them if I can.

(First questioner: About three years ago Béla C. Nagy wrote two articles about the two sections of the ancient type of Hungarian folk music: the Finno-Ugrian one and the Mongol–Turkish one. With a colleague I tried to put his results to practical use. Last December the author declared that they had already gone far beyond that stage. We who believed him have been left stranded.)

Kodály: This question throws light upon a strange contrast. On the one hand there is the complaint that there is no periodical in which research can be published. This case reveals that too much is being published before it is really ready and mature for publication, and then the authors withdraw their statements. It is a tragedy of science that every scientific matter, once they begin to write it down, begins to grow obsolete and in one year's time or in ten it is proved wrong. But this is part and parcel of the development of science. Science keeps on changing and fluctuating: it is perhaps only in mathematics that eternal truths which do not change in thousands of years can be set forth. In every other science the ground is very shaky and new data may disprove present conclusions. In any case, it was rash of Béla C. Nagy to publish the fruits of his first enthusiasm if he himself withdrew them so soon. I do not think that from a practical point of view the matter is of great significance. When new tunes emerge, they are either beautiful, and singable, and we like them—or not. If not, it is no good insisting on them and proving their value, with however scholarly a set-up. If they are alive and attractive they will get on without science and will fertilise the fantasy and soul of the singers. Theoretical-historical research is a field better left to scholars; let them take all its odium or glory. Thus practice is here to be separated from theory. I think that choir leaders need theory to provide a firm basis only for their own knowledge; but in most cases they had better keep it to themselves and not advertise it; or, if they do, only as much as is absolutely necessary to clarify the essence of things.

As far as the rhythm of songs of the masses is concerned—in connection with another matter—this, as is well known, is mainly a question of the text. There have been innumerable conferences on this but those very writers who should be most qualified to help did not even come to most of the conferences. By no means could they be persuaded to come and listen to the musicians' wishes, to hear what was wrong with the texts they had written so far. The way they tried to arrange this, by writing the melody first without the words and then writing the words to the tune succeeds only with difficulty; sometimes it works, sometimes not; more often not. Anyway, the natural process would be to write the text well, in a rhythm to which it would be possible to write a good melody and not in iambics or dactyls; we are sick and tired of the incessant dactylic rhythms of these movement songs to be heard in the streets, a rhythmic structure considerably opposed to the Hungarian language. The language cannot put up with this for long, at least not in songs. True, the writers of our epics used this structure but their epics never became truly the treasure of the people. Simple people are always ill at ease with an alien rhythm, which they do not feel to be a rhythm. The epic *Zalán futása* (Zalán's Rout) is poetry only for somebody who has completed grammar-school studies, children of the soil will feel it to be prose.

A heartening change became apparent at the latest session of the Writers' Congress. The speeches made there, as well as some articles, reveal that two truths are beginning to dawn upon the writers. The fact is that if somebody wants to be a Hungarian writer he must, on the one hand, know Hungarian and, on the other hand, he must know how to write. *(Laughter.)* No more is needed to write good texts and once we have these, music will join them more easily than before. Up to now the trouble was that it was from a great distance that they stretched their hands out to each other and in most cases they were unable to merge.

(First questioner: I was interested in general in the perspective and relationship between Hungarian folk music and songs of the labour movement still to be written.)

Kodály: It is well known that certain tunes of ours are 1500 years old. This shows that there is an unchangeable layer which will be the same in 1500 years' time as it is now, and if the new songs of the labour movement want to maintain some connection with the people, they must at all costs be based on this aspect. This will mean their further development, since for all that they have developed in the course of the 1500 years; not only have the oldest tunes survived but innumerable tunes of a new type have also come into being. Thus, there will be new tunes emerging in the future, too, but they must keep in some kind of touch with this ancient foundation or else they will appear to be crude and foreign.

Often original texts do not sound any better than translations. This trouble was present in operas, too. Hungarian operas were composed to Hungarian texts but they sounded just as if they were translations. Why? Because the musical phraseology which evolved through translated operas came to possess composers to such an extent that they were unable to free themselves from it and because the verses of the libretti were usually of a foreign—iambic—structure and to them no other music could be written. In this respect the writers must come to some radical decision, for they cannot turn a deaf ear to the fact that there is an enormous difference between the Hungarian and the Indo-Germanic linguistic systems. Thus, for example, in the question of accents, the Hungarian text practically always demands a stress and the melody an upward line or emphasis precisely where Indo-Germanic languages would demand the very opposite. These are irreconcilable opposites, they cannot be surmounted unless melodies conceived in the spirit of Hungarian music are written to texts conceived in the spirit of the Hungarian language. Then that music, though not identical with folksongs, will be more or less close to it in its basic characteristics and will never deny that it has originated from them. Thus, it is first of all a question of texts, because there are composers who would be able to write in this spirit, but they have not yet got suitable texts.

(Second questioner: Would you give us some idea how the folksongs discovered while folk dances are being collected could be saved from getting lost?)

176

Kodály: Of course, side by side with the collecting of dances, the collection of tunes not suitable for being danced to can also be carried out, particularly if we start from the point that what the people sing is not bad. Thus, if you go to villages it is indeed the best course if you establish a reciprocal arrangement with the peasantry and are not content with simply giving your performance for the people's benefit but strive to merit something from them, too. Exchange what you have and then the choir leaders will see what the people know, for unknown things can turn up anywhere. I think the choir leaders have reached a stage where they are able to write down what emerges, and here and there even a local schoolmaster may be found who has the ability to do this but has not applied it so far because he considered it useless. It is best to persuade such local people to deal with the matter all the time. Thus there is hope of even more results because a stirred imagination will often come into action only days later and come up with pieces that did not come to mind at the first encounter.

(Third questioner: I should like to ask three questions. The first: do the text and tune of the folksong constitute an organic, artistic unity and if so, is it permissible to touch the texts of folksongs? The second question: Is there a pure form of the so-called "Hungarian composed song" which can justifiably exist side by side with the folksong? The third: What is the course of the further development of the folksong? In the course of this evolution will the difference between folksongs and movement songs continue to exist, in view of the fact that in a socialist society the emergence of a folksong is no longer the most unconscious creative process but a conscious one?)

Kodály: Folksongs themselves answer the first question, because one and the same song has a certain text in one place and a different one in another. The folksong entitles us to exchange the text for another one, if it is less suitable for one reason or other, particularly if the new text matches the character of the tune better. Rural people are in any case not too fastidious in this respect. If they like a tune and want to sing it more, they may use texts with it whose emotional contents do not suit the melody very well. Such an intervention is quite justified, even desirable, if we want to save a melody which has a poor text, by finding a good one for it.

Here a question arises which you have not put, although it is included in the question: is it permissible to write a new text for a folksong? I consider even this to be permissible provided that it is written by a talented writer and that it is poetry he creates. In a different sense this is the same as happens spontaneously in the folksong. There, too, the texts multiply so that now and again a text emerges that has not yet been written down. As a rule these texts are not radically new; there is a slow change song by song. So it is allowed if somebody has a good idea and can put a text underneath a tune which does not clash with its musical characteristics but sets them off even better than the original words. Of course, there are texts that fit the melody perfectly well. We can easily put aside the ones that for one reason or another do not go well together with the music.

The second question is whether the existence of "Hungarian composed songs" is justified. This again is a matter that cannot be settled by regulations. We can see that it is owing to some mysterious internal vitality that tunes survive for decades or centuries. There are some ephemeral melodies, to be forgotten a few weeks after their first performance and there are some that live for hundreds and even thousands of years. If a melody is so much alive that there are people who feel like singing it even today, it would be no good to prohibit it: it will be sung.

"Justified" is not the right word in this case because it is in itself and in its vitality that every tune carries the degree of its justification. If it goes out or withers, the song is over and cannot be revived by any means.

There is a section of these composed songs that has been irretrievably lost in any case as a result of the changes in the way of life and social forms. These are the so-called carousing songs which used to be sung in the course of revelry and drinking bouts lasting till the morning. I think this kind of merry-making has ceased everywhere and with it the kind of songs most fitted to such occasions have irredeemably vanished. Besides, not all the composed songs are bad; there are tunes among them which are musically valuable and interesting. No objection can be raised to their being sung even today. But enlightenment should proceed in such a way that the singers should know better and better what it is they are singing.

The third question demands prophetic gifts; it cannot be answered. It is unforeseeable how things will take shape. On the one hand, it depends on the forms of life and, on the other, on future talent what they will be able to add to traditions. One thing is sure. The identity of the line will remain as long as there are Hungarians in the world, as long as the Hungarian language is alive. Until then, as a matter of course, certain types of tunes and rhythmic formulae closely connected with the idioms of the language will survive.

(Fourth questioner: How do you visualise, Professor, the development of the instruments in popular orchestras? Are we and the Hungarian State Folk Ensemble pursuing the right course— or should other instruments be included?)

Kodály: You have to start from what there is; adventurous innovations are to be steered clear of. It takes a long time for a certain tone colour—a type of ensemble—to become permanent, to strike roots, to grow into a national characteristic. Our folk ensembles are like this, too. This small ensemble (we might call it a chamber orchestra), which has gone along with Hungarians for centuries, is a contrast to the brass band, that German import which, though gaining ground even in rural parts here and there, has never become really dear to Hungarians' hearts. Nor are brass bands suited to bring out the special accents of Hungarian music. Here the instruments themselves take the whole practice of music over to an alien territory, different from that pointed to by the direction of Hungarian development so far.

I do not say that wind orchestras are to be exterminated. They, too, are needed. On the one hand, in military bands for marching, a purpose they are highly suited to because the instruments are easy to carry, and, on the other, for open air music-making, because their sound carries a long way and can be heard well at greater distances, too. But until now I have not heard music of a Hungarian character transferred so successfully to wind orchestras that one might say they will have a dominant role in the future.

Smaller groups of the chamber orchestra kind are what Hungarians like best. Ever since they have existed their make up has been the same as today—indeed, they used to be even smaller than at present. In old pictures one can see gipsy bands of three–four–five–six musicians, playing in even very grand places. True, they mostly played indoors and through this the slight sound was sufficient. If they are to play out of doors, of course, the number of the players is to be increased, but the character of the sound remains the same. To invent and propagate new instruments is an adventurous enterprise, which proceeds very slowly. We can see the same thing in music history. If a new instrument emerges it is sometimes used and sometimes not, and it takes a long time before it is accepted among the old, traditional instruments. It needs centuries for an instrumental culture to develop and change thoroughly.

The saxophone is the most characteristic example of this. The saxophone was constructed about a hundred years ago and composers of those times, precisely those most sensitive to tone colours—like Berlioz—took it up with great enthusiasm and used it in their symphonic works, but soon they had no followers and after a few decades the instrument came to be neglected. It found its way into wind orchestras, particularly with Latin peoples. It had in fact been invented in France and mostly manufactured there. It was increasingly introduced into French, Belgian and Spanish military orchestras. Suddenly it appeared in a not too appealing role as one of the chief instruments in jazz music. In this way it adopted the characteristics of this music so much that it became practically useless in higher symphonic compositions, for anyone who hears it will immediately think of jazz music. This is a pity because it is a good instrument with a colour unlike that of any other wind instrument, so it only enriches the tone colour range. But it has been branded—so to speak—by its use in jazz, and this effect is long-lasting. Perhaps, by the time jazz is worn out and vanishes from the world to cede its place to something else, the saxophone will be rid of such associations and be available again for symphonic music.

The pipe (furulya) is a special instrument of Hungarian herdsmen. So far it has not been used much in orchestras, since it was not to be found in gipsy bands, and the efforts being made with it at present are still in the initial stages. It seems to be spreading, which is desirable. The bagpipe is an incompatible instrument, because, as the proverb puts it, there is no room for two bagpipe players in one tavern. This does not mean so much that they would fight but rather that two bagpipes cannot be equally tuned: the pitch depends so much on chance that it cannot be regulated. That is why a bagpipe can only be used as a solo instrument, or as a curiosity, as a special instrument.

(Fourth questioner: When speaking of the pipe, Professor, have you the Blockflöte type in mind?)

179

Kodály: I mean the common Hungarian peasant's pipe. Peasant pipers used to handle it with a virtuosity that is not to be found anywhere with more recent players.

(Fifth questioner: Although a great number of our male choirs have been transformed into choirs for mixed voices, there are still many male voice choirs in the country, and they feel that the literature for male choirs is very poor and incomplete. In the name of the male choirs of the country I would ask you, Professor Kodály, to write for us a good few choral works like *The Songs of Karád*.)

Kodály: I should have to live a very long time to do everything I have been asked to do. Indeed, we have tried everything possible to make choruses for mixed voices more fashionable in Hungary and therefore we have consciously somewhat neglected the writing of choral works for male voices. At the beginning I started writing an article "How to write for male choirs". I wanted the right course to be pursued not only by my direct pupils. But I did not write the article. I thought we had enough male voice choirs and we should rather go in for mixed choirs. So I only got as far as the first sentence: "How to write for male choirs" I would say; not at all—let us write for mixed voices. But we fully realise that there are groups where it is physically impossible to create a mixed choir; where there are only men and they, too, want to sing; indeed they deserve to sing well. I think that the upswing in recent choral literature will contain enough choruses for male voices, too.

(Sixth questioner: Not long ago I was in Bulgaria, where the bagpipe is a common instrument, not only in solos but in orchestras, too. It occurs also in ensembles of a high artistic level. In answer to my question I was told that an extendable part is placed in the blow-pipe section of the bagpipe and by this the bagpipe has become an instrument which can be tuned. My question is whether in your opinion, Professor, the bagpipe has any chance in our orchestras where it would represent an additional tone colour.)

Kodály: South-Slav bagpipes are factory-made, their tuning is regulated and much more perfect. Besides, they are operated by bellows. The players press the bellows under their arms and do not blow them up with their mouths, which considerably facilitates the business. It is the same in Southern Italy. With the Scots, too, a great bagpipe cult prevails, where this instrument is turned out by a great industry. These instruments have much greater volume and are more regulated in pitch. However, there they have a tradition of several centuries and they have also military use, for Scottish regiments have bagpipe and pipe bands. They have no brass instruments. With us the bagpipe has always been a subsidiary, "fringe" instrument, an instrument of herdsmen. They made it with their own hands and naturally it turned out as it turned out. That is why we can never find two bagpipes with identical sounds. But I do not think that the bagpipe would particularly suit the specific features of Hungarian music. As is well known, the harmony of the bagpipe is based on the circumstance that one of its fundamental notes is continuously sounded. Only in very few tunes would Hungarian music tolerate this. If the bagpipe were to be introduced on a large scale the menace would loom up that people would want every melody to be accompanied by this instrument and thus it would lose its original character. Hungarian tunes, if polyphony can be applied to them at all, prefer a more mobile bass, not one that is static all the time. Music-making with the bagpipe is rather of the South-Slav type. Of course, we have no links whatever with the Scots, but they, too, have tunes dating back a thousand years which not only bear this bagpipe bass well, but it is difficult to imagine them being accompanied by any other bass. The overwhelming majority of our tunes can not tolerate the bagpipe bass, so even if more perfect instruments were made a greater bagpipe culture would not seem to be advisable. It may stay, however, as a curiosity, as a special production with one bagpipe, presented for the sake of variety. Besides, it is so loud that it can fill a large hall alone.

(Seventh questioner: In connection with gipsy orchestras I should like to ask about one of our important problems: that of orchestras of string instruments plucked with a plectrum. Recently new masses have joined in the practice of music, actively too. Instruments with strings to be plucked with a plectrum are available at relatively low prices, one can easily learn to play them. But while there is no doubt that orchestras of plucked strings are suitable for a great many purposes, the performance of Hungarian folk music is not one of them. How do you, Professor, see the solution of this serious problem, in view of the fact that we have already some traditions in these instruments?)

Kodály: The only instrument that has some traditions with us is the zither. This again is not a factory-made instrument, people make it themselves, and its use is fairly widespread. Here and there it is used for accompanying dancing. But to introduce it further is not desirable, for it is unsuitable for Hungarian music.

Besides, it is no more difficult to learn to play the clarinet than these plucked instruments. I have in mind particularly the guitar-like instruments, which are quite alien to the people, although for a time they were in favour with the educated classes. We know that at the beginning of the last century, in the *Biedermeier* period, the guitar was the dilettante's instrument, used either independently or for accompanying singing. We have a number of transcriptions for the guitar in old manuscripts; even Hungarian songs were transcribed for the guitar or given a guitar accompaniment. Nevertheless, the guitar was not able to gain a greater popularity, although there was a period about 150 years ago when the performance of a sentimental Biedermeier song was unthinkable without guitar accompaniment. We know that János Arany, too, played the guitar in his youth, and took it up again in his old age. In his poem *"Tamburás öreg úr"* (Old Gentleman with Tambura) he even depicted himself as a guitar-player. But, of course, one should differentiate here. As an accompaniment for singing it cannot spoil the Hungarian character much, for most of this character is in the voice part. It does not make a great difference whether a slight accompaniment is provided by a piano or a guitar, for it consists of only a few chords and a basic bass. Indeed in this respect the guitar may even be better than the piano, for the tone colour of the piano has become so neutral and general that whatever small

181

amount of national character there is in the instrumental accompaniment would merely fade away on the piano. I cannot imagine that whole orchestras of plucked string instruments could ever express Hungarian character. I am thinking of the balalaika orchestras. In some factories they have gained great popularity. This is an ephemeral fashion, because it has no close link whatever with the Hungarian soil. Wind instruments—as I said—are just as easy. It is as easy to learn the clarinet or the pipe, and these instruments offer a greater chance of expressing and emphasising the Hungarian character.

(Eighth questioner: Is it imaginable that ancient laments or folk ballads be performed in their original unison with an appropriate choir, or should we, perhaps, try to make arrangements of them?)

Kodály: This is a purely artistic field where nothing can be said. Everything depends on talent and success. If somebody has an idea by which he can make this acceptable, he can do anything; if he can solve the problem monodistically or polyphonically. He has complete and boundless freedom and can set to work courageously. But it must not be forgotten that laments are songs connected with quite rare occasions. They must not become hackneyed or they will lose all their effect.

There have been very few experiments in arranging ballads although this is a very fruitful field offering a lot of possibilities, beginning with unison performances, of which we have already seen instances. They can be coloured by an alternation of high and low voices, by dynamics or other means; they offer possibilities for polyphonic arrangements, too.

Unison transcriptions, unless they are done by an artist, can very soon become boring on account of the number of repetitions.

(Ninth questioner: I have been appointed to a region where the members of the choir do not speak the mother-tongue of Hungarian music. I am in Sopron, where the cultural influence of Vienna makes itself felt more than that of Hungary. They take Hungarian folksongs, as well as transcriptions and particularly unison folksongs with bad grace. On the other hand, they like unison folksongs with piano accompaniment. But, apart from *Twenty Hungarian Folksongs* I hardly know of any other collection suitable for this purpose. Would you kindly tell us, Professor, whether you think the publication of such a collection necessary?)

Kodály: To tell the truth, I do not very much like choral singing to be accompanied by the piano. The chief reason is that since the singers are not trained artists, good at keeping their pitch, they sing out of tune, almost without any exception. I, at least, have never heard a performance without their moving out of tune sooner or later. They either rise or fall in comparison with the pitch of the piano and a cacophony emerges, not to mention the fact that with a bigger choir the squeaking of the piano does not have the same power, and what is more, it does not blend with the singing. Orchestral accompaniment would be better. In the case of less practised choirs, there is always the danger of singing out of tune. With things as they are, I admit that such choirs are to be led with the greatest of tact and must not be forced to sing folksongs.

In this way, they might be made to understand at the same time that piano accompaniment is not an indispensable accessory, moreover, that from a certain aspect it is disturbing, because it is all in vain—they cannot keep in tune correctly and sooner or later they will deviate from the piano. In the past the singing of folksongs with piano accompaniment was a necessary evil: we wanted to introduce the Hungarian folksong to the concert hall, which had previously happened rather rarely, and it had to be adjusted to the atmosphere of the auditorium. If somebody is accompanied by the piano all evening, this is more acceptable, because the atmosphere of the piano will not cause any hitch, but it will cause a very awkward hitch if during an evening of choral singing, a song with piano accompaniment follows three or four a cappella choruses. The clattering of the piano causes almost physical pain even if there is none of the out-of-tune singing which is so difficult to avoid.

I do not think that accompaniment of choruses on the piano should be favoured too much and I have grave doubts as to whether piano accompaniment would be particularly suited to making people who do not like the songs grow fond of them. I think that if they become more engrossed in unison singing they will grow familiar with that rather than with the piano, which, when all is said and done, is a foreign element as opposed to the folksong—indeed to achieve a fully satisfactory effect with piano accompaniment will seldom succeed and even then only with a great deal of artistic tact.

(Tenth questioner: What is positive in the cultural competitions recently held?)

Kodály: To be honest, I am not a great friend of competitions, because I know from the time of the old singing contests that there was more annoyance, anger, hatred and squabbles because of them than there was positive value in them, because adjudications at a competition can never give satisfaction to everybody; there are always those—and they are in the majority—who will complain about injustice. Whether it is justified or not does not matter. A certain feeling spoiling the mood and atmosphere always lingers on after such competitions. This may become less distinct if there are such masses of contests as now; perhaps contests encourage ambition in those who otherwise do not have any ambition or at least not enough. This effect should not be overestimated and maybe we should strive for having singing festivals—as we had them in the Singers' Federation—instead of competitions. (Approval.) At festivals there are no adjudications, no marking, for, after all, every musical production cannot be measured by the inch as at a horse-race, where there is no problem: the horse's nose is this much or that much longer, so it came in first. (Laughter.) At a choral production the results would have to be measured and summed up by so many short heads that it would take a year to work out the results. Such a competition cannot be judged justly. Most adjudicators decide on the basis of an impression, and their judgment also depends on their mood. It is impossible to reach an absolutely realistic, positive judgment.

Thus I should prefer if these competitions turned into festivals at which everyone showed what he was able to do. Ensembles considered to be better may get a certificate or some object as an award, but there should not be strict grading between the first, second and third. Thus the third would not think, "You can say what you like, I know that I am the best"; and there would be no second feeling that he deserved first place. We had better abolish such bitter moods from these meetings. Then every participant would come away from them with better and more harmonious memories.

(1951)

WHO IS A GOOD MUSICIAN?

Address Delivered at the Ceremony Marking the End of the Academy of Music's 1953 Academic Year

Dear Students, I should like to say a few words to you as a send-off for the long vacation. Two or three months is a long time, and only a few students know what to do during that period. Most of them, left to their own devices, stagnate or regress. And yet, every organic development is continuous; if interrupted by something, it stops altogether. In musical studies our customary long vacation is a particular hindrance. Let us just imagine in what state a gardener would find his garden if he left it to its fate for two or three months.

The decree (No. 68/1952) of the Council of Ministers has forced a development of our Institution to an extent which could not previously have been imagined. The Academy can now admit nobody who is not appropriately prepared, nor can it issue a diploma to anybody not fully trained in his or her profession. On the other hand, the decree requires the special music schools to provide first-class tuition at a level which enables the pupil to continue his studies at the Academy without any hitch.

For the Academy, the decree has come too soon. Because amidst the turbulent circumstances of the past few years pupils have been admitted here who are now unable to meet the enhanced requirements because of inadequate preparatory training. And the present state of the special music schools is such that it will take years for them to reach the level at which they can provide adequate preparatory training.

But what is the development of an institution if not the development of its pupils? What is the finest vessel worth if it is empty? In vain will bees produce regular hexagonal cells if there are no flowers to provide the nectar to fill them with.

In the past better musicians emerged from here than emerge today. Why? There is a general reason: the slow but continual decline of Hungarian intellectual life since the First World War.

Efforts made in the field of music alone will not suffice to end this decline. Nevertheless we must do our best to start off once again on an upward course. Moreover, the decree, which makes the Academy the highest musical training institution in Hungary, binds us to make this effort. From now on we must produce a far greater number of good musicians. This means harder work on the part of students and teachers alike.

But *who is a good musician?* This question must be dealt with, since I see that not every student and not even every teacher is clear about this matter.

A hundred years ago Schumann told us in a few apt sentences who the good musician is. I was appalled to learn that our students have not yet read even this, although it has appeared in two Hungarian translations. During the whole year it was taken out of the library only once.

To be sure we—some music-loving pupils of a provincial secondary school—wanted to know what *Kreisleriana, Davidsbündler,* and so on, meant. We had neither money nor a library, but we managed to raise a few pennies, the price of a cheap German edition of Schumann's writings. There was no Hungarian edition then. We had a smattering of German—we had started studying it only a couple of years before—but we learned from the book and the enthusiastic, fresh writings left a life-long impression. Indeed, following his advice we tried to become better musicians. What can we say now, when even our most intelligent students do not take advantage of what a well-equipped library offers? I don't say that the whole library is to be read. In fact, I'll let you in on something: for practising musicians who do not intend to become musical scholars very few books on music are worth reading—but Schumann's writings are among them.

Let us look at some of the "home and life rules" of the *Jugend-Album.* If you know even a little German you should not deprive yourself of the distinctive vitality of the original wording. If not, you should read it at least in translation.

Developing the ear is the most important thing of all. Concentrate first of all on recognising note and key. Try to determine the note of a bell, a pane of glass, a cuckoo, a motor car, etc. The myth of "perfect pitch"! It is not innate but a question of practice, just like measuring by eye. In fact, before pitch was defined by international convention, the note A was different in every city.

Practise scales and five finger exercises assiduously. Many people, however, think that they can achieve everything if they spend enough years practising automatic exercises for hours and hours every day. This would roughly be like reciting the alphabet faster and faster every day. Make better use of time! (To acquire a technique and money—are necessary evils. Leschetizky.)

Mute keyboard? Try it to convince yourself that it is good for nothing. You cannot learn to speak from a deaf-and-dumb person.

Play in time! Some virtuosi play the way a drunk man walks: not an example to follow!

Learn the basic laws of harmony early. Do not be frightened by words like: theory, figured bass, counterpoint. They will welcome you in a friendly way if you approach them amicably.

186

Never strum; play with fresh impetus and do not stop playing before finishing the piece!

To drag and to rush are equally great mistakes.

Rather play an easy piece well and beautifully than a difficult one in a mediocre way.

Your instrument should always be correctly tuned.

Your pieces must not be in your ten fingers only: you must also be able to hum them without a piano. Train your imagination until you are able to retain not only the melody but also its corresponding harmony. In his noteworthy book *Wer ist musikalisch?* Billroth, the famous surgeon, tells (p. 83) of a young girl who had been studying the piano for two years: she had practised a piece by Mozart for three weeks before performing it for her teacher. She was late for her lesson and found him playing the piano. "What is that you are playing?" she asked. The teacher was surprised: 'Why, this is what you've prepared for today's lesson!' She did not recognise it but proceeded to play it faultlessly. Behold the result of German music teaching of the time (and, unfortunately, to a great extent, of Hungarian teaching even today). — In his posthumous notes (Anton Grigorevich) Rubinstein wrote the following: *"Klavierspiel ist eine Fingerbewegung, Klaviervortrag eine Seelenbewegung. Man hört jetzt meistens das Erstere."* (*Gedankenkorb,* 1897, p. 56.)

Try to sing, however small your voice, from written music without the aid of an instrument. This will sharpen your ear. But if you have a fine, sonorous voice do not hesitate to train it; consider it the most beautiful gift of Heaven.

You must learn to understand music on paper, too.

When you are playing, do not be concerned about who is listening to you.

Always play as though a master were listening to you.

If you are given an unknown piece of music read it first and play it only afterwards. (This assures that you will have understood it while reading it.)

If you have done your daily work in music and you feel tired, do not persist. It is better to rest than to work without freshness and the right mood. To rest, read poetry. (On this point Brahms later added: "He who wants to play well must not only practise much but must also read many books." His correspondence with L. Billroth, p. 60.)

Walk often in the open air. (This—the musician's health—would deserve a separate chapter. Music is a dangerous occupation. Many fine careers have been wrecked after a promising start because the artist had neglected his physical condition. Clara Schumann wrote: "Along with artistic education my father took care, first of all, of physical education. In my childhood I never practised more than two hours and later more than four a day; but I had to walk as long with him every day, so that my nerves would get stronger." Litzmann: *Clara Schumann,* Vol. III. p. 434.)

Do not play "fashionable" pieces! What is fashionable will soon be out of fashion. A hundred lifetimes would not be enough to get to know all the good work that exists. Nevertheless, you must get to know all significant works of all significant masters.

With sweets and candy one cannot rear healthy people. The food of the soul should also be simple and strength-giving. The masters have provided plenty of such nourishment. Feed on this.

Do not propagate bad works; on the contrary, fight against them with might and main. (Of course, to do this you must know what is bad.)

Manual skill is not an end in itself: it is only valuable if it serves higher purposes. With every work try to achieve the effect the author has imagined; anything beyond gives a distorted picture.

You will save time if you follow the advice of your elders in choosing your pieces.

Do not be dazzled by the great success of the so-called virtuosi. Consider the appreciation of artists more worthwhile than that of the masses. In Schumann's time a number of superficial virtuosi scored easy successes. That is why he said the following:

When you are bigger, spend your time with music rather than with virtuosi. ("Le pianiste qui n'est que bon pianiste, est un mauvais pianiste." Lavignac, p. 117.) This, of course, applies to every instrument.

Do not miss any opportunity to play with others. Thus will your playing become fluent and buoyant. Also accompany singers. (Today only a few people appreciate the valuable effect of playing with and accompanying each other on a musician's development.)

You can learn much from singers, but do not take their word for everything. (In his memoirs Rubinstein describes the impact of Rubini's singing on him and how he tried to imitate his style on the piano [*Erinnerungen,* p. 22]. Wagner mentions enthusiastically how much he learned from Madame Schröder-Devrient, the great singer of his time. Schubert would not have written a number of his *Lieder* if Vogl's enchanting recitation had not introduced him to the texts. But this Vogl, during the pauses between his appearances on stage, used to read Greek and Roman classics in the original. Where can one find such singers today? With the passing of time the opera—from Mozart through Wagner to Puccini—has settled for less and less adequate musical training. Good performers in other genres are very hard to find. There is a world crisis in singing. See Lavignac's cited work and Vol. 1951 of *Sovietskaya Musica.*)

Love your instrument but do not deem it, in your vanity, to be the first and only one. Just consider that other instruments and singing are as beautiful each in their own place and that the most superb music is expressed by choir or orchestra.

If everybody wanted to play first violin, there could not be an orchestra. Honour every musician in his own place.

Play diligently the fugues of good masters—first and foremost of Bach. The *Wohltemperiertes Klavier* should be your daily bread. Then you will surely become a good musician. On this point, Backhaus was greatly admired because he could play any piece of the *Wohltemperiertes Klavier* in any key. This, however, mainly requires getting used to thinking relatively. He who has learned from the beginning to play his small pieces in other keys, will not find it difficult by the time he reaches the *Wohltemperiertes Klavier*. This is the real test of the good musician. After many requests, Beethoven permitted little Liszt to visit him; after a Bach fugue he asked the boy whether he could also play it in another key. Liszt was able to do so, and it was only then that the initial rigidity of the great master began to ease. It eased to such an extent that he honoured Liszt by attending his public concert.

Make friends with those who know more than you.

Be modest! You have not yet devised anything that was not thought of before by others. And if you succeed in inventing something new consider it as a gift from above, a gift you have to share with others. A study of the history of music and listening to masterpieces of different periods are the best remedy against vanity and conceit.

Thiraut's fine book *(Über Reinheit der Tonkunst)* you should read often once you are older. (Today we can omit this.) In another passage Schumann himself writes:

Beethoven did not have to learn everything that Mozart did; nor Mozart what

Handel had to learn, nor Handel what Palestrina had had to—because they had absorbed their predecessors. There is only one source to be drawn upon again and again: Bach.

If you pass by a church and hear the organ, go in and listen to it. And if you are lucky enough to be allowed to sit at it, try to play it with your little hands and admire the infinite power of music. Do not miss any opportunity to practise on the organ. This instrument avenges immediately all impurities, both in the playing and in the composition.

Sing in choirs often, particularly the middle parts. This will help you to become a better and better musician.

So who is the good musician? You are not one if you worry about the piece and play it to the end with your eyes glued to the music; you are not one if you stop because someone accidentally turns two pages at once (and even worse if you stop without any turning at all!). But you are one if you guess in a new piece and know in a familiar piece what is coming—in other words, if the music lives not only in your fingers, but in your head and your heart, too.

But who is a good musician? My dear child, the most important thing: a keen ear and a quick appreciation here, as in everything, are natural endowments. But talent can be trained and enhanced. You will not be a good musician if you shut yourself up like a hermit and pursue mechanical exercises, but only if you live a many-sided musical life and have particularly close contact with choirs and orchestras.

Get to know the kinds and compass of the human voice as soon as possible; listen to choruses to find out in which pitch they are most powerful and in which they are best able to express tender and gentle feelings.

Listen to all folksongs attentively, for they are the treasure trove of the most beautiful melodies and through them you can get to know the character of peoples.

Begin early to practise the reading of old clefs. Without them many of the treasures of the past will remain inaccessible to you. (If for no other reason, this is the secret of quick and sure reading, a part of musical training not to be neglected. There are no old clefs and new ones: there are only seven clefs. Only he who knows the seven can read well.)

Observe early the tone and character of different instruments and learn to remember their particular tone colours. (Keep this up until you are able to imagine a melody on any instrument whatsoever.)

Do not judge at first hearing. What one likes at first hearing is not always the best. The masters must be studied. There are many things you will understand only as you get older.

"Melody" is the battle-cry of dilettanti. Certainly, there is no music without a melody. But bear in mind what they mean by it: only what is easily apprehensible and of pleasing rhythm counts with them. But there are other kinds of melody as well: wherever you open Bach, Mozart or Beethoven it rushes at you in a thousand forms. I hope you will soon get fed up with the paltry uniformity of recent Italian operas. (This refers to the commonplace operas that overwhelmed everything at that time. "Puppet Theatre music!"—Schumann remarked about a work of Donizetti's. He appreciated Rossini, although he wrote the following about Rossini's visit to Beethoven: "The butterfly flew into the path of the eagle, but the latter gave him room lest he crush him with the beat of his wings." — For a time Rossini was more highly thought of than Beethoven in Vienna.)

To try to pick out small tunes on the piano is charming. But it is a matter for real rejoicing if they come by themselves, without the piano, because then the inner sense of sounds has stirred. The fingers should follow the will of the head and not the other way round. (This was the great flaw in Schumann's own training. He admitted himself that he had produced everything up to op. 50 at the piano. He wrote the following to Clara about Mendelssohn (On the 13th of April, 1838): "Had I grown up under similar circumstances, destined for music from my childhood, I would have achieved more than any of you!... *würde ich Euch samt und sonders überflügeln!*"—Justified self-esteem: his talent is deeper and more original than Mendelssohn's.)

When you start composing do everything in your mind first. Only when the piece is quite ready should you try it out on an instrument. (We could add: only then put it into writing.) If the music has come from the core of your being, if you have really felt it, it will have the same effect on others, too.

If heaven has endowed you with a vivid imagination you will spend your lonely hours sitting as though chained to the piano, trying to express your inner self in harmonies. The vaguer the magic circle of harmonies is before you, the more mysteriously will you be attracted by it. These are the happy hours of youth. But do not indulge this tendency too much since it will lead you to squander your time and strength on phantoms. Only recording in writing will teach you to mould forms and to design lucidly. Thus, write rather than indulge in fantasies.

Learn to conduct early; watch good conductors. You are allowed to conduct along with them in your mind. This will create light within you.

191

Look into all aspects of life, other arts and sciences too. Leschetizky said something similar:

Keine Kunst ohne Leben,
Kein Leben ohne Kunst.

The laws of morals and the laws of art are the same.

Without enthusiasm nothing good can be born in art.

Art is not a means of gathering riches. Be an ever better artist, the rest will come by itself.

Only when the form is quite clear to you will the spirit be clear.

Perhaps only a genius can wholly understand a genius.

A perfect musician, somebody said, is able to see any complex orchestral work in his mind's eye, as though it were in a score. This is the highest level one can reach. In another passage he expresses this in the following way:

A young music student was seen zealously reading the score during a rehearsal. "This could be a good musician!" Eusebius said. "Not at all!" replied Florestan. "The good musician understands the music without a score as well and understands the score without the music. The ear should not need the eye nor the eye the (outer) ear."
   (This is what every musician should strive for. It is advisable to read music silently and to check often with a tuning fork whether we have not strayed from the pitch.) "Read a lot of music, too; this will develop the internal ear to its keenest. Do not play a piece before hearing it very clearly in your mind." (From a letter of Schumann's dated 4th August, 1824.)

   These aphoristic pieces of advice show the way to good musicianship quite clearly. To whom are they addressed? First of all to children who play the piano and compose. Just count how often he tells the children: "Early! Soon!" At the same time, the whole is a criticism of German music-teaching of the time. Schumann himself was affected by its shortcomings and the awareness of this oppressed him all his life. That is why he thought it necessary to include good advice in the album destined for German youth. It would have been superfluous to do so if music was already being taught this way in Germany. Schumann had not travelled much; he had never been to Paris or to Rome and he did not know how music was taught by Latin peoples, but he instinctively recognised what was wrong with the German method. Wagner, who admitted having finally understood the *Ninth Symphony* only when he heard it per-

192

formed in Paris by a French orchestra, sharply criticised German music-teaching in his *"Über das Dirigieren"* and set forth in detail the reasons for the difference. Music-teaching in Latin countries starts with singing and therefore their instrumental playing also has the nature of singing. It is based on the teaching of sol-fa, which has several centuries of tradition behind it and is improving all the time. Only by practising this for a long time does the musician develop his ability to transform the notes seen into sounds and the sounds heard into written notes. In no one is this ability innate; it can be acquired by hard work only, taking a shorter or longer time depending on the person. As a matter of fact, this is the only thing that can be taught. For talent, be it that of the creative or the performing artist, is an innate gift. Its development depends on the development of the power to imagine sounds. Without it even the ship that has the finest start is exposed to perilous journeys and even shipwreck.

Since that time the most eminent German musicians have continually drawn attention to this. There is a well-known saying of Bülow's: "He who cannot sing, be his voice good or bad, should not play the piano either." What did Bülow mean by this? He did not mean that every movement and part of a Beethoven sonata should be sung before it is played. But that nobody can play it well if he does not feel and know where the essence of the melody is, and if he cannot bring it to life with his voice whatever his voice may be like. I heard the finest singing in the world by the world's worst voice—Toscanini's, when at rehearsal he demonstrated a phrase in his blunt, hoarse voice for his players and singers. And this is why they could sing so beautifully under his baton. His most frequent comment to the orchestra was *"Cantare! Cantare!"*

Bülow was not the first or only person to warn pianists of this. For a time Thalberg was considered a serious rival of Liszt, and not really without reason. On 26th October, 1838, Schumann wrote of him to Clara: "...*ein prächtiger Spieler, der es mit Euch allen aufnimmt."* Although it is difficult today to form an idea of what his playing was like, it is impossible that his studies, as he gave an account of them, left no trace on it. In the preface of his work *L'art du chant appliqué au piano* (another publication I have never seen in the hands of any student) we read the following: "It might encourage young artists to know that I studied singing for five years, under one of the most famous masters of the Italian school."

Our music-teaching methods were developed on a purely German pattern, but without the warning of the Wagners, the Bülows and the Thalbergs. At Debrecen Szotyori-Nagy, who had been to Switzerland, began something of the kind, translating *"technique générale"* into "general training". This means that all kinds of musicians must know how to read and write music; this training, initiated by the French, has been intensified since 1870 by the practice of dictating music, a practice now pursued everywhere.

Only after 1882 were Wüllner's *Chorübungen der Münchner Musikschule* used at the Budapest Academy of Music. It was a poor substitute for sol-fa, used in small choirs only; in addition, only its first part was applied and even this was not compulsory for everybody. The turn of the second part never came. It was designed to prepare for big choruses and not for basic music tuition. The dictation of music was introduced only in 1903 and then only at a primitive level.

When I was a young teacher I gave the worst mark in harmony to a pupil of David Popper's. He had never attended classes through the year and had never studied. Popper asked me to give him a better mark so that he might continue without being obliged to repeat the year, arguing that the young man would be a clever *"Musikant"*. *"Lieber Meister"*, I said, *"ich dächte, wir hätten Musiker zu erziehen, nicht Musikanten."* We should do him no good unless we taught him everything a good musician needs.

Obviously, Popper did not urge his pupils to try to acquire a full training in music. Unfortunately lesser men took the same approach. Through neglect of the so-called subsidiary subjects a great many half-musicians with skilled hands but empty heads have emerged from this institution. To a large extent this was why society did not consider them to be persons of full value.

I do not want to go into the details of the Sisyphean efforts I have made since 1907 to improve the situation. In the faculty of those times I was left to my own resources and in my own class I succeeded in achieving some very little results. In 1918 I agreed to take part in the running of the institution only because I hoped that basic tuition might be improved by general measures.

Then I had to look on with folded arms as the level sank year after year. As time went on hosts of poorly prepared students were admitted to the Academy. The number of "charity diplomas" rose, the standards got lower and lower. In the department for training music teachers "musical science" had to be introduced because it turned out that the students' learning in harmony and knowledge of form had been minimal and by the time they came to be trained as music teachers, they had forgotten the little they had learned and could hardly even read.

It was a treatment of symptoms—it was necessary to make up for the deficiencies in the basic tuition. The difference between the nominal and real value of diplomas grew by leaps and bounds. The institution cheated its students by issuing diplomas which implied qualifications far surpassing their knowledge. There were more and more qualified music teachers who were unable to read even a simple folksong faultlessly.

During the years until 1945 any serious suggestion was simply out of the question. Then reconstruction from the physical and spiritual ruins of the institution began: silently, without any grand words and, as far as possible, independently of the topical personal squabbles of the times. The "reform" of 1949 interfered greatly with this process, by stopping the teaching of sol-fa... It became obvious within a few years that efforts to train musicians without it were doomed to utter failure, and since 1952–3 it has been included in the curriculum again. The effects of years of neglect cannot be repaired overnight. But the work improves year by year and all will be in order again when the special music schools start sending us impeccably prepared pupils. For the time being we have a number of students who are like houses without cellars. For them the digging and building of foundations at this late date will require a truly great effort. But the effort must be made: the walls of a building without foundations crack and soon collapse. The lack of basic training in youth takes its revenge later on. This is why we have so many musicians at odds with themselves and with the world. This can and must be forestalled. He for whom *music* is not the principal subject will never become a good musician. The instrument is only the first subsidiary subject; it can change in the course of time quite a few people do take up another one. But music, which the player wants to express on his instrument, will not come to him unless he studies *music,* day after day, with continuous ardent attention.

Last year, while preparing the new decree, we took a survey of the students' musical apprehension. It turned out that less than half of them could read and write at the level demanded by the standard of their playing. The effects of abolishing sol-fa three years earlier had clearly been disastrous. It is significant that the students of the so-called "artists' training class" wanted to instigate a rebellion against their examination; as if school-children protested against pulmonary screening or the examination of their teeth.

At first there was a protest even against vaccination. Human stupidity will often rebel against its own interests.

The intensified sol-fa teaching of the past school-year (1952–3) improved matters a bit, but the lion's share of the work is still to be done. Everybody must understand that to modernise our music teaching a complete shift is needed.

In cultures without writing there were illiterate classic authors and musicians who did not know the notations. There were and there are skilful instrumentalists who are illiterate. Oriental music is not written down but learned by ear even today. Bihari did not know the written notes and yet his playing enchanted even trained musicians. The most valuable part of our musical culture, the folksong, has survived for thousands of years on the lips of illiterate people and continues to spread thus to this very day. Nonetheless, the struggle to move from an illiterate culture into one with writing is our most urgent task. To reach a written, up-to-date culture, the outdated type of musician—half-gipsy and half-illiterate—must be eliminated most urgently.

Who needs sure and quick musical reading and writing and what for? Every professional musician, on different levels. There can be no good conductor below the summit mentioned by Schumann. So far, our conductors' training section has not sparkled at the sol-fa competitions. (In 1910 Frederick Delius, the eminent English composer, complained that German conductors were "amazingly stupid; they could not imagine the composition away from the written notes and always wanted me to play it. On the piano(!) an orchestral composition, although I cannot play the piano!") An indirect proof of how right he was is provided by Guido Adler who writes on p. 121 of *Der Stil in der Musik* that "only few can reach the highest level".

195

Of course, it is first and foremost the composer who needs an internal ear as keen as possible. Its lack is an appalling obstacle to his development. How can he hear and write down accurately what is sounding within him if he is unable to perceive quickly and surely the sounds coming from outside?

How often has it happened that pupils studying composition without a trained ear write down something quite different from what they have imagined? Lavignac mentions that Massenet had once sent back to a sol-fa course a pupil who was studying composition but making no progress at all. (*L'éducation musicale,* p. 40. This excellent book quotes much of Schumann's advice in Franz Liszt's French translation...) The further fate of this pupil is also instructive. He did not achieve anything—proving that basic training acquired at the cost of great effort after the age of 18 is neither firm nor durable enough. Here, too, we have seen often enough what a struggle the study of composition, and even of simple harmony, is for one who failed to learn the reading and writing of music early enough.

The pianist needs somewhat less. The whole work is condensed in two staves, but he is lost if he does not hear the harmony even away from his instrument. If necessary the violinist or wind instrumentalist can manage if he masters his part thoroughly. But he will play it in a different way if he can hear the other parts along with his own even if he does not see them in writing. He cannot clearly intone a more complex work if he does not know the score and is not aware of the tonal function of every single note. Although the violin solo of the *Psalmus Hungaricus* is just a few notes, only he can play it correctly whose training in harmony is sufficient to enable him to interpret clearly the role played by every single note in the harmony.

What shall we say about singers, among whom good readers are few and far between? Just imagine the National Theatre if the members could not read and the director had to cram every single sentence of their roles into their heads in the way customary in the Opera House today.

At the sol-fa competition we looked into a shocking void. Brilliant pianists are unable to write down or to sing faultlessly a simple one-part tune after hearing it fifteen or twenty times. How do they expect to imagine an intricate piece of several parts if their internal ear is so undeveloped? They only play with their fingers and not with their heads and hearts. They are not musicians but machine operators. It cannot be the aim of the Academy or even of special music schools to train genteel misses to strum on the piano. They used to play the "Virgin's Prayer", today they may play the *Allegro barbaro,* but in neither case do they have anything to do with music.

Today there is much talk of overburdening the students. It is true that the musician finds burdensome the learning of subjects whose direct use in his career he cannot see. If he realised, however, how much easier it is to learn every *music* subject, and how much time is won if he first trains himself to be a quick and sure reader, he would not rest day or night until he had achieved this. To teach a child an instrument without first giving him preparatory training and without developing singing, reading and dictating to the highest level along with the playing is to build upon sand.

One can even attain a virtuoso's skill without reading: we can still find singing or recorder virtuosi among older people of the peasantry. The Gipsies of old accomplished wonders on the violin, clarinet and cimbalom even without written notes. But such can be considered only half-musicians today; they can never become conscious, cultured musicians.

On the other hand, an exaggeratedly one-sided concern with writing is also something we must guard against. There are few music students today who could sing a tune after the first hearing, or write it down quickly. Only the well-conducted teaching of sol-fa can develop the ability to connect tone-image with written note to the point where the one will evoke the other instantly. Today's musician, if he wants to make his way, must unite in himself all values of content and form both of folk culture and of written culture.

As a general rule, only someone who has been taught well can teach well. Yet it can happen that someone who has been taught badly becomes a good teacher because he wants to save his pupils from the mistakes of his own training. I have watched the trial teaching of some "artist-teacher" trainees. It was as if they felt this work to be rather beneath their dignity. However, "with the people for the people" is bound to remain an empty platitude for anyone who is not equipped to establish a firm bond of sympathy with the people so as to bring music into their lives. How can we teach what we do not know ourselves? One or another of the trainees failed to notice when an interval was wrongly intonated and left it at that. He should take pains in his own interests if for no other reason. A new generation is growing up and—in the hands of good and faithful teachers—is approaching music in the right way. By the time those who are seven or eight years old today have grown up, those who are twenty now will be active musicians in their prime. Those not good enough as artists or as teachers will be swept aside by the younger generation. For there is one thing of which we should be fully aware: only one in a hundred will prove good enough to be an artist and live exclusively from being an artist. On the other hand, the history of music shows that in many cases the greater somebody is the greater is his desire to pass his knowledge on to others.

You have here a faculty composed of many teachers, all of whom desire to equip you as well as possible for the hard battles of life. You can fully repay this anxious affection only by applying yourself with the utmost diligence to the achievement of this aim. After all, it is a question of your own success.

On the basis of what has been said, the characteristics of a good musician can be summarised as follows:

1. A well-trained ear 3. A well-trained heart
2. A well-trained intelligence 4. A well-trained hand.

All four must develop together, in constant equilibrium. As soon as one lags behind or rushes ahead, there is something wrong.

So far most of you have met only the requirements of the fourth point: the training of your fingers has left the rest far behind. You would have achieved the same results

197

more quickly and easily, however, if your training in the other three had kept pace. If elementary mistakes in rhythm did not have to be corrected in the instrument classes. If you had the analysis of the content and form of the composition at your finger-tips. If you approach the work with an understanding of its spirit the intellect will guide your fingers and you will find the right path much sooner than if you try to get at the spirit by means of the fingers. Short-lived successes or the semblance of success can be achieved by imitation of the master or of another artist. However, without the first three points, nobody can create independent work.

Sol-fa, and the science of form and harmony together teach the first two points. To complete this teaching, a musical experience as varied as possible is indispensable; without playing chamber music and singing in chamber choirs nobody can become a good musician.

As for the third point, I cannot find lessons in the curriculum of any school. And yet, most of the shortcomings are in this area. But it cannot be taught in classes. Psychology might help, and that can be taught, but the rest is supplied by life; the reading of great writers' works, the study of great artists' creations: "Look into all aspects of life, other arts and sciences too..." Every art offers something that is its own and cannot be found in any other. "A cultured musician can study Raphael's Madonnas as profitably as a cultured painter can study Mozart's symphonies," Schumann wrote in another passage. A musician must immerse himself, first of all, in his own art. The majority of pupils studying music hardly know anything that is not included in their curriculum, in the strict sense of the term. This is because, as a result of their poor reading abilities, it requires so much time for them to get to know a composition. It is not enough to listen once, fleetingly, to great works; one has to prepare for them and to follow the notes through the pages both before and after hearing them in order to implant them abidingly in one's mind. Personal participation is worth more than anything else. It is a pity that for years we have had no choir; in the past, the choir's memorable performances of great masterpieces contributed much to the development of the students' music, and of their hearts as well. Although we already have a string quartet the mass of students do not know what can be gained by listening to this superior kind of music. Only a few of them listened to the beautiful performance of Schubert's *Quartet in A Minor,* though with its richness of feelings this work is of outstanding value in cultivating the heart. For such works it is worth going on long pilgrimages. And yet it was played here on the premises—and they did not listen.

We have seen that the title of good musician can be earned only by a sustained many-sided effort. Nothing can be knocked off this price: if one misses something it will show, whatever course one pursues as a musician. Basic training missed in youth cannot be made up for later on. Happy is he who is young and has not missed anything yet; but time flies swiftly, and he who has not learned to read and write fluently by the age of fourteen, can learn to do so later only with great difficulty, if at all.

198

The title of good musician also implies an educated taste. Schumann waged his war only against Herz and Hünten. But in the overwhelming chaos of music produced today only a past master can find his bearings. It is a hundred times more difficult to acquire sureness of taste today than it was a hundred years ago. Often the genuine can scarcely be distinguished from the counterfeit. But a good musician knows what good music is. He is guided by his familiarity with literature, his theoretical and practical knowledge and his educated taste—all acquired over the course of many years.

And what is the aim of all this long and tiring work? To win competitions? To outshine one's fellow-musicians, to obtain fame and renown?—No. It is the bounden duty of the talented to cultivate their talent to the highest degree, to be of as much use as possible to their fellow men. For every person's worth is measured by how much he can help his fellow men and serve his country. Real art is one of the most powerful forces in the rise of mankind and he who renders it accessible to as many people as possible is a benefactor of humanity.

Obviously, a perfect musician is an unattainable ideal; even the best can find shortcomings in themselves. But seeing the goal, they can measure the distance and understand what is still to be done to approach it. For such people Schumann's last sentence is not depressing but encouraging:

> *"Es ist des Lernens kein Ende"*
> (There is no end to learning)

Appendix

A short speech could not cover all the questions involved in the learning of music. Only a couple of sentences have been added to the second printing. But it is worth mentioning that in the 1953/4 academic year attempts have been made at the Academy to organise groups of three pupils for extra-mural practising. Practising two parts without a third companion observing and beating time is not worth much, for the singers do not notice the mistakes they make nor do they keep time exactly. Among hundreds of pupils only a couple of groups could be organised and even they did not work systematically.

This was due partly to the pupils being overburdened with their studies; mostly to the great distances and to the thousand trials of the capital—time consuming, distracting, sometimes amusing—and, last but not least, to financial worries. Because of all this, a music student of the capital, even if born good-natured, turns into an egocentric hermit. He rushes home from his lessons to do his homework; he doesn't care about his fellow-students, in fact he hardly knows them; finally, for lack of social life, he becomes an anti-social being. He is aware only of the disadvantages of the capital, and enjoys none of its advantages: he doesn't find time to go to the theatre, to the art-gallery, or even to do some serious reading. He does not take advantage of the opportunities offered by the school for increasing his awareness of his own field: he hardly visits the library, and usually only a couple of dozen students attend the Academy concerts, although the programmes often contain important works that are rarely heard.

The one students' hostel in the capital is no help. It is an overcrowded building, not fit for this purpose; the residents only disturb one another instead of helping each other; mutual help is impossible because their professions and ages are so different.

The smaller the town, the less possible it is for an individual to hide; all the more is he obliged to live a social life. Feelings of mutual dependence, a sense of "help others, for by doing so you help yourself", have so far developed best at Békéscsaba. The measurable achievements in music are also adequate there. In three different schools I made a test using a short piece for three voices. Only at Tarhos did they sing it faultlessly at first sight. In Pécs they sang it somewhat haltingly, and the secondary music school in Budapest trailed far behind.

It is in the capital that it is most difficult to develop better musicians and more social human beings. Students should go there only when their foundations, both professional and human, are firm.

(1953–1954)

PREFACE

to the Volume "Musical Reading and Writing" by Erzsébet Szőnyi

It is a long-accepted truth that singing provides the best start to music education; moreover, children should learn to read music before they are provided with any instrument. Recently in Hungary not only has this been accepted as fact, but every effort has been made to put it into practice. Nevertheless, it is still not a universally held precept. This is due to two factors.

Among other things, we are still living in a musical culture that exists without writing. And yet it is indeed a real culture: one which includes instrumental music after the oral tradition—playing by ear. Our magnificent treasury of folksongs is part of our culture. Its custodians, the people, have never learned to read or write music, and yet they can produce brilliant performances. In their own time, Hungarian Gipsy and non-Gipsy virtuosi of instrumental music also represented culture, although they, too, were unable to read or write music.

But the time for a culture of handed-down oral tradition is over, and outside Hungary the world has long since entered into the era of a written culture. In our own country, there is no more urgent task than the hastening of this transition if we do not want to be left behind for good. Without literacy today there can no more be a musical culture than there can be a literary one. Thus the promotion of musical literacy is as pressing now as was the promotion of linguistic literacy between one and two hundred years ago. In 1690 Miklós Tótfalusi Kis's idea that everybody could learn to read and write their own language was at least as bold as the idea today that everybody should learn to read music. Nevertheless, this is something no less possible.

Let us consider musicians *per se*. Are they musically literate? By no means! Or, if musical literacy is a basic criterion of musicianship, then the majority of our professionals in music are not musicians.

The other factor providing a reason for our musical backwardness in this respect is the whole historical development of our music-making. Consider how music has been taught in Hungary, and by whom. Ignoring for the moment earlier periods, in the nineteenth century there appeared in some of the houses of the distinguished landowners and successful businessmen the *Klavier-master*. (It was only later that the name *Klavier* was replaced by the Hungarian for piano.)

These masters were usually second or third-rate German or Czech musicians who were unable to make a living at home. Their aim was to train the young ladies and gentlemen entrusted to their care in the art of musical pyrotechnics—usually in as short a time as possible. Nor did their employers demand any more than that. Up to the end of the century—indeed, in country districts to this very day—this spirit prevails in the private teaching of music. The result? Instrumental practice half by ear, and without any theoretical knowledge: music-making by the fingers, but not by the soul.

Although as early as 1840 Liszt urged the establishment of a National Conservatoire to produce higher standards—one which would affect the education of the whole nation—even starting and campaigning for a fund to this end, on account of unfavourable circumstances, the Academy of Music could only be realised in 1875. Even then it did not have the right organisation. Is was built from the top and was, at first, only an institution for the very ablest. However, as there were not enough advanced pupils to attend it, it developed downwards. Slowly and unsystematically it began to teach beginners and, in its practice-teaching classes, even small children.

From 1893 onwards it issued diplomas for music teachers, although not providing candidates with the right method for elementary stages—as had been developed in the Latin countries—because it followed exclusively German examples.

The results of German and Latin (or Italian–French) music education were most sharply criticised by a German, Richard Wagner himself in *Über das Dirigieren*, 1869.

In this work he relates that, although he had known Beethoven's symphonies very well indeed, and had even copied the score of the *Ninth* by hand and had made a piano solo arrangement of it, the confused performances of this work in Leipzig put him off to such an extent that he became assailed by doubts about Beethoven himself, and stopped studying his works for a while. Only in 1839, at a performance by the Paris orchestra, did the scales fall from his eyes. What was that orchestra's secret that it recognised in every bar the Beethovenian melody and sang it? The secret that led to this recognition lay in its education, since the French–Italian school approached music through singing, and under this school, instrumental playing was the equivalent of singing. On the other hand: "I have never met a German conductor who was really able to sing a melody—be it with either a good voice or a bad one. For him music exists as some peculiar abstract thing, floating between grammar, arithmetic and gymnastics."

Thus Wagner himself was a victim of German education. Had he but learned to read soon enough, to imagine the written notes as the actual sound, he would never have doubted the value of the *Ninth Symphony*. These doubts were never known by Habeneck who, at the price of several years' untiring work, finally fashioned this "unperformable" work, realising the way he had imagined it. Wagner needed Habeneck in order to have his faith in Beethoven restored. Even before then, in 1865, in a work called *Bericht über eine in München zu errichtende deutsche Musikschule*, he stressed the superiority of the French education and the performing arts, setting them as an example to be followed by his compatriots. Since that time German music education has greatly improved, but some of the very basic contrasts have survived even up to the present, and we do not know whether it would wholly satisfy Wagner.

Education played a great role in Italy's having produced so many outstanding musicians. For example, about 1750 Bertalotti was teaching in the ordinary schools in Bologna his *Solfeggi*—a work which has become established only in the past fifty years as a set item in the special music schools of Northern Europe.

We can read in Berlioz's autobiography that the music master invited to the small provincial town from Lyons first trained him to become an intrepid sight-reader—*lecteur intrépide*.

As early as 1810 a modest second violinist from Lyons knew how to educate his pupils in music. In Hungary, even today, musicians in much higher positions do not know this. The French and Italian schools have practised the right methods with increasing care, yet always finding something to be improved upon. In 1870 they introduced music dictation. Yet, in his preface to his great work *Solfège Universel*, Émile Artaud wrote in 1878 the following:

"The world of music is indebted to A. Thomas (Composer of *Mignon, Hamlet*, etc., at that time director of the Conservatoire), for having established special solfeggio classes for the singing pupils. To raise singers—whose ignorance had been proverbial for so long—to the rank of musicians; this was the most urgent reform needed for the revival of the teaching of singing. Thus in the matter of a few years every musician —even the singer—would really become a musician: someone who could write down a dictated melody, and read with facility every rhythm, clef and key, in addition to answering questions on elementary theory including the foundations of harmony."

He went on: "For good singers are not rare due to nature not producing good voices—they are created every day—but because well-qualified singing masters have disappeared."

The gradual neglect of solfeggio as the serious basis of music training has directly caused the decline of singing, together with the ineptness of artists overestimating their abilities, and the attitude of the dilettanti.

"From the example of the Paris Conservatoire it will be seen that the time is approaching when it is acknowledged that, just as writing cannot be learned unless reading has been learned first, singing or playing an instrument cannot be mastered unless solfège has itself been mastered first."

Indeed, since 1878 his (Thomas's) example has been followed everywhere except in Hungary. Artaud sent his work to Liszt, dedicating it to him in his own hand; even today his book is preserved in the library of the Academy. Liszt, however, had no time for reforms, and for decades after his time there was no tuition in any way resembling solfège provided by the Academy of Music. It was not until 1903 that dictation of music at an elementary level was introduced. Even then, on account of diverse obstacles, real and methodical teaching of solfeggio was not built up until now. Nor is the principle widely accepted all over the country that sol-fa needs to be continued right up to the highest grade of tuition in both singing and instrumental work in order that we should read music in the same way that an educated adult will read a book: in silence, but imagining the sound.

If, at long last, we wish to put our music education in order, we must take up the threads where Liszt dropped them. Fortunate indeed is the child who creates with his own voice the first association linking it with the picture of the notes.

If he starts singing based on the concepts of instrumental techniques, then our endeavours to make the singing and aural concepts primary can hardly succeed. And if he does not sing at all, it will be nearly impossible for him to achieve free and intimate "singing" on any instrument.

Even the most talented artist can never overcome the disadvantages of an education without singing.

Erzsébet Szőnyi's book describes the best way, and explores fully the child's happy musical development. It is a common starting point for the musical education of both musicians and the general public. Of course, this book cannot be anything but a sketch of her peerless, practical teaching; filling it with life requires the skill and artistry of the teacher, who, nevertheless, can learn the method from it.

Every lesson should be built in such a way that at its end the child should feel his strength increased rather than any sense of tiredness; moreover he should look forward to the next. Today such teachers are as rare as blue diamonds, and it will be a long time before the preparatory and sol-fa lessons, existing only on paper, fulfil the promise of their contents. Once the number of good teachers has risen sufficiently, Hungary can achieve a golden age never before hoped for, reflected also in the teaching of our professionals.

Let us not delude ourselves with vain hopes: no musical culture can be created with deaf-and-dumb musicians. It is only after directing the training of such professionals into the right course that we can think about really bringing music nearer to the people. The only practical course towards making an elementary knowledge of music into public property is through the development of hearing.

With these aims in view, we must rear a great number of good musicians. Anyone who studies carefully these one hundred lessons cannot stray from the path to good musicianship. Nor should he despair at not having completed them by the age of twelve; he can still win laurels. Even an adult musician will experience renewed discovery through studying these lessons, which may indeed overcome many small shortcomings in his proficiency.

It is the richness of both the musical experiences themselves and the memory of them that makes a good musician. Individual singing plus listening to music (by means of active and passive well-arranged experiences) develops the ear to such an extent that one understands music one has heard with as much clarity as though one were looking at a score; if necessary—and if time permits—one should be able to reproduce such a score.

This, and certainly no less, is what we expect from the student of a language; and music is a manifestation of the human spirit similar to a language. Its great men have conveyed to mankind things unutterable in any other language. If we do not want such things to remain dead treasures, we must do our utmost to make the greatest possible number of people understand their secrets.

(1954)

INTRODUCTION

to the Volume "Musical Education in Hungary", Edited by Frigyes Sándor

The present volume is evidence that musical education in Hungary is on the right path: it is designed not only to train musicians but audiences as well.

Continuing on the same line it will have achieved its purpose when matters are managed by those who have experienced the advantages of this education themselves, namely—those who are now about ten years old.

If one were to attempt to express the essence of this education in one word, it could only be—*singing*. The most frequent word to be heard on Toscanini's lips during his orchestral rehearsals was *"Cantare!"* expressed in a thousand and one shades of meaning.

Such encouragement is wasted on those who have never sung. Are there any such people? I refused to believe it, but I have been convinced by innumerable proofs that they exist. Indeed, why should anyone sing who has not been hushed to sleep in his cradle by his mother's lullabies, who has grown up in the presence of the radio and the gramophone and can hear much better singing by turning a knob than he can ever hope to produce himself?

Our age of mechanisation leads along a road ending with man himself as a machine; only the spirit of singing can save us from this fate.

Twice in our century the sound of soft Hungarian singing rising again has been stilled by the roar of cannon and the sound of bombs exploding. Were we not confident this cannot happen again, we should despair.

It is our firm conviction that mankind will live the happier when it has learnt to live with music more worthily.

Whoever works to promote this end, in one way or another, has not lived in vain.

(1966)

IV
ON HIMSELF AND HIS WORKS

CONFESSION

A Lecture Given to the Nyugat* Circle of Friends

When the organisers of the Nyugat Circle of Friends invited me to give a lecture this afternoon, I at first declined the honour, because I am a man of old times and do not like to talk about myself. In my time girls still stayed at home to wait for their fiancés and we waited for the critic. Today all this has changed and what was once an exception, namely that the girl would say to the boy, may God give me to you, is now the regular thing. Literature and art have also been influenced by new trends, the new objectivity, which exhorts us not only to speak ill of others but to speak well of ourselves and not to wait for others to verse their opinions, for they are bound to be bad. Considering all this I have decided, nevertheless, to speak, but I must ask for your forbearance if this ill-fitting guise does not suit me.

The piece Tivadar Országh played has been picked out again—although many of you have probably heard it already—as it is my most successful work. None of my other works has been played so often as it is still broadcast weekly even today by one radio station or another. It is, however, a very old work of mine originating from the times when I knew nothing about folksongs; no more than what was present in the air and visible on the surface. Socon clusions could be drawn from this as to how I would have written later on if, for example, I had not found my way to the countryside, or if folksongs had not existed, or if I had not come into contact with them. In the course of the afternoon I should like to contrast this most successful piece of mine with a group of the least successful ones, which will be sung by Mária Basilides, and then I shall try to explore the reason for this difference. Maybe this venture of mine can be excused because we are dealing with a phase of my work that has come to an end; after all, at fifty one should discard one's lyre and not wait for it to emit scraping sounds.

You will certainly have noticed that this Adagio does not show any traces of Hungarian folk music; here at long last is a piece in which there is no folk music, some of my friends may say who object even today to my having gone to the country-side to bring back such things. This is a fairly clear, fluent and internationally comprehensive style; it has not been stolen from anybody, so that there must be something

---

* *Nyugat* (West), was a significant literary journal founded in 1908 which played an important role in the development of modern Hungarian literature. As its name suggests, the periodical proclaimed a revival that was based on the literary spirit in Western Europe.

individual in it and, as its success has proved, it is easily accessible. If I had pursued this style, I would have been treading on the path that leads to easier and swifter successes. But man is guided by his desires, and my desires lead me to where lesser results were to be achieved by even harder work.

To understand this you must recall what the world was like here in Pest in our young days. At that time the Wagner cult was at its climax here. If it had not been for the fact that the programme was in Hungarian, the music played at concerts would have made one think that one was in a small German town; besides, it is only a few years ago that the German text was omitted from the back page of the philharmonic concert programmes. (Anyone who wanted could consider the Hungarian text as being on the back page.) This was self-evident in view of the fact that the majority of professional musicians did not know Hungarian, and even the lovers of finer music—not the opera-goers, but those who practised music at home, the performers of classical chamber music—preferred talking German to Hungarian. No wonder that in this great German world we were overcome by a terrific longing for the real Hungary, which could not be found anywhere in Pest, for here German was virtually the official language of music. We were amazed at this for Budapest had been (at least in the newspapers from which we had known it until then) the focal point of Hungarian life reflected in the glory of the millennium. We were unable to reconcile ourselves to this great disappointment. We were astonished to see that one had only to scratch the surface of Budapest for the old German town to show through immediately. We did not understand why one had to speak German in order to practise classical music, for we knew that it was practised in Russia, France and England, too. I was brought up on classical music, it was the music that first fell to my ear—my father had found some students in Kecskemét with whom he played Haydn quartets though none of them knew German. Knowing German was not a prerequisite for playing classical music, but the fact that this had been entrusted to Germans had grave consequences upon the development of Hungarian music. The understanding of music with a text is linked to the language used so that those who practised classical music in Hungary lived, where music with words was concerned, in the world of Schubert, Schumann, and their companions, and regarded the Hungarian songs which they happened to encounter as trivial, vulgar, a product of uneducated and useless dillettantism. They were right up to a point, and so the elevation and development of the Hungarian song from its ancient roots to an artistic level equivalent to foreign songs emerged as an urgent and crucial problem.

The road leading to this could be sought only in the musical atmosphere of the villages. Many people cannot see clearly even today what the point in these journeys to the countryside was, because to them, the village is the scene of ignorance, rowdyism and coarseness. This is where their mistake lies. The tenderest flowers of the Hungarian spirit blossomed in the villages, and what is more, most of them did not even reach the towns. Not only did we find a lot of songs in the villages—and it doesn't matter whether it was a hundred or a thousand—material in other words that could be collected, taken away and used, but also something else without which these tunes would never have come into being: and that is culture. However strange this may sound, we found a homogeneous culture, with the tunes forming an insepar- able part, its summit as it were, but most definitely its organic blossom. We must think here of a culture that can be understood without reading or writing, which does however contain the main quality of culture, for it arms each participant against all eventualities and makes him a happy being until he leaves the circle of life that is suited to him. It is a long time since I have read anything as stimulating as the novel of the same title (*A boldog ember* [The Happy Man])*; the first piece of writing that at long last illuminated the greater depths of this world. I could not but exclaim in innumerable passages that it was true, that that was how I saw it myself; and that anyone who wished to form an idea about this dying culture, should look through the pages of this book. I should add that in those days there were quite a few villages in Hungary where no schoolmaster, priest or village notary lived, in short there were no "gentlefolk" at all and it was precisely in these villages where nothing disturbed homogeneity that folk culture and folksongs flourished most.

I shall illustrate with four examples how little feeling for folk culture was shown in bygone days. One was the case of a parish priest, who tried to persuade me on one of my journeys that it was quite useless and superfluous to collect the songs sung by the village people for they were nothing but distorted and ruined versions of songs that had come from the towns, from the educated classes. Then there was Count Albert Apponyi, who bluntly expressed his conviction that it was not worth dealing with folksongs by refusing to grant any funds for the promotion of collecting material during his post as Minister of Culture. It must be admitted that since then he has come a long way, by way of his present political attitude up to the *Spinning Room*. The third random example refers to Endre Nagy. Once Vilma Medgyaszay, accompanied by some girls in Palóc attire, appeared on the stage of the Endre Nagy Cabaret. They sang prettily and then Endre Nagy came forth and expounded his opinion on the folksong, which, naturally, reflected the view of his own period. He said that every provincial region must surely have its own poet who wrote the songs, which then spread among the people. The evening meetings of the Friends of Nyugat had not yet begun so that I could only argue with Endre Nagy in myself, thinking that anyone who could write even three lines of the kind we had found would be worth his weight in gold. The fourth example concerns Mihály Babits*, who often wrote wise and profound articles on the problem of folksongs; according to one of his articles folksongs were nothing but the poetry of people who were uneducated in literature. It is an apt and exact definition, except that it is not true of genuine folk poetry; but it is correct of the songs and authors of the Hungarian middle classes, which are still popular today. There is nothing offensive in my saying—what they incidentally admit themselves—that the Balázs-s and Fráters could not write poetry;

* A novel written by Zsigmond Móricz, an eminent prose writer who belonged to the Nyugat Literary Circle.
* Hungarian poet, novelist and translator (1883–1941).

as for possessing any musical culture, which would mean knowing the classics, they proudly declare that they do not even want to know them. Babits's definition fits them; but it should be added that their songs *no longer* belong to folk culture and are *not yet* part of a higher culture. They are dubious, whether viewed from the folk culture or higher culture aspects, and as opposed to these, the songs of the people in their own way are perfect and unsurpassable. High aims had been set to achieve such perfection and excellence; this will be understood by all who have ever been enchanted by Negro art. This, too, is an old art rooted in folk culture, without any trace of literary culture—but I am sure you will accept that our own art which is of a similar rank and order is, nevertheless, somewhat nearer to us; and, indeed, that nothing could have provided a better starting point for the creation of the artistic Hungarian song.

And here is the Rubicon that separates us from European peoples: the language. In spite of their great differences the European languages stand nearer to each other than any one of them to the Hungarian language; their system of stresses and their natural melodies are so different that they may be considered diametrically opposed to Hungarian. What follows is that music written to a Hungarian text—if it follows the natural intonation of the language—is virtually impossible to translate into a European language and furthermore the melodic line flowing from a Hungarian text will sound alien to the European. And here lies the explanation as to why artistic Hungarian songs have no audience. The rhythm of the German language is deeply rooted and the melodies following the German text appear natural in the souls of our audiences well-versed in music—not because they are of German descent, though some of them are, but rather as a result of everyday practice. On the other hand, audiences with a good sense of the Hungarian language feel alienated from these songs on account of their artistic qualities; they find them burdensome and cannot accept them. It is interesting to note that both groups rather prefer the Hungarian songs that pursue alien melodic lines.

And here are the tragic consequences of the exaggerated cult of the iambus practised by our nineteenth-century poets. The iambus is an absolutely natural rhythm for the English language, less so for German, French and Italian—but it is diametrically opposed to the Hungarian language. And yet, in the nineteenth century our poets surrendered unconditionally to the iambus, with the result that innumerable masterpieces in our literature were irredeemably lost to music. János Arany* already claimed that it was impossible to write Hungarian tunes to iambuses or trochees, and that if we put them to music foreign melodies would emerge unless we used violence and ignored the iambus as Egressy did with the *Szózat* ("Appeal"), producing a very distorted rhythm. Those who nevertheless tried to compose Hungarian songs on a higher level were faced with almost insurmountable difficulties. The road was long; the form and treasured quality of the Hungarian folksong had to be discovered, and

* A great nineteenth-century poet, who based his language on the colloquial speech of the people.

learned; only then could one cautiously attempt to write a melody that did not conflict with the natural melodic line of the Hungarian language to a poem that was non-Hungarian in form. And at this point it was discovered that the Greek and Latin forms stand nearer to the nature of the Hungarian language, for they form uneven and more varied groups of syllables than the iambus or trochee. Thus, however improbable this may sound, it was through the songs of simple Magyars that we learned how to put some of the masterpieces of Hungarian literature to music.

It was in a small village, where Berzsenyi's* name had not even been heard, that it became clear to me how Berzsenyi could be expressed in songs; that is how the songs, some of which you are going to hear now, came into being; songs that, for the time being, have no audience. When will they have an audience? Let us hope that some time in the future they will be popular; and first and foremost at a time when it will have become a matter of common knowledge that our peasant culture is not only the ancestor of Hungarian culture in its entirety, but a living, organic part of it and that without it Hungarian culture would be incomplete. I shall give just one example to illustrate this. On one occasion a highly cultured man with a fine sense of literature told me that he did not understand Ady's** phrase: *"Beágyazott a villás Vénség"* (Pitchforked Old Age has turned me in). In this single line it becomes clear that, whether we like it or not, the idiom and imagery of our greatest poets are identical with the vocabulary of the country folk. I wonder what would remain of Petőfi,*** Arany or Ady if we eradicated the lines from their poetry that are incomprehensible without some knowledge of rural life?

Nevertheless the increasing number of signs reveals that the time is approaching when we will understand the significance of folk culture. A lot of water has flowed under the bridge already: if we watch the daily press, the most sensitive seismograph of public life, we will notice that it is full of village life. Árpád Pásztor has written enough monographs of villages to compile a volume—if only he had done so when he went to America. The yearbook of the *Est***** is also full of dancing peasant figures (though they kick their legs a bit higher than they do in real life); but at the back of the same volume there are over a hundred advertisements for foreign boarding schools without as much as a thought that if we send our children to such places, they will have to discover their Hungarian blood when they are grown up. Never mind, interest is being shown and will perhaps increase. It may bring fruit in the field of music, too; and from another aspect the spread of musical culture may eventually reach responsible Hungarian circles and open up paths there, too. Then there will be more people practising Hungarian songs; for today there are very few, and they cannot counteract what is happening on the other side, where a thousand tiny rodents are industriously gnawing away at the surviving ruins of the Hungarian song. I am thinking here of so-called light music, which contains at least one offence against

* Dániel Berzsenyi (1795–1836) poet inspired by classical poetry.
** Endre Ady (1877–1919), poet and prose writer, one of the Nyugat Circle and the greatest figure of this period.
*** Sándor Petőfi (1823–1849), a lyric poet, who died while fighting for the War of Independence.
**** A contemporary Budapest daily.

Hungarian intonation in every line. Many people find this amusing; indeed, some authors intend it to be so; but if the Hungarian language dances for much longer on its head it is possible that it will forget how to walk on its legs. I think we should be careful with this laughter lest we dig the grave of the language with it for good. I wish the Hungarian language to have other kinds of friends, whose souls have been pervaded at least once by the pealing of bells that has been continuous in the Hungarian language from the *"Halotti beszéd"* (Funeral Oration)* right up to Ady. I wanted to record some of the pealing of the bells. It was hard work and has no more results than a few crudely carved slabs of stone. But some day the ringing tower of Hungarian music is going to stand. And if, in its pedestal some of these stones will be lying intact and the rest destroyed I shall—to use Berzsenyi's words—regard with safety the night of my deep grave.

(1932)

* The oldest Hungarian literary record, dating from the twelfth century.

BICINIA HUNGARICA

Preface to the Hungarian Edition

I wrote these songs in memory of my school friends of Galánta, whose voices I still hear after the passing of fifty and more years.

I see you still, as you were when we were children: barefooted rascals, fighting among yourselves, throwing stones into the air, exploring the countryside for birds' eggs, but ever sturdy and fearless; and the girls—demure, and always busy at home. I remember your singing and your dancing; but where have you all gone?

If in those far-off days we had been taught what I try to teach in this book (as well as some other important things), life would have been very different in our little country. It is left with you who use this book to show that while singing in itself is good, the real reward comes to those who sing, and feel, and think, with others. This is what harmony means.

We must look forward to the time when all people in all lands are brought together through singing, and when there is a universal harmony.

(1937)

LET US SING CORRECTLY!

Most singing teachers and chorus masters believe in controlling the pitch of the voices by the piano. But singing depends on the acoustically correct "natural" intervals, and not on the tempered system. Even a perfectly tuned piano can never be a criterion of singing, not to speak of the ever "out-of-tune" pianos available at schools and rehearsal rooms. Yet how often have I found chorus masters attempting to restore the shaky intonation of their choirs with the help of a mistuned piano! And how often does a teacher, lost amid the waves of the piano accompaniment, not even notice that the pitch of his singing class has gone wrong. Usually the voices drop, in spite of the piano... The beginners' first steps in the endless realm of notes should be supported not by any instrument of tempered tuning and dissimilar tone-colour, but by another voice. The advantages of singing in two parts can hardly be overestimated, but unfortunately it is often left until far too late. It assists aural development in every way, even in unison singing. In fact, those who always sing in unison never learn to sing in correct pitch. Correct unison singing can, paradoxically, be learned only by singing in two parts: the voices adjust and balance each other. Those who have a clear aural concept of the sound C—G will sing the interval C—G correctly.

If the concord is felt to be correct by each of the two groups who sing it—and that is only felt when the tempered pianoforte remains silent—then the interval will also be correct; first one group sing C and the other G, then one sing C—G and the other C—G. The teacher must see to it that the ear is trained accordingly. The simultaneous sound is the guarantee of correct attack, not the method of stepwise climbing up the scale; for, when we reach the fifth or sixth note, the first will have been forgotten; and the uncertainty of the intermediate notes will render also the fifth and sixth notes uncertain. The "C-major-scale method" is the enemy of correct singing. Every interval must be memorised separately, and each in its particular characteristic tonal function, not fitted together as steps of a scale. Those who try to sing the larger intervals by climbing up the scale will find them but slowly and vaguely. The scale will sound correct only when its "pillars" are established in advance, and these "pillars" are the notes of the pentatonic scale: C—D—E—G—A, or in solmisation doh-ray-me-soh-lah (d-r-m-s-l).

I cannot see any reason why the first exercises in two-part singing should not be done with the aid of solmisation or words; solmisation, I think, should even precede acquaintance with musical notation.

The syllables used for solmisation are as follows:

doh(d) ray(r) me(m) fah(f) soh(s) lah(l) te(t)
(tonic)   *(leading note)*

These syllables are used irrespective of the actual scale, "doh" always meaning tonic and "t" the leading (seventh) note of the scale. In the minor the first note is always called "lah" with "doh" remaining the tonic of the relative major scale.

The pupil will advance more quickly with the reading of music if he has learned to find the correct pitch. Rhythmic exercises should have begun much earlier, also in two parts, as physical exercises in pairs; musical work in two parts offers possibilities that unison cannot provide. And if the nursery school contributes its share in developing the sense of rhythm, music reading in the elementary school will become practicable.

Correct intonation is the main purpose of the present exercises; rhythmic difficulties are therefore avoided. Only choirs that sing correctly have colour and brightness; and children's choruses will become capable of low notes which they could not sing otherwise. The proof and reward of correct singing is beauty of sound, caused by the appearance of combination tones, and, in the higher registers, by the increased brightness of the overtones.

With the exception of the last two, these exercises do not contain semitones. Correct intonation can better be achieved if semitones are postponed until whole tones are sung with sufficient assurance.

Finally: relative solmisation can be of great help and should not be dismissed. Successions of syllables are easier and more reliably memorised than letters; in addition, the syllable indicates at the same time the tonal function and, by memorising the interval, we develop our sense of the tonal function. It is a common experience that singing is more correct in countries and schools where solmisation is practised.

After these exercises have been mastered it will not be difficult to sing semitones, because, then, we shall be supported by the solid "pillars" of the pentatonic scale.

First "fah" (the fourth note of the major scale) should be learned. After having properly memorised a number of melodies within the hexachord d—l we may begin applying it in two parts, like this:

d-f-m	m-f-m	m-f-m	s-m-s-f-m	s-l-f-m
d-f,-d	d-f,-d	m-r-d	d-d-d-r-d	d-l,-l,-d

217

s-l-d'	l-f-m	d'-l-d'	s-d'-s-l-d'	s-l-s-l-l-d'
d-f-m	f-r-d	m-f-m	s-m-s-f-m	d-f-m-f-r-m

"Te" (the leading note) should be learned from melodies with the compass t,—l and s,—m and also from melodies in the minor ranging from l,—f.
Exercises in two parts should follow, similar to these:

d'-t-d'	d'-t-d'	d'-t-d'	d'-t-d'	d-r-m	m-s-m	m-r-d
d-s-d	d-s,-d	d-r-d	d-r-m	d-t,-d	d-t,-d	d-t,-d

l,-m-f-m	l-s-f-m	l-s-l-f-m
l,-	l,-d-r-m	l,-t,-d-r-m

Only after each of these two notes has become firmly rooted in the aural memory should they be attempted simultaneously; at first only one at a time should be introduced and the approach should be by steps; later they may be approached by leaps.

m-s-f-m	d'-t-t-d'	m-f-f-m	s-f-f-m	s-l-t-d'
d-t,-t,-d	m-s-f-m	d-l,-t,-d	s,-l,-t,-d	s-f-f-m

d'-t-l-s	m-f-m	d'-t-d'
d-r-f-m	d-t,-d	m-f-m

s-l-s-t-d'	d-f-m-r-d	l-f-f-m	l-f-m	m-d'-l-f-m
d-f-m-r-d	d-l,-s,-t,-d	l,-l,-t,-d	l,-t,-d	l,-l,-d-r-m

$$\left\{\begin{array}{l|l} \text{m-l-d'-f-m} & \text{m-d'-r'-f-m} \\[3em] \text{l,-d-l,-r-m} & \text{l,-m-f-r-l,} \end{array}\right.$$

In this way we shall gradually learn to sing diatonic music in two parts. In order to achieve satisfactory results care must be taken

(1) that at each lesson no more than one or two new exercises should be learned. The old ones should always be repeated.
(2) That no instrument is used. The pitch should be given orally.
(3) If, at the beginning, simultaneous attack in two parts is too difficult, the second part may enter later, i.e., after half the value of the note (cf. exercises Nos. 82–85); if necessary, the semibreves of the first part may also be sung at half their value, followed by minim rests; the part with less movement should begin; at first the exercises should be practised at a slow pace, breath being taken after every note; even later the speed should never be too fast, so as to allow for proper control of every note.
(4) Every exercise should be repeated at once with exchanged parts, at the same pitch if the range permits, otherwise at a different pitch, higher or lower.
(5) As preparation for the exercises let us practise the major and minor triads (d-m-s and l,-d-m) in various positions (m-s-d', s,-d-m, d-m-l, m-l-d,); and also as chords of four notes (doubling "doh" at the octave): there are twenty-four different ways in which the four notes can be grouped. For every exercise in which the melodic line rises two should be practised in which it falls. The latter are more difficult, since we are less accustomed to them (this is one of the reasons why the reading of music is so unsatisfactory). Finally let us also practise in canon.

$$\left\{\begin{array}{l|l|l|l} \text{d-d-d-d-m-d} & \text{s-s-s-s-d'-s} & \text{m-s-m-d-m-d} & \text{s,} \\[3em] & \text{d-d-d-d-m-d} & \text{s-s-s-s-d'-s} & \text{m-s-m-d-m-d} \end{array}\right.$$

$$\left\{\begin{array}{l|l|l|l|l} \text{d-d-d-d-m-d} & \text{s-s-s-s} & \text{s-m-m-m-s} & \text{d-d-d-d} & \text{d-d-d-d} \\[3em] \text{s,} & \text{d-d-d-d-m-d} & \text{s-s-s-s} & \text{s-m-m-m-s} & \end{array}\right.$$

This traditional children's tune on the five-note bugle signal could be sung even as an eight-part canon, with the entries on the strong beats only. However, let us be content with two parts to begin with.

(1952)

FIFTEEN TWO-PART EXERCISES

Preface to the English Edition

These fifteen exercises constitute a progressive course in two-part singing following the two-part Exercises in Intonation. What I said there about the usefulness, and indeed necessity, of two-part singing at an early stage applies here with even greater force.

Moreover, these exercises will serve as an introduction to the style of the greatest epoch of choral singing.

(1961)

PENTATONIC MUSIC

Postscript to the Hungarian Edition

While pondering on the music of the Kindergarten, I decided that mere criticism would not bring about any real improvement. It was thus that these little pieces were written in order to make some small contribution to replacing the awful marching and walking songs then customary in such classes. "What is the need for them? Why, there are already folksongs available", somebody might say. Indeed there are, but, as I have declared many times, we have very few pentatonic folksongs of sufficiently limited compass and rhythm. For this reason smaller children need tunes written in the spirit of folksongs but without their difficulties. In such pieces, by making them into games, we can prepare the ground for genuine folksongs. With much the same object in view I wrote *333 Elementary Exercises,* where most of the pieces can be used as tunes for marching and so on.

The most suitable instrument for playing these *100 Little Marches* is a pentatonic wooden xylophone. The reason for my waiting to issue these pieces was that I hoped that we could find someone who could mass-produce this instrument...

Until this instrument is produced these pieces can be played on the diatonic wooden xylophone which is in use now, although it is slightly more difficult to find the notes on it due to *fa* and *ti* which must be omitted; also more notes will sound in glissandos—the only objections. (The glissandos, marked here and there, concern instrumental playing only, and not singing.)

However, these pieces can be played on any other instrument or can be sung unaccompanied, wordlessly or with a text if a suitable one can be invented. If this cannot be done, it will be enough to sing them in *sol-fa*. The "bird-language" of the *sol-fa* names is entertaining for children, and moreover it creates a basis for musical thinking in a playful way.

There is no reason why a six or seven-year-old child should not learn to sing in *sol-fa*. If he could begin school with this knowledge, school music-teaching would progress at great speed and without particular effort.

Nowadays it is no longer necessary to explain why it is better to start teaching music to small children through pentatonic tunes: first, it is easier to sing in tune without having to use semitones (half-steps), second, the musical thinking and the ability to sound the notes can develop better using tunes which employ leaps rather than stepwise tunes based on the diatonic scale often used by teachers.

(1947)

221

INTRODUCTION TO
THE PERFORMANCE
OF THE "PEACOCK VARIATIONS"

The national culture of music of every people rests on a healthy relationship between folk music and composed music.

Only the music which has sprung from the ancient musical traditions of a people can reach the masses of that people.

A long series of endeavours in Hungarian composed music was unsuccessful because they were not rooted in folk music but tried to imitate various foreign forms as did literature a long time ago with German, French and Latin schools.

In the beginning the Hungarian school was disdained, until finally, achieving a victory with Petőfi and Arany, it pointed to a path that has not been abandoned ever since by any real Hungarian writer.

Nor was it only to literature that they showed the right way; they pointed to it in every other art as well.

This is the path we have pursued in music for decades and on this the work to be heard now has set out. To understand it no special musical knowledge whatever is needed.

But we must know the folksong out of which it has grown like a flower from a seed. We only know a tune really well if we know it by heart. In this the Budapest Chorus will help us now.

When we then mutely sing the tune to ourselves while the music is being played, we shall hear it from amidst even the most colourful variations and by this we shall hold the line in our hand to the end.

Variation is the most natural development of folk music, for folk music itself is nothing but an endless series of melodies developing from each other and changing from one to the other in unnoticeable transitions. It is a pity that our composers do not write variations on folksongs more often. By this they would promote more efficiently than by anything else the bringing of folk music and composed music closer to each other.

(1950)

"I MADE MY FIRST INSTRUMENT MYSELF"

Statement

Kecskemét, Szob, Galánta, Nagyszombat: the dwelling places of my childhood. Much coming and going, and flitting. I was hardly a few months old when we got to Galánta and that is where I spent the finest seven years of my childhood.

The shaping of my life was as natural as breathing itself. I sang before I could speak, and I sang more than I spoke. I got to know the instruments and classical masterpieces early in my life.

I made my first instrument myself. I was hardly four years old when I took Mother's draining-ladle, threaded strings into its holes and fastened them to the end of the ladle. On these strings I played the guitar and sang improvised songs to this accompaniment. These improvisations made me happy as no later work of mine ever did.

At Nagyszombat my first orchestral work—an overture—was performed when I was a pupil of the sixth form of the grammar school. I had never heard an orchestra apart from the fire-brigade's orchestra and the church orchestra, both of them very small. Béla Toldy, leader of the orchestra, prepared for the première with great affection; he borrowed brass players from the local fire-brigade orchestra. There was only one flautist among the pupils of the school.

The first performance met with resounding applause.

The enthusiastic audience demanded that the composer should come onto the platform.

And the first review, written by a music critic from Pozsony, appeared:

"The work sounds well, the ideas are treated logically, the piece is vigorous and bears witness to talent."

(1950)

FIFTY-FIVE TWO-PART EXERCISES

Preface to the Hungarian Edition

We should perhaps be allowed to make an effort to help our musicians to become as outstanding as our football players. The possibilities exist for we certainly possess abundant talent. But few achieve the level of perfection, because there are many shortcomings in the fundamentals of musical education, and because studies are abandoned much too early. Today, every intelligent musician is beginning to realise that if a higher level is to be attained we must change our working methods. We can produce better musicians only if we can bring about a thorough reorganisation in our methods of teaching music. How valuable are "brilliant" pianists if they cannot sing simple folksongs without making errors? There must be a strenuous attempt to replace music that comes from the fingers and the mechanical playing of instruments with music from the soul and based on singing. We should not allow anyone even to go near an instrument until he or she can read and sing correctly. It is our only hope that one day our musicians will be able also to "sing" on their instruments.

Many pupils recognise the advantages of the method (of which this volume is part) in the earliest stages of their musical studies. Everyone, however, has not yet fully understood the importance of continuing singing in two or more parts, without the aid of an instrument, until the highest level is attained. At least three people should cooperate even though there are only two singing parts, because only a third person, "the outsider" (who may, of course, be the teacher) is able to notice mistakes in intonation and to ensure that the rhythm is kept.

The two parts were issued in separate part-book for two reasons: one is to teach each pupil to listen to his partner without seeing the other part, and the other is to enable our young musicians to carry their singing books with them into the open air. Music is a profession which compels the student to spend far too much time indoors and this is detrimental to health. So let them carry on what studies they can out in the open air. I do not say they should disturb the reverent peace and quiet of the woods, but in the open air, on the banks of some river or spring they can counter the many unattractive noises of nature (as well as other more unattractive sounds not perpetrated by nature) with something that is both more pleasant and more profitable.

It is naturally understood that the various positions of "doh" must be defined beforehand, as a result of which students also study harmony without observing the fact that they are doing so. The position of "doh" is a matter of choice. In the case of a mixed choir both parts may be doubled an octave lower. If an all-male section is to sing the lower part it will be necessary to take both parts a few notes down. Under no condition should the upper part (soprano) be left in its original position and only the lower part (alto) taken down, for in such a case the two parts would be too far from one another.

There is a need for better musicians, and only those will become good musicians who work at it every day. The better a musician is the easier it is for him to draw others into the happy, magic circle of music. Thus will he serve the great cause of helping music to belong to everyone.

(1954)

A LITTLE BIOGRAPHY

I was born in Kecskemét but as my parents moved from there when I was only a few months old, I can scarcely claim the proud title "Son of Kecskemét". I was nevertheless forced to take advantage of it when I was asked during my wanderings from village to village, "Where were you born?" The very name of Kecskemét always produced gleaming eyes and fellow-feeling.

But for all that I grew up a lowlander: the Galánta district, where I began to find myself, is just as open as the Great Plain itself. Even my brief stay in Szob did not make a highlander out of me, although it was there that I first came into contact with mountains—but not on my own feet: I was carried on someone's back up to the top of Hegyestető.

There was always a longing for mountains in me, but it was only after a long, long time that it was satisfied. From Galánta I could see the Carpathians looming blue in the distance, from Nagyszombat they were a little nearer, but it was years later before I could actually set foot on them. At that time to go out on excursions was far from customary. My student colleagues never budged out of the town. The children of the vine-growers lived in their Szuha vineyards during the summer, and I also moved around there as a guest, but to go further afield, especially on foot, was a rare thing. We looked on one of our number as a complete crank simply because he travelled right round the Balaton during a vacation. Even later, when I roamed a great deal in our mountains, before I had the chance to go to Switzerland, it was only on one single occasion on my solitary tours that I met with three Debrecen students, at the foot of the Gyömbér, but they did not go to the summit.

It was a serious defect in our education at that time that it never inspired us to move about the country. My student colleagues did not know the country apart from their immediate surroundings. Our father, as a railwayman, took me and my younger brother off on tours from time to time in the summer. We saw the Vág valley, Kassa, Kolozsvár, Brassó, Pest. By spending one summer with relations in Resicza, I got an appetite for the mountains there. But serious mountain roaming was reserved for later years.

(1966)

APPENDIX

NOTES

I ON FOLK MUSIC

Hungarian Folksongs
The foreword to a folksong publication of great significance in Hungarian music history, the first joint publication by Bartók and Kodály. The foreword was written by Zoltán Kodály and then signed by both. (Rozsnyai, Budapest, 1906.)

The Pentatonic Scale in Hungarian Folk Music
The article first appeared in the first season of the *Zenei Szemle* in 1917. The translation was made on the basis of the final version which was included in the anthology *Visszatekintés* (In Retrospect), edited by Ferenc Bónis, Zeneműkiadó, Budapest, 1964.

Hungarian Folk Music
Zeneközlöny X, No. 9 (1925).

What Is Hungarian in Music?
Apollo IV (1939).

The Role of the Folksong in Russian and Hungarian Music
Lecture at the Hungaro—Soviet Cultural Society's Congress held in 1946. *Visszatekintés* (In Retrospect), Zeneműkiadó, Budapest, 1964.

Children's Games
Foreword to Volume I of the *Corpus Musicae Popularis Hungaricae* (the very important series of publications by the Hungarian Academy of Sciences' Folk Music Research Group under the leadership of Kodály). Zeneműkiadó, Budapest, 1951.

Calendar Customs Songs
Foreword to Volume II of the *Corpus Musicae Popularis Hungaricae*. Akadémiai Kiadó, Budapest, 1953.

Wedding Songs
Foreword to Volume III of the *Corpus Musicae Popularis Hungaricae*. Akadémiai Kiadó, Budapest, 1955.

Pairing Songs
Foreword to Volume IV of the *Corpus Musicae Popularis Hungaricae*. Akadémiai Kiadó, Budapest, 1959.

Message to the International Folk Music Council's Quebec Conference
Bulletin of the International Folk Music Council, No. XX (1962).

II ON PREDECESSORS AND CONTEMPORARIES

Claude Debussy
The article was written when Debussy died. *Nyugat* XI (1918).

Thirteen Young Hungarian Composers
Kodály's composition students, and thus Kodály himself as their teacher, were attacked in the *Neues Pester Journal* (28th May, 1925). Kodály's article in reply in German was not published by the paper. In Hungarian it first appeared in the *Budapesti Hírlap* (14th June, 1925).

To Yehudi Menuhin's Budapest Concerts
This first appeared in June, 1946, in the programme for the concerts.

On the Anniversary of Beethoven's Death
Opening address at the gala concert in the Budapest Academy of Music on 25th March, 1952. *Visszatekintés* (In Retrospect). Zeneműkiadó, Budapest, 1964.

In Memory of Haydn
Presidential opening address at the memorial session of the Hungarian Academy of Sciences in February, 1959. *Zenetudományi Tanulmányok* (Musicological Studies). Volume VIII, Akadémiai Kiadó, Budapest, 1960.

Letter to Pablo Casals
Foreword to the Hungarian edition of J. M. Corredor's book: *Beszélgetéseim Pablo Casalsszal* (My Talks with Pablo Casals), Gondolat Könyvkiadó, Budapest, 1960.

Béla Bartók's First Opera
Written on the occasion of the Budapest première *A kékszakállú herceg vára* (Bluebeard's Castle). *Nyugat* XI (1918).

Béla Bartók
Zoltán Kodály wrote this study at the request of *La Revue Musicale* II (1921). In Hungarian: *Visszatekintés* (In Retrospect). Zeneműkiadó, Budapest, 1964.

Bartók's Compositions for Children
This article first appeared in German in the 1921 Bartók Number of *Musikblätter des Anbruch,* under the title "Bartóks Kinderstücke". In Hungarian: *Visszatekintés* (In Retrospect), Zeneműkiadó, Budapest, 1964.

Béla Bartók the Man
Lecture to the Hungarian Musicians' Trade Union, 22nd February, 1946. *Zenei Szemle* I (1947).

Bartók the Folklorist
Új Zenei Szemle I (1950). (Bartók Number)

In Memory of Bartók
Speech on Hungarian Radio as opening address for the Bartók-Year (Kossuth station, Hungarian Radio, 1st January, 1955). *Visszatekintés* (In Retrospect), Zeneműkiadó, Budapest, 1964.

On Béla Bartók
Presidential opening address at the memorial session of the Hungarian Béla Bartók Memorial Committee on 26th September, 1956. *Visszatekintés* (In Retrospect), Zeneműkiadó, Budapest, 1964.

Opening Address
Given in the scientific lecture series organised on the occasion of the eightieth anniversary of Bartók's birth, 17th March, 1961. *Visszatekintés* (In Retrospect), Zeneműkiadó, Budapest, 1964.

Liszt and Bartók
Opening address at the second International Musicological Conference in Budapest, September, 1961. *Visszatekintés* (In Retrospect), Zeneműkiadó, Budapest, 1964.

III ON MUSIC EDUCATION

Children's Choirs
Zenei Szemle III (1929).

Music in the Kindergarten
Lecture on 3rd December, 1940. *Magyar Zenei Szemle* I (1941). The postscript was written in 1957. Zeneműkiadó, Budapest, 1958.

Hungarian Music Education
Lecture in Pécs on 19th November, 1945, before the Kodály concert there. *Visszatekintés* (In Retrospect), Zeneműkiadó, Budapest, 1964.

The National Importance of the Workers' Chorus
Éneklő Munkás I (1947).

A Hundred Year Plan
Énekszó XIV (1947).

After the First Solfège Competition
Speech made in the Academy of Music in Budapest in June, 1949. *Visszatekintés* (In Retrospect), Zeneműkiadó, Budapest, 1964.

Ancient Traditions—Today's Musical Life
Lecture in the school of the Budapest Folk Art Institute, on 12th July, 1951. *Visszatekintés* (In Retrospect), Zeneműkiadó, Budapest, 1964.

Who Is a Good Musician?
Speech at the end-of-session ceremony in the Budapest Academy of Music, 1953. Zeneműkiadó, Budapest, 1954.

Musical Reading and Writing
Preface to Erzsébet Szőnyi's book, volumes I–III, Zeneműkiadó, Budapest, 1956. In English volumes I–II, Boosey & Hawkes, London –Corvina Press, Budapest, 1973 and 1974.

Musical Education in Hungary
Introduction to the book, edited by Frigyes Sándor. It appeared first in English: Barrie and Rockliff, London–Corvina Press, Budapest, 1966.

IV ON HIMSELF AND HIS WORKS

Confession
Lecture to the "Nyugat Circle of Friends", 23 December, 1932. *Nyugat,* XXVI (1933).

Bicinia Hungarica
Preface to volume I, Magyar Kórus, Budapest, 1937. Second edition of volume I, Magyar Kórus, 1941. Volumes II–III, Magyar Kórus, 1941. Volume IV, Magyar Kórus, 1942. In English: Boosey & Hawkes, London, 1957.

Let Us Sing Correctly!
Foreword. Magyar Kórus, Budapest, 1941. In English: Boosey & Hawkes, London, 1952.

Fifteen Two-Part Exercises
Magyar Kórus, Budapest, 1941. New edition, Zeneműkiadó, Budapest, 1962. In English: Boosey & Hawkes, London, 1962.

Pentatonic Music
Volume I, Magyar Kórus, Budapest, 1945. Postscript to volume II, Magyar Kórus, Budapest, 1947. Volumes III–IV, Magyar Kórus Budapest, 1947. In English: Boosey & Hawkes, London, 1970–1972.

Introduction to the Performance of the "Peacock Variations"
In the City Theatre, at the concert arranged in March, 1950, when the composer conducted the *Peacock Variations* and the *Concerto.* *Énekszó,* XII, (1950).

"I made my first instrument myself"
Statement for the paper *Család és Iskola,* (Budapest), 1950.

Fifty-Five Two-Part Exercises
Preface. Zeneműkiadó, Budapest, 1954. In English: Boosey & Hawkes, London, 1965.

A Little Biography
Published in László Eősze's book: *Zoltán Kodály – His Life in Pictures.* Belwin and Mills Publishers, New York – Corvina Press, Budapest, 1971, facsimile Nos. 226–227.

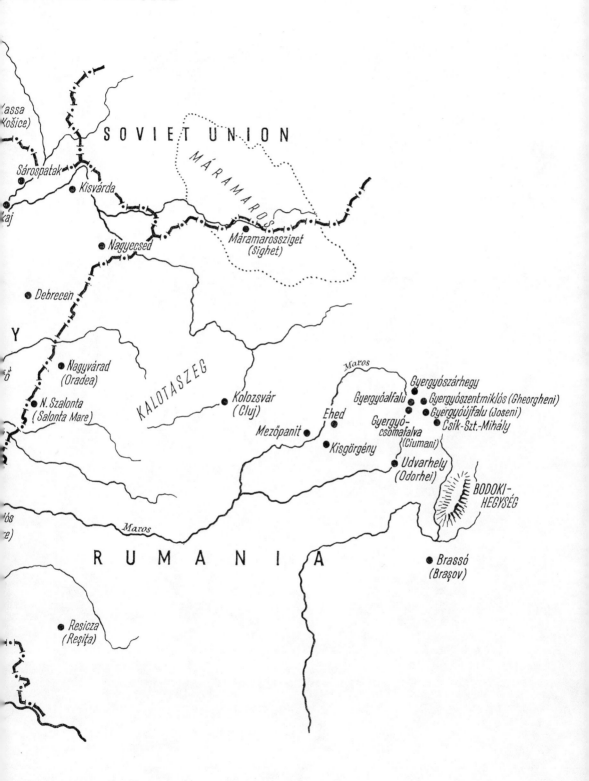

Vassa
(Košice)

Sárospatak

Kisvárda

Saj

SOVIET UNION

MÁRAMAROS

Máramarossziget
(Sighet)

Nagyecsed

Debrecen

Y

Nagyvárad
(Oradea)

ó

KALOTASZEG

Kolozsvár
(Cluj)

Maros

Gyergyószárhegy

Gyergyóalfalu

Gyergyószentmiklós (Gheorgheni)

Gyergyóújfalu (Joseni)

N. Szalonta
(Salonta Mare)

Ehed

Gyergyó-
csomafalva
(Ciumani)

Csík-Szt.-Mihály

Mezőpanit

Kisgörgény

Udvarhely
(Odorhei)

BODOKI-
HEGYSÉG

lós

e)

Maros

R U M A N I A

Brassó
(Brașov)

Resicza
(Reșița)

INDEX

(Persons of Hungarian nationality are marked by asteriks.)